SURVIVING THE LAW

FROM UNDOCUMENTED IMMIGRATION TO DOCTORS, LAWYERS AND SCIENTISTS

Jose R. Campos

TRUE STORIES

The Philemon Foundation
thephilemon.com
Washington, DC

Paperback English: 979-8-9921105-0-0
Paperback Spanish: 979-8-9921105-2-4
Casebound (Hardcover) English: 979-8-9921105-3-1
Casebound (Hardcover) Spanish: 979-8-9921105-1-7
Ebook English: 979-8-9921105-4-8
Ebook Spanish: 979-8-9921105-5-5
Audiobook English: 979-8-9921105-6-2
Audiobook Spanish:979-8-9921105-7-9

Library of Congress Control Number: 2024925889

Copyediting: Katherine Pickett, popediting.net
Fellow illustrations: Brigette Solatorio
Art direction, coaching, and interior design: n-kcreative.com

First Edition 2025

The Philemon Foundation Inc.
thephilemon.com
Washington, DC

Printed in the United States.

Disclaimer: I have to write this because of the lawyers. Everything I write is based on my memory. I changed some names and details to protect people. I really think that everything I wrote is true. I really don't think that anyone actually reads this tiny print. Some of the things are super serious but I still make a joke out of it because laughter is the best defense mechanism to pain.

This is for those of you who are still in the struggle.

For you, special *Fellow*, keep going.

I hope these words give you energy.

CONTENTS

PART II

Meet the **Fellows**

STORIES OF EXCEPTIONAL PEOPLE WHO PURSUED THEIR GOALS

Prologue

IN FEBRUARY 2013, I FOUND MYSELF wide awake, wandering through downtown Baltimore's Inner Harbor. The touristy side of town was asleep, not a person in sight to watch the bay. I mindlessly found myself strolling through the brick roads one last time before having to face the morning.

It was freezing. I was wearing my usual black trench coat. I forgot my standard-issue black hat, so after a while my ears began to burn. There was no time for me to think about my comfort. What mattered was that for the past twelve years I had suffered a lot to get to this point. The following morning, I would face the hardest test of my life: the bar exam.

As I walked, I reflected on the life I'd just lived. I thought about how I had trained for the past twelve years for the exam I would take the next day. I could not believe a person like me pulled this off. I wasn't supposed to go to college, let alone law school, or even exist in this country. Just two weeks ago I was undocumented and tomorrow I would sit for the bar exam.

For the past twelve years, I survived in this country by hustling. At seventeen, I came to the United States with only $110 in my pocket, a farewell gift from my family. I heard stories of people working undocumented in America. Working long hours, getting little pay, watching over your shoulder so that *La Migra* wouldn't catch you and deport you. I knew that life wasn't going to be easy, but I did not know how hard it was going to get. I thought, "Yeah, people work hard and that is what people do." However, I wasn't ready to experience eating Cheerios for breakfast, lunch, and dinner every day in college because that was all I could afford to do for months. I didn't realize that a good jacket can prevent you from getting sick. I wasn't expecting to let go of my emotions to combat depression and loneliness. Not in the most affluent country in the world. I left El Salvador seeking the American Dream. I wanted to learn English and improve myself. My parents had emigrated a year earlier and I wanted to join them. At home in El Salvador, I had the basics—pupusas and tostadas to eat and a roof over my head. Up until I came to America, I was in my comfort zone and there were always people I could talk to. I had friends and family readily available in case I wanted to bother them with something. Part of my American adventure was the uncertainty. The journey wasn't full of suffering either. Along the way I also experienced hope, joy, and the care of a few loving people.

After all these painful challenges, would I do it all over again? Absolutely.

Walking in the middle of the Inner Harbor, my nose was numb, and I could see my breath when I exhaled. I recalled all the things I had experienced since I arrived in the US, the jobs I'd had, the couple incidents where I almost died, the women I'd loved, and the friends who helped me.

After a brief review of my memory, I looked down at the water and shed a tear that I tried to hold without success. I went through a lot to earn my law degree. I remembered all the sacrifices I made. I was proud of what I'd done, but it took a toll on my soul. That tear was a proud tear that reflected a win after excruciating pain. I could not believe I'd made it this far with absolutely no papers. I had no immigration status whatsoever. Looking back at all the relationships I made along the way, the places I saw, the important people I talked to; it made everything feel like a dream.

How the hell did I do it? I had no money, no title, no family connections, like a lone wolf proving to myself that things could be done if I worked hard for it. This was the definition of grit. Regardless of your immigration status or where you're from, people care about you and want to see you succeed. There is a common human principle that makes decent people value you and appreciate the hard work you do. The government and its terrible immigration policies are one thing, but friendly people you meet on your journey are what make the American Dream a reality. In America, you can come from "nothing" and make yourself into anything. Yes, it is hard, but it's possible. I can say with confidence that is not possible in at least 80% of the world. The difference in the US is that this society rewards those willing to take risks, work hard, and learn how to play the game. Ultimately, if I could do it, anyone can do it. It took a Molotov cocktail of luck, hard work, help from others, help *to* others, sacrifice, perseverance, passion, and faith.

All the crazy stories that you are about to read are true. After you read this book, you may not believe that everything I did was possible, but I wasn't the only one who went to grad school without papers. When I decided to write this book, I started by writing my story and jotting down all the crazy memories. However, having my story alone didn't feel complete. I decided to tell the stories of other exceptional people who did the same thing. I wanted to find people who decided to attend grad school despite being undocumented. I learned about young folks who went on to become lawyers, doctors, scientists, psychologists, and those who pursued a life that was better than what they had. I enjoyed having one-on-one conversations with them. These people refused to stay seated, pouting about how life could be. They pursued and conquered. I had doubts about how they did it, but by studying their lives, talking to them, and spending hours and hours researching their trajectories, I corroborated that a situation always looks impossible until it becomes possible. Throughout these conversations I learned there is still so much more to learn from them—they taught me a lot.

It wasn't easy to find all of these extraordinary individuals. They are highly educated, highly intelligent, and highly humble. I was like

Professor X, and they were my X-Men. I had to look through all of America for these powerful mutants. It was challenging to get them to talk and meet in person. It was challenging to get them to talk to *me* about their most guarded secrets. I clearly told them, "My goal is to inspire other undocumented students to continue with their education, and to do that, I have to show them what you and I have done so that they believe it is possible. In order for me to achieve this goal, I need you to give me power. In order for you to give me power, you have to be vulnerable and open up. The more vulnerable you are with me in this interview, the more powerful the story will be and the more power I will be able to transmit to others. I will ask you the most uncomfortable questions that you have never answered to anyone in the past, and I probably will ask you about things that caused pain in you." With that speech, they opened up to me because they related to my story. They joined me in my quest. They became my Fellows.

These Fellows are super powerful now, but they were not always this powerful. In fact, some of them started out super weak. You will meet Tony, a man who came from nowhere with no self-confidence, yet became a person with a higher net worth than royalty and the self-confidence to lead others and inspire others. You will meet Healer, a little girl who grew up on the poor side of Los Angeles who became a recognized doctor from Harvard Medical School and is saving lives in a prestigious hospital in the San Francisco area. You will be impressed by Mighty, a powerful scientist from Yale who worked from 6:00 p.m. to 6:00 a.m. making sandwiches to put himself through college.

You will also learn my story. How I was destined to become a negative bully in life, but instead I became a human with a positive attitude. I was on my way to becoming a Sith Lord. There was a burning hatred in my heart. I couldn't understand why life was so draining in the most powerful country in the world. You will see that Life did not give me power until I deserved it. For twelve years I was oppressed and I couldn't wait for it to be my turn to oppress others. But I didn't. It was the love of friends, family, and lovers that pulled me to the light side.

These people appeared in my mind that night in Baltimore. I looked at my phone and realized it was 2:00 a.m. I started my walk back to my room. Tomorrow was the day. Even on my way back, I knew I wouldn't be able to fall asleep. That night I lay in bed trying to keep my eyes closed to get some rest. *I've been training all my life for this moment; I don't know what is going to happen tomorrow.* The clock on my left glared in the room, letting me know it was now 4:00 a.m. *In a few hours I'm taking the bar exam.*

Read on to find out how I got here and what happened after I took the most important exam of my life. By the end of this book, I will tell you a secret that not many people know. I will reveal to you a purpose that Life revealed to me by writing this book. When you're finished, I hope you give this book to a person you care about.

PART I

1

Starting Life

Do not take life too seriously.
You will never get out of it alive.
—Elbert Hubbard

I WAS ABOUT EIGHT YEARS OLD when I saw *Return of the Jedi* for the first time. I was so impressed with "the Force" that I had to find out how I could use it. I wanted to become a superhero. I went straight to Dad, as he was the most knowledgeable person in the entire world, and I said to him:

"Dad, when I grow up, I want to be a superhero. I want to save everyone in danger."

"How are you going to do that?" Dad asked.

"I will use the Force. But I need to know if the Force is real."

Dad looked at me, not dismissively, but with a matter-of-fact tone and said, "Lito, if you set your mind to it, you will be able to accomplish anything you really want. You have to keep thinking and thinking and eventually you will figure it out. Maybe not today, or tomorrow. Maybe it will take you years, but I believe you can do whatever you set your mind to."

"That's great, Dad! But seriously, I need the Force right now. How can I make objects float in the air?"

"In life, you will find that the Force is real. You probably don't believe that right now, but I am sure you will understand its presence one day. Scientists make airplanes float in the air, and, in a way, they use the Force. Now, go on, Lito. Go find the Force."

I wasn't that excited after that conversation, as Dad didn't make anything float before me right there. But my dream of becoming a superhero started that day.

I landed on earth on September 4, 1984, in a middle-class family in El Salvador. Mom and Dad married at the age of twenty and had me when they were twenty-eight. I am the youngest of four children. Looking at my parents' example, I don't know what I would do with four children at the age of twenty-eight.

At the time of my birth, El Salvador was in the middle of a freaking civil war that nobody understood. Capitalism vs Communism—that Cold War type of shit. Russia and Cuba financed guerrilla insurgents, and the US financed the military dictatorship. This is the definition of a proxy war. Both sides did a lot of damage.

The only thing this conflict accomplished was that it left my country in ruins. There was a lot of killing and in the end nobody won. Each side believed they were right by the standards and morals they created for themselves. To this date, some old men that managed to survive still believe their cause was justified.

I felt fear in the hearts of my parents. My earliest memory, from when I was around four years old, is the sound of machine guns crackling at 1:00 a.m. I would wake up to the sound of gunfire, but shortly thereafter I would fall back asleep when I saw that nobody in my family had been shot. That wasn't for us. It was probably a guard shift or a cue to let the general know that the soldiers were still awake. In the mornings, I would venture out to town with my family and count the bullet holes in the walls nearby.

"What if the guerrilla guys come to our house?" I asked Dad.

"If they do, I'll give you and your brother some cement to fix the holes left in the wall the following day."

I prayed that that would never happen. Oh yeah, I also didn't want to get shot. Mom and Dad tried not to show us that they were afraid, but little kids perceive a lot of things like Jedi Force-sensitive younglings. I'm not going to lie; I felt scared.

When I was five years old, I used to see the helicopters circling the San Salvador volcano from the top of my house in Santa Tecla. The choppers were throwing flares and shooting bullets like they were fireworks. I was amazed. It was a live-action Fourth of July American movie from my rooftop. At five years old, flares and bullets were fireworks. Little did I know that those fireworks were intended to kill humans.

The blackouts were normal in the evenings. The entire city would lose power, leaving everyone in the dark. Back then, I would stay up late with my cousins. The adults always came by the room with the bigger mattresses and would lay them on top of us.

"How about you kids play house?" an uncle would suggest. "Use the mattresses as the roof of your house." And just like that, he would walk out of the room, and we played house until we fell asleep. To have a big sleepover with all my cousins was the coolest thing at five years old. The truth is that my cousins couldn't travel past dusk because of the country's curfew.

The country had a curfew in place to keep people off the streets at night. People would get shot from wandering out too late. I later realized that the mattresses weren't for playing house, they were for the stray bullets that could accidentally hit us. I'm still not sure today how a thin mattress could protect from a 7.62 x 39 mm Soviet bullet, but it was the best cover the adults in the house could figure out.

■

I would listen to the adults talking about the dangers of war. At the time, my heart was broken and *it hurt*. It literally started to hurt. One day I fell on the ground in front of my parents. I was holding on to my chest, I couldn't take the pain anymore. My mom and dad were scared and looked at each other expecting the worst. They immediately took me to the doctor. The doctor diagnosed me with tachycardia—a rapid heartbeat due to anxiety. Basically, I worried so much about the dangers of war that my heart rate accelerated to the point that I felt pain. The doctor explained that I was absorbing the "adult talks" like a sponge and how all of that caused my heart to beat faster. Because of this my parents decided it was best to move out of El Salvador to Guatemala City, where things were supposed to be "better." Sure, Guatemala City was safer and much better, but Guatemala, our neighbor to the north, was going through a similar conflict in the countryside.

My family didn't have much, but we made it work. I remember we rented a small house and it was fully equipped with boxes. There was a big cardboard box as a table and small cardboard boxes as stools. The living room was also fully furnished with cardboard boxes. A big box as the sofa and a medium box as the centerpiece table. We had plenty of cardboard boxes to sit on. I think we almost developed a new cardboard box fashion in the neighborhood. Our home was a decent place to live, we even had a few mattresses on the floor to sleep on at night. We were luckier than many people in Latin America who don't have a home in the good parts of town.

My dad commuted back and forth from El Salvador to Guatemala, working in the accounting department for a big business with American owners. He was providing for the family to keep us in a safer location.

One day, at the end of my first grade, Dad decided to go to the United States. He left my mom and four kids in Guatemala in order to make money and pay the bills. I can only imagine what went through his mind leaving his family behind. But it was a bottom-line decision like the one that most immigrants make. Dad took a plane to the US, and a few months later he would send for us. In the meantime, Mom would take care of the four children in Guatemala.

My First Time in America

After a couple of years of having Dad in and out of my life, the whole family was going to reunite in Florida. I was so excited. My first time boarding a plane to America! The only America I'd seen was the one from the movies. We flew into the States with a tourist visa and started living in Ruskin, Florida—a small town near Tampa. My family and I were finally together.

My three siblings, my parents, and I stayed in a two-bedroom apartment. My parents took the master bedroom, my two sisters took the other bedroom, and my brother and I shared an inflatable mattress in the living room. That was my first time witnessing the art of an inflatable mattress. The futuristic technology of the flat rubber material that blows up into a bed. America is another world of odd amenities—there was always plenty of food stocked in the markets, and the water came out of the tap crystal clear.

I spent six months in sunny Florida. My parents put me in an elementary school nearby. I took ESL classes to learn English. I picked up a few words here and there. Slowly, I was becoming an American boy. But right when I was going to grasp onto the English language, my parents decided to cut my dreams short. "Okay, children, we had enough fun, now we have to go back to El Salvador."

My siblings and I were in shock.

My oldest sister Mari said, "What the heck, Mom? Dad, what is this all about? We have it all here. What are you talking about? You have to be kidding."

My parents explained, "Hey, guys, we are not allowed to live inside this country for more than six months."

I said, "Why not? Look at all the other people around us. They are doing it." I pointed at the Mexican neighbors. "If they can do it, we can do it too."

Mom: "There are some laws that say we cannot do it."

Me: "What kind of stupid law is that?" *I did ask really good questions as a kid.*

My sister Pepa came to my rescue: "What do other people have that we don't? Look at the family across the street. They are no better than us. In fact, I'm much smarter than the kid across the street who is two years older than me. Can we stay, please?"

My brother Pepe: "Right when things are getting better, we have to leave?"

My mom got tired of arguing with us. We were definitely winning the argument. We had all the parts of a winning argument; we used logic, facts, evidence, and reason to convince my mom and dad that they were making a mistake.

Then Dad said: "The law is the law and we can't change it."

That was the end of the story. We had to do as Dad said. He would have the last word in everything. No matter how good our logic, facts, evidence, and reasoning were, my dad had the Law. My first introduction to the American judicial system. Mom and Dad ran out of patience and stopped arguing with us. Apparently, we could not "understand" the reason we had to leave the States. Or maybe they wanted to protect us.

If I were a parent in this situation, this is the conversation I would have had with my kid:

Here's the deal, there are laws in this country that don't allow for everyone to come here to live. People in this country don't want a lot of people from all over because they think that bad things will happen to them. We can't control the way they make decisions; we can only react to the decisions they make. We can obey their laws or disobey them and submit to the consequences. If we obey, they accept us—we can come back and visit when we have enough money saved up. If we disobey the laws then we're going to have to live in hiding and not talk to many people about our situation. We would not be able to go back and

see our family in El Salvador. By the way, attending college
will be very hard for you.

See, how simple. Take notes, moms and dads.

Had I been given this rational and well-thought-out explanation at the age of seven, I would have definitely concluded to *still remain* in this country. Screw your reasoning. We had it all here. College? I didn't need college for another ten years. My family in El Salvador? I didn't know much about them. I didn't need my extended family. All I wanted was my mom, dad, and siblings. I was cool about not going back to El Salvador.

■

The real story about us leaving the US had to do with my dad's work in Florida. While my siblings and I went to school, my father worked at a flower nursery—under the table of course, getting paid cash and working without authorization. He saved good money and life was beautiful. Then, my father had the entrepreneurial idea to open a business importing merchandise into the US from El Salvador and Guatemala. He wanted to sell handcrafted vases, wooden furniture, and any item that was crafted by hand. It was a great idea. Had it worked, we would be superrich now. Unfortunately, it wasn't so simple. It turned out that you needed a bunch of permits and paperwork to import merchandise to the US.

My father went to El Salvador by himself, leaving us in Florida. When he came back to Florida he brought a bunch of merchandise with him. When he tried to reenter the US, Customs officials questioned why he had stayed in the US for six months and then wanted to return to the US so soon with a bunch of merchandise. My father was adamant to come in, arguing that his visa allowed him to do business and tourism. It was a good try. I admire the courage he had to open an international enterprise at the age of thirty-five, but my dad lacked the sophistication and knowledge to protect his business. This became the beginning of the end of Dad's first business.

The immigration agents gave my father an option to go back to El Salvador with the merchandise right there and then, or to wait for an immigration judge and fight his case. My dad chose to fight his case. It would take him four weeks to see a judge while he remained detained. All of a sudden, my dad became trapped in the immigration detention system. It sucked not having my dad around. Without my father's support, my mom was taking care of four kids by herself again, and in a foreign country. She was worried. Many nights I would come out of my bed to see her crying by herself alone in the dark. Dad was in jail with a bunch of strangers and indifferent guards. I would come up to my mom and try to hug her to make her feel better. That made her cry even more.

A friend from church saw my mother's situation and offered help. She let us into her home. It was a complete act of kindness. This friend had two children and a Native American husband who spoke Spanish. She just took a mother with four children into her house for a month and a half. My brother and I stayed in her living room and my two sisters stayed in a room with my mom. Not many people would do what she did for us. I was seven—I didn't think much of it at the time. I was just happy to be playing with the video game console that belonged to another kid. Mom had shelter. Dad would call here and there, happy to hear from us while he was in immigration jail. I would ask him: "Dad, when are you coming home?"

All he would say was, "I have to take care of this international business trip, but I'll see you soon!"

I was cool with that answer. I went to school and life was okay to me. Mom wasn't alone anymore, and she stopped crying. Or she at least stopped letting me see her cry. But deep down she was scared. She was in a foreign land away from her family at the mercy of good church people. I understand why she wanted to go back home.

My father talked to a lawyer, and the lawyer explained to him that it wasn't so simple to bring merchandise just like that. That there were laws and regulations to follow. "You can't just bring stuff and sell it on the street, blah blah blah." You know how lawyers are. My father argued with his own lawyer about freedom and the US Constitution. Of course, he did—he thought he knew the law much better. Dad even went on a period of rebellion while in detention. He went on a hunger strike and didn't shave in protest to this unjust treatment from the Empire. The immigration agents laughed at him telling him, "You want to go on a hunger strike? Sure, let's see how long you last." My dad was eating the following morning.

My father got tired of fighting his case and decided to take voluntary departure. He could have continued fighting while staying in jail for an undefined amount of time, or he could just go back and be free. His family was without him and he was without us, so it was an easy decision. The rest of us followed him a month later.

My family returned to El Salvador and life wasn't better for me. Danger and suffering were waiting for me.

Fighter

THE VERY FIRST PERSON I INTERVIEWED for this book was a lawyer who graduated law school the same year as I did, in 2012. We have a picture together from 2011 receiving a fellowship from the Hispanic Bar Association of DC, giving us money to complete a summer internship providing services to the less fortunate. Neither of us knew that the other was undocumented when we received the prize. Ten years later we reunited through mutual friends. We were at a wedding sipping beer and celebrating the end of the pandemic in a beautiful venue located in the countryside of Virginia. I want you to meet Fighter.

Fighter was brought to the US from Mexico when he was two years old. He grew up in a predominantly Latino population in Arizona and was raised by a single mother. He does not like talking about his biological father. He does not invite many people into his heart. He keeps most things to himself. I tried getting deeper and asked him to talk about his father, but I touched a nerve that hurt too much for him, so he immediately shot me down and pushed back defensively.

Fighter is a light-skinned Mexican. He recalls that in elementary school they separated the white kids from the Latino kids in order to have segregated classes. Fighter was placed with the white kids. He got a better schoolteacher and more resources than the other Latino kids. Now Fighter has a thick beard and mustache. I saw him clean shaven back in 2011, and I can see how he could pass as a white kid.

Fighter

Growing up, Fighter had to take care of his two other siblings who were born in the US. At the age of ten he was helping change diapers and slept on the couch because the entire family of three boys and a single mother could only afford to live in a one-bedroom apartment. Fighter's mother had multiple jobs cleaning places and babysitting. Fighter was often tasked with staying home to care for his younger siblings while his mother worked to support the family. This guy had to grow up fast. Fighter's mother kept telling him that education was the way to improve his life. That stayed with Fighter, and he applied himself to his studies and got a scholarship to a private high school that prepared him for college and later for law school. Fighter got really good grades in the private high school. All he did was study hard and babysit his siblings. That provided Fighter with a full ride to all three Arizona colleges where he applied. However, a storm was brewing.

The Arizona legislature, in their jealous and evil spirit to quash enlightenment, decided that it was time to stop undocumented kids from paying in-state tuition and thus stop them from going to college. In the infamous Proposition 300 they said: "Well, these illegal kids are too smart, and we don't want smart kids in our schools. If they're so smart, how about they pay three times the normal tuition?" Suddenly Fighter was in the dilemma of whether he could go to college.

Fighter was desperate. Frustrated. The whole state of Arizona was against his dream, working not as a bridge but as an obstacle. This led Fighter to join a nonprofit called Chicanos por la Causa. Their mission is to fight this injustice and advocate for these kids to go to college. After the fight, movement, and outcry, Fighter was able to use the full ride he earned to attend college. On top of that, he got a cash stipend for living expenses!

In college the attacks on undocumented students continued. A group of undocumented college students formed the Arizona Dream Act Coalition. It was an organization to help those current students in Arizona and it was run by undocumented students themselves.

Let me remind you that this was 2006; undocumented people were very much in hiding and afraid. At the time there were about two hundred undocumented students in Arizona and forty to fifty decided to organize. These folks in Arizona saw how much pressure they were under just because they wanted to study. It was a sin to want to know more in Arizona. I'm telling you, these Arizona legislators were like the Viet Cong who suppressed education after the Vietnam War.

Fighter studied business and was on the path to be a businessman, but this crisis led him to be an advocate. Fighter saw how much power the law wielded. The law could change people's lives. It was 2006 and these kids were *open* about being undocumented when most undocumented folks would put their heads down and live in the shadows. These kids were out on the front lines. I call it the Gladiator Effect. When they saw big challenges coming their way, they decided to unite. If they stayed together, they would have a chance to survive. If they ran around on their own, they would die. (You should watch *Gladiator*; Russell Crow explains it better.)

After college, Fighter decided to go to law school. He studied a lot for the LSAT (Law School Admissions Test) and got a super score, which led him to a nice scholarship at Baylor University Law School in Texas. Fighter's advice for those who want to go to law school is to invest the time in this one test and to do the best you can. This single score will open doors and will be the only reference that some people will use to judge you.

Day and night, Fighter was on a mission. Fighter applied to over forty law schools and got accepted to most of them, but Baylor gave him the most money. At first, Fighter did not know where Baylor was. He found out it was in Waco, Texas. Where is Waco? Fighter did not know where Waco was, either. He found out it was a small town in Texas where a massacre occurred in 1993. Despite all that, he decided to go there, as the cost of living was low.

While in college, Fighter had joined a debate team and had leftovers of special debate supplies such as pens and notepads. In law school, he saw a market for these debate supplies, and he opened an online business to sell them. He created a website and sold supplies to the debate teams at other universities. This is how he paid his bills during law school. At the end of law school, he sold this business for $40,000!

Fighter also waited tables while in law school. He was a hustler. He worked in his business. He took his law classes and slept very little. Fighter graduated from law school without papers. In 2012, right after Fighter graduated law school, President Obama announced the Deferred Action for Childhood Arrivals (DACA), a program that gave Fighter a work permit.

Fighter is doing well now; his entrepreneurship and wits continue to take this man far. Now he is the founder of a Washington, DC–based consulting firm that engages in immigration advocacy on behalf of state, local, and national immigration nonprofit organizations.

Fighter became a public policy warrior who never rests. He continues with his DACA status without any options for a permanent status. He has fought all his life and that is what he knows best. There is no resting for him now, life is not easy. However, he never gave up and will not give up anytime soon. In the meantime, he will continue to be a fighter.

2

Back in El Salvador with the Bullies

There are many good seeds in you.
Therefore, you must avoid every bad soil in
the world.

—Israelmore Ayivor

IT WAS 1992 AND A PEACE treaty was signed that ended the civil war in El Salvador. No more war, so my family went home. El Salvador, a tropical nation full of smiles. As soon as I exited the airplane the suffocating heat touched my face. That was a warm welcome. A crowd had accumulated outside of the airport doors, with everyone waiting to welcome their returning relatives. It was like the entire town came to welcome *El Hermano Lejano*, that dude that went away long ago to make it in the US and now returns with success and presents for everyone. Girls put on their best dresses. I saw a lot of *quinceañera* dresses—that is the best dress that most girls had in a poor country like El Salvador. It sure was different from the US. I was seven and I did not remember much of this country since I left at the age of five. I saw the paved roads with the painted yellow dashed lines coming out of the airport and then a bunch of cracked, pothole-ridden streets. I did not like it, but it was what it was.

This time we rented a house with actual furniture instead of boxes. We had a kitchen and a living room, and the house was in a nice location. After all, Dad worked in the US for six months and he had savings. By Salvadoran standards, we were rich.

You Need a Haircut

It was 1995 and I was in the fifth grade. My parents enrolled me in a good Catholic school from the neighborhood. It was a private school and most of the good private schools in El Salvador were Catholic. My aunt came to my house and saw I had long hair, so she decided to cut my hair. She used a razor on the bottom of my head, making a border the size of the razor from one ear, across my neck, all the way to the other ear. I was a kid and did not think much of it. My older brother, Pepe, being the bully he was, made fun of me for my newly acquired haircut. He told me he would shave my whole head. I said, "Yeah, I've seen Shaolin monks with shaved heads, that'd be cool."

I got a shaved head.

Next day on my way to school a couple of kids stared at me. For me, having a shaved head was a normal thing, but then more kids came and saw me and started laughing. I really could not understand why they were laughing. Then kids from other grades came to see this freak with a shaved head. It was a lot of teasing. I cried. I cried because I did not understand why people enjoyed making fun of something that wasn't that extraordinary.

Now, I understand that some humans enjoy causing pain upon others and that is a fact of life. From that moment on, I learned that to fit into this society I had to become a bully or be the one bullied. It's not a proud moment in my life. But survival was essential for me.

The next three weeks, my teacher let me use a cap while my hair grew back. I never let my aunt cut my hair again.

My Brother the Bully

Pepe—a typical older brother, smarter and stronger—is seven years older than me. Growing up, I worshiped him and wanted to be just like him, largely because he was more worldly and also because I saw others treating him like the coolest guy around. I emulated the way he spoke, dressed, and behaved, going where he went, talking the way he talked, and eating what he ate. My parents forced my brother to share everything with me—closet space, clothing, toys, you name it. Pepe didn't like that one bit; although he was still my hero, he now saw me as a burden.

One day, our shared room became "his room," and I was transformed into the unwanted mosquito, one that he couldn't get rid of, no matter how hard he swung. When I was fast asleep, he would come into the room and turn on all the lights, startling me awake each time. I tried one night to do the same to him, but he immediately took a swing at my shoulder, smacking me hard enough to send a clear message. When I went crying to my parents, Dad just dismissed my concerns. "What's a little punch here or there?" he said.

My parents began to treat me like a crybaby who complained about everything, but truthfully, I was just a nine-year-old, needy kid who frequently wanted his mommy to do things for him and who craved her attention. It probably didn't help matters that my parents saw my three older siblings acting similarly when they were my same age. By the time I came along, their "patience tank" was out of gas. Added to that, my parents both lived through a Central American civil war where atrocities were an everyday affair. At this point, their minds were likely occupied with bigger problems, such as how to put food on the table, survive, and remain safe. In an effort to make me feel better about being picked on, they would periodically scold my brother in front of me. This move, however, was mostly for show, and more often than not, they would simply pay no attention at all, painting what they were witnessing as some silly sibling rivalry that would improve when we aged and matured.

Sensing that it was useless to present my side of the story, I learned instead to respect my brother's commands. After all, I was nine and he was sixteen; I was completely overpowered, so I learned to accept that I had to walk on eggshells when Pepe was nearby. Catering to him in this way, though, instead of appeasing him, made him even meaner. Little by little, my brother changed from being my hero to becoming my sworn enemy. I fought back, silently planning it so that all my moves targeted him, snitching on him when he ate the cake my mom had saved for another day, when he missed his curfew, or when he broke our grandma's vase. I operated in the shadows, looking for opportunities to make my brother's life as difficult as he had made mine.

When I was playing video games, he would grab my controller and start playing as if I wasn't there, ignoring my demands to give it back. If I persisted, he would strike me in the chest, stunning me and ending the argument. Rarely did he hesitate to use my arms or face as a punching bag; bloody noses and bodily aches and pains began to appear regularly on and in my slight nine-year-old body. Pepe was crafty, however; he would only hit me hard enough to leave temporary bruises, most or all of which healed or disappeared before I could present them to my parents as testimony to his bullying. The divide between us grew.

Pepe's cruelty worsened; he would bait or hurt me outside the house, making me cry in front of my neighbors just to prove to them that he could do so. One of his schemes involved chanting "Cry, cry, cry" repeatedly when we would lose a basketball game to neighborhood friends. When I tried to walk away from this form of humiliation, he would follow me, continuing to harass me. Seeing that his chanting didn't produce the desired result, he would then pin me to the ground, arms behind me, and continue his taunt until his torture got the better of me and I would burst into tears. Walking away, trying to fight back, or taking my complaint to my parents had all failed to resolve the problem. My long-suffering Salvadoran mom and dad didn't take me seriously, and so the physical and psychological abuse persisted. I felt more scared, unprotected, and alone as time went on.

A Punch to the Ribs

I was about fourteen years old when my brother and I got into a big fight. He was twenty-one. I was a bit older and going into puberty, but still no match for an adult. This time it was a fight for the TV remote control. I was watching TV having a good time when he came in grabbing the remote from me just because he could. He changed the channel. I stood up for my right to watch TV in peace and grabbed the remote back from him. I negotiated with him to take turns. I told him, "Hey, I am watching, I'm in the middle of a show, if you want to watch, wait for the show to end and then it will be your turn." We had a little struggle for the remote and I pushed him and then he pushed me. I had gotten stronger and his little push did not do much. Then I grabbed his neck with my arm the way he did to me many times. My brother did not like my act of rebellion. He felt his authority challenged, so he took the biggest swing at my ribs without holding back. A full-capacity punch to my ribs that I did not believe he was capable of. I felt the most excruciating pain I have ever felt. I heard a crack. I felt the crack. The little skirmish I had with him was instantly over. It took me months to recover. To get out of bed I had to lift my leg, hold it, and then put it down in order to lift my body. The pain was too much. I was broken.

I told my parents that my ribs were broken and they thought I was exaggerating. My father actually believed me two months later when he perceived that I could not lift my backpack. He felt sorry for me that time. He did not take me to the doctor, though. That day he pulled my brother to the side. My dad's normal nonchalant scold was replaced by this rigid look. Dad began to believe that my brother was crossing the line with me. His eyes were different this time. He was mad.

"You have to protect your brother," was all I heard from my dad. For Dad that was enough for now. I was used to the bare minimum at this point. I learned to survive by staying quiet. Maybe if I was back in Florida, I would have had child services called on my parents because my teachers would be concerned. But Dad lacked the sophistication and knowledge to protect me.

An Elbow to the Upper Cheek

I was fifteen years old. I was playing Mario Brothers in the original Nintendo minding my own business when my brother entered the living room and took my controller away from me. He told me I had been playing enough and it was his turn. I told him: "But I'm about to beat the game, please give me a few minutes. I'll give it to you in just twenty minutes." Then he turned the Nintendo off without warning. All my game effort for that day went away. I told him, "Why do you do this, this is not just for you, we have to share, now I have to start from the beginning." I turned the Nintendo back on. He looked at me with rage and I stood up and glared at him in defiance. I was fifteen, so I could pretend to put on a fight with him. Next thing I felt was his elbow on my cheekbone. There was no warning. No skirmish. A full nuclear bomb without a battle. He threw at me everything he had, knocking me to the floor. His elbow hurt. I lay on the ground with the rage of not being able to fight him.

With every punch I cried out, "Why? Why do you keep doing this?"

He just looked at me with his eyes staring at me. Not caring that I was his only little brother. Not smiling, just a plain emotionless face.

Later, I told my parents about this and I had a big bruise on my cheek as evidence of the abuse. My parents couldn't deny it this time. Finally, they had no choice but to punish my brother. I wanted a real punishment. He was twenty-two and I was fifteen. My father wanted to kick my brother out of the house and told him they would stop paying for college. My father told me it was up to me when he could take the punishment away. My brother begged me to lift his punishment. This meant he would have to work to go to school. I didn't care. All I wanted was for that son of a bitch to get away from me. The years of abuse from him had finally caught up to him.

I looked down at my begging brother. "Fuck you. I couldn't care less about what happens to you. There will be no college for you. Your punishment is to be stupid for the rest of your life."

I meant that. That was a real curse I cast upon him which materialized later in life.

In the end, the punishment wasn't up to me. A few weeks later I learned that my father continued paying for his college and Pepe was living at home like nothing happened. The 90's Salvadoran criminal justice was alive in my own household. Nothing gets done and the criminal gets to keep doing what they want. I was outraged at my parents for not protecting me.

All I wanted was to escape his physical abuse. I longed to be older so I could beat up my brother. Just one time would be enough to gain my freedom. This wish came true. The big match against my brother was epic. I was sixteen years old. I almost killed him.

Mentalist

TO LEARN MORE ABOUT THE ARIZONA struggle I went to Bethlehem, Pennsylvania, where I met with Mentalist. He is a big-shot professor at Lehigh University in their psychology program. While talking with him next to Harry Potter–like dining halls and libraries that made me feel like I traveled two hundred years back in time, I could see he is a humble man. He is not cocky or presumptuous. He is down to earth. This man has published lots of academic papers and is a leader in psychology. I felt his peaceful presence. And with his kind eyes, he told me his story.

Mentalist was born in Venezuela and his family was middle-class under Venezuelan standards, meaning that they struggled, not as much as others but they did. It was 2002 and Hugo Chavez was getting radicalized. Mentalist was fifteen years old and his father had a tourist visa to come to the US. Mentalist's father overstayed his visa and sent money to the family back in Venezuela. Mentalist's father was apart from the family for two years. Mentalist, his mother, and his younger brother lived with Grandma.

The family got tired of being apart, so they took a twelve-hour bus ride from their city of Merida to Caracas in order to get a visa at the American embassy. They got the visa, but the country was in such political turmoil that there was a massive national strike of workers protesting against the government, and the very next day after Mentalist got his tourist visa, the American embassy closed

operations and stopped issuing visas. The Americans knew if they kept giving visas to the Venezuelans, everyone would flee that country for the US. Mentalist got lucky, and at the age of fifteen, he escaped Venezuela's messed-up government.

Mentalist thought he was just coming to the US for a couple of months to visit his father during the Christmas break. However, when the family saw the news about Venezuela, they thought that a civil war was about to start there, so they decided to stay together and try their luck in Arizona. They overstayed their visas.

Mentalist's father and mother worked hard at different jobs while he went to high school. He liked school and worked hard too. Mentalist did not have much, but he hit the books hard. At the age of seventeen he wanted to contribute to the family, so he got a job at Taco Bell. The best people work at Taco Bell.

Mentalist graduated high school and wanted to go to college, but he did not have a student visa. He tried getting into Arizona State University (ASU). They told him he could not enroll despite having the grades. The staff at ASU wanted to see Mentalist's passport, so Mentalist gave them his Venezuelan passport and told them straight up that he did not have papers. The staff incorrectly said, "Even if you pay out of pocket yourself, we can't take you." That wasn't true; they could take him if he paid full out-of-state price. However, Mentalist did not have that kind of money. Someone suggested he should apply for a student visa. That is not how it works, man. Had he done that as an undocumented student, his student visa application would have been denied and probably he would have been placed in deportation court. Mentalist did not give up and enrolled in community college. This was cheaper than ASU, but he still had to pay three times the in-state cost as an out-of-state resident.

To cover his expenses, Mentalist worked at a furniture store selling furniture. He got paid in cash. He worked long hours and went to school at the same time. He got home late to do homework. Some people would say that he had no life. Others would say that he had no life. Mentalist was done with his two-year community college and wanted to go to ASU despite the cost. The Arizona legislature kept pushing against immigrants and they said that no public services would go to undocumented people—those bastards. But Mentalist did not care, he was a soldier. He paid out-of-state tuition himself and took a couple classes a semester at ASU.

Mentalist's perseverance at ASU paid off and he found a scholarship called the American Dream Fund that paid for the rest of his education. Any other guy would have given up and not seen the purpose of schooling, but not Mentalist, no sir! He paid for the rest of college that way. This scholarship gave Mentalist a break and he stopped working so hard at the furniture store. He concentrated on school. He didn't know how long this scholarship was going to last, so he took six classes per semester to take advantage of the full ride. One semester he took seven classes. This dude was a workhorse.

Mentalist decided to go to a master's program after double majoring at ASU. He saved some money tutoring here and there, getting paid cash. He could not get a teaching assistant job because he had no papers. Instead, he got involved in activism around the immigrant community and saw Sage, a big-time undocumented student who did a fundraising campaign to go to Harvard and study for a master's degree in social work. I'll tell you about Sage later.

Mentalist did what Sage did: he organized a fundraising event. He was out there being vocal and public about his undocumented situation. He did a golf tournament so that rich folks would donate to his master's degree fund. He wasn't shy about this; he was out there promoting his cause and letting people know about his goals without shame. He said to anyone willing to listen: "Hey, I'm undocumented and I want to go to grad school. I'm working hard and I have no shame sharing my story." Shame will get you nowhere. He got some money and paid for his first semester of the master's program.

While in grad school he met a Jewish girl from New York who also worked in favor of the immigrant community. They met fighting against the infamous SB 1070 law, or the "police-can-check-your-papers-if-they-feel-like-it" law. This basically legalized racial profiling for police. Their fight gave Mentalist and this woman a purpose. This fight gave them time to struggle together. Day after day, they enjoyed their company and got closer and closer. They noticed each other and a smile turned into a flirt. They fell in love. Mentalist married her. Through marriage, Mentalist got his green card, and as a green card holder he got a student loan to finish his master's degree. Then he went on to study for his PhD in psychology. If you did not know this, PhD students get paid by the universities to do research. At that point Mentalist had a green card and could be hired by the university to do research work.

Mentalist went into activism because he felt like he had no other option. That is how most legendary leaders are created. In times of hardship, they take a stand. Mentalist took a stand and fought against Arizona's unjust laws that took scholarships away from immigrants just because they didn't have papers. Had life been easy for Mentalist he probably would be another boring guy working in the stock market, soulless and emotionless. Instead, Mentalist got so involved with immigrants' rights that he served as president of the activist organization to push for in-state tuition in Arizona for students who qualify for DACA. It wasn't until 2022 that Arizona finally agreed to grant in-state tuition for undocumented students.

Mentalist even showed his tax returns on national TV to combat the myth that undocumented immigrants don't pay taxes. Can you imagine if every US president would show their tax returns?

Now Mentalist is working on the psychology of undocumented students, and he is the leader in that field. He is a tenure-track professor at a top-50 university in the country. He is living the dream.

Mentalist gave me a tour of Lehigh University while sipping coffee. We walked through its small town, climbed the hill, and walked through its castle-like architecture, passing through other modern buildings. After that, I went home thinking about how other folks struggled so much but that struggle was part of their growth.

The next Fellow you'll learn about is Sage. She disagrees with the way I did things. She doesn't believe that hardship should exist. Sage challenged the whole premise of my book and she wasn't happy with my theory. I'll tell you about our big argument.

3

Growing Up

The biggest adventure you can take is to live
the life of your dreams.
—Oprah Winfrey

MY FATHER RAISED US AS VEGETARIANS. As a teenager he joined a philosophical fraternity called the Great Universal Fraternity, where they compiled all major philosophical beliefs, extracted the best teachings of the world's religions, and combined them into one big fraternity. It was almost like a cult, but its members were relaxed.

My dad found shelter in that fraternity because of his rough childhood. Let me talk to you about my dad. He began his life in poverty and worked his way up to become an accountant in a midsize corporation. His father was an alcoholic and a wife beater. Grandpa was a functional alcoholic and respected accountant during the day, but Mr. Hyde during the nights and weekends. He used to leave the family and be gone for days. Often, he passed out on the sidewalks crapping his pants. Those were the good old days when a man could drink himself away and sleep in the comfort and safety of the convenient sidewalk.

The fraternity provided guidance to my father, and one of their teachings was that you should be vegetarian, so Dad forced us into it. This belief had to do with not intoxicating our bodies and not making other living beings suffer.

When I would go to my friends' homes, everyone looked at me like I was crazy when I told them I was vegetarian. It was El Salvador in the 1990s, these ideas were radical. I didn't mind at first, but later on I was annoyed that I couldn't eat a burger like most of my friends.

The good that came out of my father's philosophical practices is that he gifted me the ability to think for myself despite living in what I considered a closed-minded society. We would have discussions about science, morality, and social issues. Once my father wanted to ground me because I wasn't doing well in school. He wanted me to quit the basketball team where I used to train every night after school. That night I told him that instead of quitting something, I should be doing something. Dad ended up cutting a deal with me. I would wash his van for four weekends as a productive member of the family and I would have the right to continue with my basketball after-school activities. Dad got a clean car and I kept playing basketball. I learned the power of a win-win situation.

Basketball was a good outlet for me. I practiced and practiced. I made the school team and then I practiced more. It became my safe haven. I hated going home. Listening to my parents' screaming matches because they were stressed from the four mouths they had to feed and dealing with my intolerable brother, wasn't exactly the best environment to live in. School was walking distance from my house, which made it easier to stay out late. But even then, I would choose the longer route home.

My dad had bought a bigger, nicer house in a new development. It was in a gated community with a series of townhouses that looked alike and had the same salmon color exterior. As a member of the auditing team for USAID (U.S. Agency for International Development) he had a better salary. He likes to tell me that the US government felt sorry for what they did to him back in Florida during his deportation proceedings, so they offered him an accounting job. I never believed that. Truth was that he was one of the few Salvadorans who could speak enough English back in the day. As a child, Dad had spent a couple of years in Los Angeles, where he learned some English. He turned that into a job.

Unfortunately for me, most of my dad's money went to pay for the mortgage and that meant he didn't have much money for food or clothing for his children. I was always the kid in class who didn't have any money on him to buy a drink or snack. My friends teased me, saying I lived in a nice house, but I was broke. I saw their point and I questioned the financial decisions my dad made throughout his life. I felt uncomfortable not having a few coins to spend like my peers did. How could an accountant not manage his money? I grew up in a "nice" house, but I walked home with holes in my shoes. I guess I was a bit angry. Or maybe I was spoiled.

Smart Mouthing

Due to the deficiency in my protein intake growing up, I was short. I wanted to be the tall kid in class like many of my classmates. But I was stuck in my five-foot-three range. Around the seventh grade, I started to get teased by the taller guys in class for being short. I would get called the midget, Polly Pocket, little shit. I started to get an attitude because of it. Eventually, I fired back at these names on this one tall guy in my class who had a bunch of pimples on his nose. One day in class, he walked over to my desk. He smirked down at me and with all his guts he called me "Midget."

I glared up at him and felt my face get red. I couldn't be silent anymore. "Stop fucking cheap whores with your nose. That's how you got herpes on your face."

The class went quiet for a single second before it erupted with laughter. I nicknamed him "Pimple." Pimple went red in the face and returned to his seat after that. He became the joke of the class. He was nice enough to not beat me up—thank God for the Catholic school I was in and to the peace values it taught. I found a new profession in entertainment.

By the eighth grade, my jokes became more sophisticated and made me likable with my classmates. One day in class, I made my way over to Pimple. He was sitting at his desk when he noticed me strolling over. I could tell he did not want me nearby. His dotted nose scrunched up with disgust. I smiled at Pimple, looking down. "Hey there, I was reading up and I saw Oxy was really good for treating acne."

Pimple stared at me with confusion. His face was asking me if this was really about to be a normal conversation. My smile quickly turned to a smirk, "But be careful, don't drop it on your dick, otherwise it's going to disappear."

Pimple's face immediately fell. Everyone started laughing. I'd succeeded in another act for my classmates. I was good at making jokes at someone's expense. As long as it wasn't mine. It gave me a high to see others laugh because of me. I felt liked by others. I felt safe.

I started to become a product of my environment. It was 1999 and I was in the ninth grade, attending a religious school in a conservative country. In El Salvador, I started school at 12:30 p.m. and left at 6:45 p.m., when it was dark. Exiting school in an all-male environment late at night was a clusterfuck. You pushed and shoved whoever was in front of you. It was like being in prison. We all wore the same uniforms and had a schedule to get to class, go to recess, and get out. Repeat the next day.

Back in the day, being gay was not acceptable in Salvadoran society. Some kids were overtly fabulous. There were three kids in my class who leaned more toward the feminine side of the spectrum. A big no-no in an extremely chauvinistic environment. A man does not cry or express emotion. He is firm, stands tall, and is strong physically and mentally. No complaining or talking about feelings.

These gay kids suffered the most every night we exited our classes. They got called all sorts of names from the crowd. I was one of the kids who would call them names. I knew it was wrong but I was part of the crowd. It takes extreme willpower to break away from bad habits and environments. Just five years before, I was the boy crying because they made fun of my bald head. Now I was the bully on the other side. I was part of the boys.

I remember one night, a guy from my class went up to one of the three boys and told him, "I think faggots should die."

One of the fabulous kids just stared and smiled. All he said was, "Then go kill yourself."

Everyone heard that and laughed at the kid. I thought it was a good comeback.

This was a constant occurrence every night after school. From time to time a guy would scream, "Here come the faggots," and the crowd would start screaming, "Queers, dick suckers, *culeros*." It's easy to be mean when it means you're safe.

To the three guys I helped bully in high school, I hope you forgive me. I hope you are well. It wasn't easy for you. I hope you moved past those barriers. I'm glad I no longer have that groupthink mentality.

After I finished the ninth grade, I got an award for "good behavior." All my friends were in complete disbelief. They gazed at me as I walked up to the front of the class to receive my certificate. After class, one of my friends came up to me. "What the hell? Who did you pay to get this? You are a complete motherfucker in class and you get this award?"

My secret to getting this award was simple. In front of my main teacher, I would do absolutely nothing inappropriate. I knew he was the one in charge of grading people and their behavior. The main teacher did not consult with other teachers as to how kids behaved. I was a complete angel to him. No jokes, no teasing, no fuck-ups. I stayed harmless for forty-five minutes a day, then I became an animal in front of the next teacher. I looked at my friend with a smirk. "Don't hate the player, hate the game."

The Girl I Liked

In ninth grade I was a complete rascal. I belonged to a church youth group, which was the only way to socialize with the opposite sex. I made girls laugh and they liked it. I really liked this one girl with whom

I talked a lot. Her name was Claudia. We always looked forward to seeing each other over the weekend. I was by no means trained in the art of flirting. I never told her exactly how I felt. Besides, I didn't work, so I had no money for dates. It's not like my parents wanted to or could fund my love life.

Three days before the school dance, Claudia called my house asking for me. My mom handed me the phone and I could instantly hear Claudia's sweet voice. "Are you going to take me to the dance?"

How cruel is it to picture yourself with your dream girl at a school dance and not be able to take her? I could see us dancing in slow motion to our favorite song. She would look up at me with her honey doe eyes and I would lean down for our first kiss. But that wasn't going to happen.

"I don't know if I would even go to the dance. I don't have money for the tickets."

"Oh…" was all I could hear her mutter. "What if I paid for half my ticket?"

"No, I don't have the money."

That was the last thing I could bring myself to say before she hung up on me. *I mean, she didn't say she would pay for her entire ticket.* No money, no honey. I could have worked in a grocery store or something but again, it was El Salvador, and there are not many jobs, and the few jobs that exist do not pay much, so I just stayed at home. The girl I liked had just asked me out, and I turned her down for lack of money. Life sucked.

Home Alone

My mom and dad took my two sisters on a trip to Florida. They left my brother and me behind. They decided that the trip would be more affordable if they left the boys at home. They had worked hard for many years, and Dad wanted to take a good vacation cruising through the Bahamas. My brother liked the authority; he was now in charge.

I had to accept the reality. If I stayed away from home most of the time, things would be okay.

I began telling my friends that I had the house to myself and we could have a party there. Word spread like wildfire. Suddenly my popularity increased. I told the guys to bring beer, liquor, and girls. They only brought beer and liquor.

My brother was on board with the party. He didn't like the idea of having strangers at the house, but he liked drinking for free. Twenty guys came, and we were loud. The booze was flowing and the music was high. My friends were walking around shirtless to get the smell of cigarettes off their clothes. The ashes dropped all over the floor. My brother would tell them, "Do as you want, drop the ashes, my little brother will clean up after." My friends assured me they would be back the following morning to help clean up.

Everyone was out of their minds drunk.

I stumbled out to the garden area and yelled at the guys, "Listen up, motherfuckers, you guys are getting out of control. If you have to throw up, do it here at the drain and do not go in the bathroom."

As soon as I finished saying that, I felt the gas from the beer in my throat. So, I took my own advice. All my friends laughed at my hunched figure over the drain. I had to do something to gain face. "And that's how you do it. So, remember, go to the drain, not the bathroom."

The next day I was hungover. There I was in the middle of a disaster zone. Ashes littered all over the floor, beer bottles and an entire pizza right there on the floor. Nobody showed up to help me clean.

Little by little I cleaned. I swept, then swept again. I mopped underneath the couch. I did a professional job. My brother came to inspect and move the furniture around and found the place spotless. He told me I did a good job and made fun of me. I felt cool. Other party invitations came my way and I felt I was part of the cool kids.

Meteor Shower

I first tried beer when I was about thirteen years old. My father was a teetotaler—he would not approve of anyone in my family drinking, probably because he saw my grandpa's alcoholism. At the age of thirteen someone gave me a can of beer at a party. I didn't like it. I also didn't want to be a wuss, so I did my best and I finished it. My classmates were impressed, so they had to drink up. Here and there I started to drink but I couldn't do it blatantly. By the time I was fifteen years old I was a short guy with a babyface. Not even Salvadoran stores would sell beer to me.

The night of my ninth-grade graduation, there was supposed to be a meteor shower. I wanted to see it, and I asked the big boys of the neighborhood to bring some alcohol, as I wanted to celebrate a job well done in school. I told my dad I was staying out late to watch the meteor shower. The older friends brought me the cheapest vodka they could find with the little money I gave them. The drink of the night was vodka and Sprite. At 10:00 p.m., in the dark waiting for the meteors to rain down, I was chugging the alcohol. Soon enough the effects of the alcohol started to make their way. The big kids ran out of beer and left to get more. I had vodka and Sprite. To be specific I had a whole 750 ml bottle of vodka, which I poured into a half-empty two-liter bottle of Sprite. What made this dangerous was that it tasted mostly like Sprite with a little kick of vodka.

Halfway down the bottle, I don't even remember seeing the meteors. Did I watch them? I couldn't tell you. It was about 2:00 a.m., and I was a complete waste. I threw up the black beans I'd had for dinner that night. Then I threw up again on an empty stomach. My friends managed to walk me back to the sofa in my house and left me there. I somehow made my way to the guest bathroom downstairs. I started throwing up my life into the toilet. Boy, was I loud. I remember hearing my dad's footsteps marching down the stairs and swinging the door open. "Lito, are you drunk?"

I responded with a slow, "Yeeeaah."

He walked out of the bathroom and came back soon after with a glass of tomato juice in his hand. He placed it on the floor next to the toilet seat. "You should drink this. We'll talk tomorrow when you're sober."

I started to throw up again, and all I could hear was a long sigh coming from his mouth. He looked up at the ceiling for a pensive moment and then walked out. I stayed barfing the Sprite.

The following morning, I was embarrassed. I was traumatized by vodka and Sprite. It took me ten years to be able to taste vodka again. Just the thought of vodka made me sick for many years. The alcohol you throw up always haunts you after.

My dad was heartbroken. He told me he took care of my grand-father shortly before he died. He said to me that Grandpa used to shit his pants and my dad would clean up after him like a baby. My grandfather would stink of alcohol in the morning. The smell would come from the pores of his skin. And there I was, his son, looking in a similar fucked-up way.

My dad wanted to sue the adults who provided liquor to a minor. I didn't like the idea at the time. I was embarrassed enough. In retro-spect, me being who I am, I definitely think a lawsuit would have been fun. After all, those guys were twenty-one-year-old adults providing a fifteen-year-old hard liquor. But he decided not to spend his time, effort, and little money on a lawsuit. I think the lack of money was a predominant factor in his decision-making process. But also, it was El Salvador, so what can you really expect from a lawsuit like this.

Due to my good performance and good behavior in the ninth grade, my parents had a surprise waiting for me. They wanted to reward me with a trip to the US to visit my aunts and uncles in the Washington, DC area. But then, I got drunk. My dad told me about the surprise he'd planned for me, but then he said he was taking it away as punishment. I negotiated with him—after all, he had already paid for the air tickets. I even suggested that he could save a lot of money by having me paint the entire house, so that lured him a little. But he came up with a greater punishment. He told me that I had to write my autobiography for him. He wanted me to not hold back, that I must share with him all my life and secrets. I was fifteen—how much did I have to hold back?

For the next month and a half, I was painting the house and doing research for my autobiography. I prepped the paint and brushes, and the other mothers in the neighborhood were telling my mom that she was so lucky to have such a hardworking kid. Here I was playing Tom Sawyer with the house but had no help from other kids. At night I was reading a file my mom kept where she had important family documents and pictures. I wrote and did my research. I pretty much told Dad everything I could in the twenty-five-page paper I wrote for him. Sure, I omitted the house party my brother and I had, but other than that I really think I did a good job for a fifteen-year-old. After six weeks of work, I handed my dad the fruits of my labor. The following night, I saw my dad and mom reading those pages in bed. My mom had tears in her eyes. I did my job as a writer—I captivated my audience.

Dad read my work and told me, "You have good writing skills." He was proud. I was proud. I worked hard on it. So off I went to the US for the second time in my life.

Life was getting better. Until my dad made a big gamble.

4

Earthquake

DECEMBER 1999, EVERYONE WAS TALKING ABOUT Y2K. How computers were going to crash because they were only programmed to have two digits to measure the years instead of four. That was going to be the end of the world. The nuclear warheads were going to take off and wipe us all out.

That was the backdrop when I visited the US for the second time, along with my brother. Dad felt bad the boys did not have a trip, so he sent us away for a month to go back and forth from Virginia to Maryland visiting relatives. After a few days, a couple of cousins, Pepe, and I drove to Vermont to pick up a third cousin at Middlebury College. Middlebury blew me away. Big dining halls, big computer centers. This was the first time I experienced a big university.

After Vermont my entire family from Maryland took us on a road trip to Chicago, and I experienced the freezing cold of the Windy City. We visited the Sears Tower and contemplated the beautiful view of the city from the top. Little did I know that thirteen years later I would be back in the same tower working.

After the thirty-day trip, I returned to El Salvador with an extra twenty pounds of pure joy.

Check Your Foundation

It was January 13, 2001. A whole year had passed and the Y2K computers hadn't blown up the world. It was during my end-of-year break, as school normally starts at the end of January in El Salvador. I was playing a computer game called Worms. I was throwing bombs killing the other team when the computer screen started shaking. I was killing it in the video and I got even more excited to see that my computer was shaking side to side and up and down. Then I felt the ground shaking—I just deployed my nuclear bombs; I was in the zone—then the walls shook hard. I snapped out of my game and saw the house shaking. I stood up quickly. The computer trembled like it was about to explode. I didn't want the computer to fall to the floor. I had to make a decision quickly, save the computer monitor or get the hell out of there. I freaking got out of there.

It was a 7.6 magnitude earthquake. The entire country was in a state of emergency. A whole neighborhood just two miles from my house got buried in mud from a hill that collapsed. The engineers built townhouses in a dangerous area without checking the foundation. Death came fast to 1,259 people that night. The subsequent tremors did not let me sleep the following nights. People were sleeping in their cars and tents outside. The next day I experienced sleep deprivation. I did not give a damn anymore. I went to my bed upstairs and every time there was a tremor, I just took it like they were rocking my bed to help me fall asleep. It was safer on the second floor than on the first floor. I could survive a fall downward, but I could not survive concrete falling on top of me.

Firetrucks, rescue squads, police, the military, and the neighbors all mobilized to help. Many lost their homes. Shelter tents were set up to give homeless people a place to sleep. Overnight, there were 1.6 million homeless victims; that was 25% of the Salvadoran population. They postponed the beginning of the school year, so during my extra free time I volunteered to help rebuild remote places. I was sixteen and I saw pain in others. I felt it necessary to help in whatever way I could. I could transport bricks from one place to another, so I did. Eight months after the earthquake, the country was still in dire condition. I started to see that there was nothing much for my future there in my country.

Sage

I TRAVELED TO LOS ANGELES FOR the first time while doing research for this book. I was excited—it was the land of Hollywood and movie stars. What better place than this to get inspiration and keep writing. The reality is that if you walk a few blocks, you will see a high concentration of homeless people, and the streets are dirty. I walked around a market and it made me feel like I was in the Central Market of El Salvador. People shouting and doing business the old-fashioned way. I met Sage in a local joint that is a safe haven for the immigrant community. A restaurant with a social purpose. A place that characterized Sage. Sage told me her story.

Sage was born in Chihuahua, Mexico. Her father came from a wealthy family that owned a lot of businesses there. The businesses were distilleries, breweries, and bars. Anything that had to do with alcohol. Sage's parents got married when her mom was twenty-three and her dad was twenty-five. Dad was the Rich Kid in town and mom was one of the few girls who got an education. They fell in love and Dad wanted to snatch up his Pretty Wife before anyone beat him to that. Sage describes how being around alcohol all the time turned this Rich Kid into an alcoholic and that meant trouble for the young couple. Rich Kid beat Pretty Wife early in the marriage. Pretty Wife had enough of these beatings and wanted to escape to the US. Pretty Wife took three-year-old Sage and moved to Arizona using her US tourist visa. Rich Kid turned into Drunk Husband and swore to Pretty Wife that he would change. Pretty Wife took him back to live with

them in the US. Drunk Husband being Drunk Husband did not stop drinking. Drunk Husband would pass out in different places, neglect the family, and forced them into poverty.

The wealthy family they once had in Mexico was no longer there for them. They cut ties. It is my hunch that the wealthy family did not see much future with the kid who turned into a drunk, so they got rid of his shares in the company and expelled him from the business. Nevertheless, Pretty Wife was such an obsession to Drunk Husband. Drunk Husband's life wasn't that pretty; his drinking gave him bad complications and he died from alcoholism a few years after Sage graduated from grad school. But before he died, he gave the family some hell. Pretty Wife got pregnant twice more in Arizona and gave birth to two more kids. Her life wasn't pretty anymore. Pretty Wife turned into Struggling Wife with three kids, a Drunk Husband, and no support system. Nevertheless, she stayed in the US thinking the future for her kids would be much better. That's how bad things were for this woman. She would rather give the kids a shot at the American Dream than go back to Mexico. The entire family overstayed their visas.

Sage wanted to seek shelter from her dysfunctional family. She found shelter in books, like so many Fellows do. When it was time to apply to college, she only applied to Arizona State University because she did not think she could go to college, since she did not have papers. But ASU accepted her for a BA in political science and even gave her a scholarship. Then the stuck-ups from the Arizona legislature passed Prop 300 forbidding scholarships to undocumented students because they were considered out of state. These clowns thought they were saving the world by forbidding people from studying. Sage had no papers and no money, but she organized with other students who also lost their scholarships and convinced the president of ASU to help them fund their education. Then, the president got in trouble for helping these bright students. The student organization continued and found a way to fund the scholarships through private donors.

Sage worked in restaurants, coffee shops, and random jobs through-out college earning money under the table. She did what she had to in order to make ends meet. She could no longer live with her father's abuse. She couch-surfed from friend to friend all over Tempe. She could not see past one year of her life. She was in full survival mode. She went to sleep in rough parts of town, but she tells me that she was not unsafe. She felt protected by her community. She was the golden girl, the pride and a symbol. A symbol that even if you are undocumented, you are able to reach educational success.

Sage graduated from ASU and applied to Harvard School of Education for her master's degree. She got in. However, she did not have funding to attend. You may have heard that Harvard has a big endowment to teach for free any students who cannot afford to pay for it. They may have a bigger endowment for the school of law and school of medicine, but it is not that big for the school of education, so Sage had to come up with her own tuition money. Sage did not have papers or money, but she was smart and a hustler. She did a fundraiser for herself. She asked for help from the people who raised her, her own community. She got $5 from the taco truck lady, $10 from the neighbor. Sage even did a five-minute documentary about her life, and more donations came her way. Everyone rallied around Sage and wanted to send an openly undocumented student to Harvard.

With living expenses, the price tag for Harvard was around $80,000 for a one-year master's degree. Harvard did give Sage $10,000. She got another $15,000 from the Mexican government through a program to send people to great schools with the condition of returning to Mexico and working for a couple years; otherwise, the scholarship recipient would have to pay back the $15,000. Sage treated the Mexican money like a student loan, since she never intended to go back to Mexico.

Sage got national exposure on Spanish-language TV by going to Don Francisco, the most popular talk-show celebrity on Univision at that time.

The following is a great story, so pay attention. Picture this. Drunk Husband is so proud that his daughter will be on Don Francisco's show. Before the TV show airs, Sage's father tells every one of their friends about it, so they organize a watch party at his house with a bunch of people. Next, Sage shows up on TV, and Don Francisco starts talking about her father being an alcoholic, how he left the family, all the domestic violence—*I can imagine the stares at the watch party.* The Dad is pissed because he looks bad on national TV. However, it is all true. Had he not beat up the family, Sage would not be telling this truth on TV. (Here's the interview www.survivingthelaw.com/videos).

Sage says to Don Francisco: "It is difficult, you can't vote, in Arizona you can't drive anywhere because there is a sheriff hunting you down, looking for us, looking at what we are doing, and how we look. We can't travel and we can't do things that many people take for granted. Also, we can't study and we want to study. People are afraid of the police because when they see the police, they don't feel safe, they feel in danger. There are raids and some small kids stay by themselves at home."

After that show, her popularity skyrocketed. Every taco stand knew her and they were willing to chip in a few dollars here and there. Churches chipped in; art galleries responded. Department stores raised money for her. The TV exposure gave Sage donations from Florida, Texas, even Germany.

Not everyone was so generous. Music artists came to Arizona to cheer the Latino population in the middle of being attacked by the legislature in 2011, but none of them donated anything to Sage. They just said, "Keep going, you should get a scholarship."

Sage raised around $50,000 to cover her expenses to move to Boston, but she could not cover 100% of the tuition. Harvard did not release her degree until she completed paying for her tuition. It took her some years to pay all she owed.

Sage had a Harvard education and she got married to a US citizen. She got her green card through this marriage. Sage was accepted into UCLA to study for a PhD in Chicano studies. Sage asked me to keep the details about her marriage off the record, so I will honor that.

While talking to Sage in LA, she was going through the divorce process. I saw she had on an engagement ring. I said, "I see you found a new guy."

She said, "Not really."

"Are you still attached to the ring from your current marriage?" I asked with skepticism.

"It is from my current partner; *she* gave it to me." I felt like a fool.

Sage talked to me about sexuality and that she is attracted to minds not bodies. She told me that she met this new woman with whom she enjoys talking and has so much in common. I was fascinated by her love story. In today's world love is love and it is cool that you can love whoever you want. I find it fascinating maybe because I did not grow up exposed to different sexual orientations living free in a community.

Even though Sage got her green card around 2011, she did not become a US citizen until after Trump got elected. She could have become a citizen three years after she got her green card, but she had conflicting ideas of what citizenship meant and whether a US citizenship really defined her. However, seeing the threat of Trump toward immigrants, she decided to be part of the American citizenry.

We were getting comfortable talking in the middle of breakfast and the following conversation happened—I'm paraphrasing a lot here:

Sage: "I am uncomfortable with your project. I think you are encouraging the cliché of advocating for the good immigrants that work hard and go to school and become successful. You are perpetuating the narrative of good immigrant versus bad immigrant. It takes a village to raise a person like a Fellow, and hardworking parents also deserve the same credit as the students who make it. It is as if you don't care about the efforts of the parents and you belittle them."

I told Sage: "Talking to you in our Zoom and phone conversations, I perceived you were against my efforts. Why would you agree to meet me and tell me all your deep secrets?"

Sage: "I was intrigued about your story and I wanted to learn about you too, but it is my task to persuade you to put humanity in your efforts."

I said: "I agree with you and I understand that nobody does the miracle of going to graduate school while undocumented alone. It takes mentors, friends, family, etc. And they all deserve credit. I understand that behind a success story there is an army of people who supported the effort of this one miracle Fellow. But it is my duty to show the tip of the iceberg as a symbol to inspire others. In this immigration struggle, we can tackle this problem through different fronts. Some people can focus on humanism, and others can focus on the merits. In the end, we have different tactics but the goal is to provide a shot at the American Dream to anyone who wants it."

I understood where she was coming from and she also got to know me. She was successful; I am now honoring the 90% of the iceberg that is beneath water. To those who helped in any way, with money, a meal, a Friday-night beer, I thank you.

Sage does not think that people should be forced to go through pain in order to be successful. I am advocating to train hard and surpass adversity. I am advocating to not give up and to keep fighting. You will get tougher. However, Sage says that anyone can train willingly, you should not be forced to train extra hard if you don't want to. I disagree; it is more effective to have an external factor forcing you to toughen up. It is easier to make a soldier with a drill sergeant during wartime instead of training on your own during peace. It is more effective to get in shape with a personal trainer if your life depends on it than to train on your own for fun. Sage's position is that it has to be a choice to become a soldier and a choice to have a drill sergeant. My position is that in wartime people have little choice and that she and I were drafted to become soldiers.

I asked Sage, "If you had magic and could make a wish, would you go back in time and erase it all in order to live a normal life?"

She said "Yes!" without hesitation. That was surprising to me, I could not believe that someone would choose to erase her existence. She said, "I wish I could have had a normal life; I wish I could have a mediocre life." I could not believe her answer, maybe her pain was too strong. Sage recognizes that she is still in the healing process. Now she is a US citizen, found love again, and has a great job she enjoys. But I could not believe that a powerful Fellow would choose mediocrity. I understand it but I do not accept it.

I had to give closure to the Arizona crowd. I left Sage and went to Arizona to meet Hardy where he is fighting the fight. I had to see what was in Arizona that made such resilient immigrants. I had to see the hard conditions there. What I saw pissed me off!

5

Dad's Gamble

Only those willing to truly risk everything
will gain everything. No person ever rose to
greatness without the willingness to lose it all.
—Dan Pearce

Only by losing everything
can you fear nothing.
—Ken Poirot

MY DAD'S JOB AT THE AMERICAN embassy as an accounting auditor was not secure. It all depended on the help that the US government sent to El Salvador. There were always negotiations that the US was going to stop the aid to El Salvador to influence policy. To this date, the United States continues to threaten to take away aid. I think the US always sends money to people one way or another. But the uncertainty was hard on my dad. He wanted to have his own accounting firm. My dad never went to college, so he couldn't sign financial documents, but he knew the business. He spent ten years auditing accounting transactions for the US government, traveling to many countries in Latin America auditing foreign governments.

Dad decided to associate with other accountants and buy an accounting franchise. Just like people buy a McDonald's franchise to sell burgers because people know what McDonald's is, Dad wanted to buy the accounting franchise to get credibility with other businesses willing to hire his accounting firm. One thing about the Salvadoran mindset is that if it comes from the US, it must be a good thing. So, Dad played with the Salvadoran marketing and traveled to Europe and the US to go to accounting conferences. He quit his nice-paying job. He stopped being a salaryman. I was fifteen and scared, of course—he was my stability. But it was my dad's dream, so he went for it.

It didn't take long before my dad's dream turned into a nightmare. The tension started to build up in the family. My dad would come home late at night and he would "forget" to pick me up from school. I would stay late after basketball practice waiting for him. Sometimes refusing rides from friends, I would often say to them, "Don't worry, my dad told me he was coming."

I got used to having Dad not show up. Instead of relying on him, I got in the habit of asking friends for rides home. Eventually, some friends told me they could not keep giving me rides all the time. Without a ride I had to walk in the middle of the night through some scary streets by myself. Go to El Salvador and walk at night by yourself and you tell me how you feel.

It turned out my dad enjoyed spending time "working late." In fact, he was working with a few women. Just a couple years ago Dad came to me while I was doing research for this book and revealed something he never told anyone: I have two half-siblings. You know, he lived his life and probably picked up a few tricks from Grandpa. I was proud that he never drank alcohol in front of us and told us that he was a teetotaler, but years later I found out that he was just hiding his drinking.

My mom was bound to find out about my dad's affairs. One time, in the middle of the night, she burst into my room waking all my siblings up. Her eyes were red and she had tearstains on her cheeks. "We're having a family meeting. Come to our room!"

I was sixteen years old. Throughout my life I had heard the bluff of my parents getting a divorce. I'd heard it since I was nine. I used to cry about my parents getting a divorce. At nine years old, the last thing you want is for your parents to separate. About four times each year, like a routine, my dad would ask my mother for a divorce in front of me. The repetition of my dad's divorce speech began to hurt less and less, year after year. Between the nights of walking home by myself, the lack of punishment for my brother hitting me, and now another stupid divorce bluff... I was tired.

The family gathered in my parents' bedroom. Mari, the eldest, was standing next to the door looking pissed for not being asleep. Pepa, sitting on one side of the bed, showed concern, her face telling me she cared about the family stability. Pepe sat on the floor just to be there because he had to, his indifference showing. And I was sitting on the other side of the bed looking at everyone. Dad was in one corner with a puppy dog face with Mom in the other corner crying.

My mom was staring at my dad now. Her eyes were cold. "Tell them why you're leaving. Go ahead and have some respect for your family."

Dad couldn't make eye contact with anyone. "I'm not happy... I found comfort in someone else. I'm sorry."

I felt the tension in the room. The family was together in one room but all of us were so distant. Pepe said aloud: "If you separate, I'll go with my dad." He probably did not quite understand that Dad wanted to live his life without us. Pepa started crying and said, "Who is this woman? I will kill her!" I felt for Pepa's willingness to save the family unit. She was always the one pulling the family together. But at that point I felt that we all were grownups and it was time to disperse. I said to my dad, "That is cool, man, all I care is that you keep paying for my school. Are you going to keep paying? You can do what you want." I am not sure if I was too sleepy and wanted to end the meeting or if I genuinely did not care anymore. Dad didn't say anything. I said, "Is that all you guys want to tell us? That my dad is banging another girl and you guys are splitting? Let me go to bed now. If you have relevant information concerning me let me know tomorrow." So, I walked away back to bed. I was proud of the balls I had telling my superiors how fucked up they were.

At some point I decided I'd had enough of them. I sure wanted the family to stay together. I wanted all of us to support each other in our endeavors. I was the youngest one. I looked up to my siblings like heroes who could help me when I needed help. They were older and more knowledgeable. Dad was strong and Mom was a loving figure. But I was sixteen now and my signs of independence started to show.

A couple days later Dad and Mom worked things out. Dad asked for forgiveness and Mom forgave. Again.

Screams at Night

One night all my siblings and I were watching TV in the living room next to my parents' bedroom. Mom was screaming, "STOP. NO. NO. I'm going to scream for everyone to hear!"

I could hear wrestling. During their verbal altercations my siblings and I knew not to get involved. That was between Dad and Mom. But this was something else. I looked at my older siblings with a look of help-me-out-here-what-should-I-do? They stared back at me with the same look. I looked again and told them, "Seriously, you guys are older than me, what the fuck?"

The yelling and screaming continued. She was suffering. I wanted to stop the screaming and stop the fight. I wanted to do something. Something, anything. But I could not come up with anything. I felt powerless and useless.

After a few minutes, Mari had had enough. She got up from the couch and made her way to our parents' door. She knocked loudly and yelled, "Mom, stop screaming like you are a crazy person!"

That was rude but maybe it was a way to let Dad know we were listening. At least she did something. The yelling and screaming continued for five more minutes and then it stopped. None of us did anything. I still recriminate myself every now and then, *"Why didn't I do something?"*

I went to see my mother the following morning. She was crying, in a fetal position curled up in her bed. Without looking at me she uttered to me, "You don't know what I go through for your well-being."

That hurt my heart. Seeing my mom curled up in bed crying. It's a sight no mother wants their child to witness. "Mom, can I do anything?"

"Just leave me alone."

From that moment on, my mom would not sleep in that bedroom again. She went to sleep in the small room next to the kitchen. I saw my mom sleeping on the floor with a couple of blankets.

I blocked this from my mind for many years. My siblings also blocked this episode. I asked them if they remember this, and one told me that they vaguely recall something like this. I accumulated resentment toward Dad. Resentment that built over time, which I would charge him later with interest.

■

My dad continued working on his business. His savings were dropping. He no longer had an income. He had read books on how to make it in business. He'd heard stories of persistent people who had nothing but perseverance and they made it. But the money was stretching more and more. The food on the table was reduced to the basics. Tortilla, rice, beans, and eggs. We went back to survival mode. Dad sold his van, and he was taking the bus to go places. He did his last samurai strike.

Dad went to the US to have one final meeting with some accounting people. While he was visiting my uncle in Maryland, he felt the need to thank him for lodging him and he grabbed the lawnmower to cut the grass in the back yard. The yard was hilly. My dad miscalculated the full force of the mower and went straight to the hill. He lost his balance. The blades of the lawnmower collided with his left foot. He felt a sting and fell. Right after, he tried to stand up but could not regain his balance. A piece of flesh and bone was on the lawn. It was his entire big toe lying raw on the ground bleeding. The paramedics came and took him to the hospital to perform emergency surgery.

Dad got out of the hospital with a medical bill in his pocket. His savings were gone. He had stopped working on the accounting franchise a few weeks before. He went to visit my family in Virginia to not be a full-time burden to the family in Maryland.

In Virginia, while recovering from his accident, he decided to play "hunting squirrels" with my thirteen-year-old cousin. The purpose of the game was to grab a BB gun and see who could kill the most squirrels. A neighbor saw that and called the cops. The cops gave him tickets as the adult in the house for animal cruelty. He had to appear in court before a judge. The judge ended up dismissing the case, but it took time from my father as he waited for his court date.

There was my dad with a mortgage, a family, hospital bills, debt, a failed business, and now legal troubles. It would make anyone crazy, and my dad was no exception. This chain of unfortunate events took a toll on his mental health. Now what was he going to do? Go back to El Salvador and start from scratch, sell the house and hope that there was money left to survive? Or stay in the US, work, send money home for his children, and pay the mortgage. It was a business decision. It was a survival decision. He stayed in the US and worked in whatever he could.

The suffering would not stop for my mother. Dad sent for her to join him. Mom, knowing what she was facing, went. Now let me tell you about how I almost killed my brother.

6

Four Siblings Coexisting

*An eye for an eye will only make the whole
world blind.*
—Mahatma Gandhi

*Sometimes you have to pick the gun up to put
the Gun down.*
—Malcom X

MOM LEFT FOR THE UNITED STATES to find work to save our house
from foreclosure. She worked hard in the States and sent money
to us. She left my siblings and me living on our own. She knew she
would be able to provide more for us if she went to the US. I was
still the youngest. I was sixteen, while my siblings were fully grown
adults. At that time, Pepa was twenty, Pepe was twenty-two, and
Mari twenty-three. Mom didn't care how old we were, in her eyes
we are always her babies. My siblings were in college and they didn't
work. The reality in El Salvador is "Either you work or you study,
you can't do both." Because of that, Mom went to fight for her kids.

Home alone with no parents meant I was sixteen with full control
over my decisions. Mom felt uneasy leaving us behind. Her four kids
who she had been with since birth. Meanwhile, I felt cool about it.
I thought it was temporary. She'll work for a bit in the States and
she'll send money over. My parents had always figured something out.

After Mom left, I avoided being at home as much as I could. I either went to school or would hang out in the neighborhood as late as possible. I got closer to my older cousin, Chus, who became my role model. Pepe was an asshole beating me up. There was no way I wanted to spend time with him. Chus was this big brother that I needed. He would play basketball with me and give me advice. He took me to my mom's hometown in the countryside of El Salvador every other weekend.

I felt like a king in that small town. All the country girls turned to look over at me. The pretty city boy. I was shocked by this attention. I would turn over to Chus and look at him amazed. "Are they seriously paying attention to me?"

I spoke with a different accent, like the preppy accent by Salvadoran standards. The only issue was that I had barely any experience with girls. Going to an all-boys school crushes any social skills picking up girls. In fact, my first kiss was still a year in the future. My game was nonexistent. These country girls were street smart and I was the visiting shy guy. All in all, I had good fun partying with friends and going to town dances.

Getting Along with My Siblings

My older sister Mari was the no-bullshit type of girl. She did not joke around much and meant what she said. Around people it would take a whole army of comedians to get her to share a Mona Lisa smile. Once, she tried to tell me that I should go to school on time. I turned toward her with my eyebrows raised. Her face immediately changed as she realized she was acting like my mother. I knew from a very young age that school was extremely important. She realized that I was a smart kid after all, and she just stopped her sermon in the middle and nodded her head. There was always something in me that made me love the act of learning, so even though I came home late on the weekends from the countryside, I always made it to school.

Pepa was the loving and charismatic girl next door whom everyone liked for the right reasons. She would show concern and listen to you genuinely. Her work ethic was the highest in school and at work. She had a job that did not pay much, but she was working hard and in college. She got little sleep. She lent me money to pay for my last year of Catholic school tuition so I could finish high school. I like her the most because of this interest-free student loan. Later in life, like way later in life, I paid her back.

My older brother Pepe. Did I mention he was an asshole? By this time, I'd learned to stay away from him. I was never in the same room with him at the same time. If he was in the kitchen, I would not go there. If I was in the kitchen and he came in, I promptly left. I imposed on myself a de facto stay-away order. I could not be close to him because he would get infuriated out of nowhere and just hit me. He got a sadistic pleasure from inflicting pain upon me. If Pepe joined me with mutual friends, I would keep quiet for a while then leave the group a few minutes later. Since my childhood, I was a victim of physical abuse from him. My resentment for my brother grew with every punch. I wanted Pepe to feel every punch I'd ever felt. The older I got the more compelled I felt to fight back. My body was growing, and Pepe's body had finished developing. We were almost on equal playing fields.

Kill or Be Killed

When Mom left, I started sleeping in my parents' room. However, my clothes were in my brother's room. My brother's room wasn't ours; it was his. I just had temporary storage space there.

One sunny Saturday morning I woke up after a good night's sleep and went downstairs to have my traditional bowl of cereal for breakfast. Then I went to watch reruns of some anime I liked. To chill was on my to-do list that day and nothing else. Noon came and I had to take a shower.

Pepe and I were sitting on a couch together. I made a comment to no one in particular, "It was a great morning, now I have to take a shower."

My brother quickly stood up from his seat and went straight to his bedroom, closing the door behind him. I heard the turn of the lock seconds later. I needed my clothes and he locked himself in the room. I marched out of my seat straight toward the door. I banged on the door. "Come on, Pepe, open the door. I need clothes so I can shower."

No response.

He locked himself in the room to stop me from getting clean clothes after showering. I decided that enough was enough. It's been years of bullshit. I decided to confront this motherfucker once and for all. I was tired of this tyranny. This psychological and physical torture was hell. I begged Pepe to please let me inside the room.

"Come on, Pepe, please, I just want a pair of pants and a shirt, I will grab them and go, please, Pepe."

He answered: "Go away, I do what I want."

I was done. My blood started boiling. My heart was racing. I was infuriated. For years I took all his shit and I was done. I went to the kitchen and looked around; my mind was clouded with rage. I went for the big kitchen knife. *Yeah, that will teach him a lesson.* I grabbed it. I looked at the big knife. But then I saw it was too extreme. I put it down. I saw a smaller steak knife. *Yes, this knife will do.* I kept the smaller knife hidden in my pocket.

I went back to his room and banged loudly on the door. This time I was demanding. "Open the door, Pepe."

I wasn't begging anymore. I was assertive. My tone changed, and my brother sensed I was talking to him with a different tone. *Today is the day I become a man*, I said to myself. I told him, "Hey, you! If you don't open the door, I know that you will eventually have to get out of there and I will do something to your clothes."

Pepe opened the door with a pissed-off face. He had a who-do-you-think-you-are face. I looked into his eyes firmly. "I will say this one last time. I will get my clothes and leave you alone." I said it in a calm tone, but with daredevil eyes. He showed me his angry face. He told me, "You don't make threats toward me! You should know that by now." Then he pushed me and grabbed me by the shirt. That was all I needed—now it was self-defense.

I grabbed the steak knife from my pocket and lashed out at him. Pepe felt a sting in his arm and he let go of me. He did not know what had caused the strange sensation in his arm. His eyes looked confused. He couldn't believe I had just cut his arm. I was standing facing him with a knife. Pepe had easily disarmed me before. But this time it was different. I acted. Rage came to me and I let him taste the first slash of the knife. He tried to block it with a karate block with his left arm. Unfortunately for him, blocking a knife with your arm is not a great idea. Pepe felt a second wound to his flesh. He took a swing at me. I moved a step behind and evaded it. Then I counterattacked with another swing of the knife. I cut his other arm. Then I thought to myself, *I'd better finish him off or he will grab the knife and finish me off.* I took as many swings as I could. I cut his flesh, here and there. Pepe was being attacked left and right and he evaded as much as he could, but all he was feeling was stings here and there. In his desperation he threw a punch randomly and it landed on my chest. I took it like a man and that fueled my rage even more. I was on the offensive. I had never been on the offensive before. Me being the aggressor was a new experience, so I continued with a combo of cuts and left punches on his body. Pepe tilted his head. I cut the left side of his neck. He continued bleeding. Pepe grabbed me and we wrestled to gain control of the knife. I managed to take back control of the knife and quickly went for his stomach in full shank mode. Pepe's elbow got in the way and the small steak knife broke as it hit his bone. Pepe was hurt. Adrenaline was rushing.

Pepe stepped behind me and tried to envelope me in a bear hug from behind to neutralize me. I bent over and let my head swing backward with a full head swing. The back of my head impacted his nose. He quickly dropped me from his arms and staggered a few steps back.

Pepe recovered and took a swing at me; I absorbed it with my arm and head. Then I took a swing at him and landed a punch on his jaw. I made some distance between us. I no longer had a weapon, and he was still bigger than me. I quickly ran to the first floor of the house, Pepe following behind me. I saw Pepe bleeding from his many wounds. *If he loses more blood, he'll get weaker. I could finally win.*

The whole commotion brought my sisters to watch the spectacle. We were gladiators in the arena. Then I saw something I never saw before—I saw him stop to catch his breath. I took that as a sign of weakness. I was winning. I launched my counterattack. I pushed and shoved; I landed another punch. "I thought you were a stronger motherfucker. You're nothing now, you piece of shit."

He said, "You are done, you faggot; you'll see."

Pepe withdrew back up the stairs and I followed him. I was on the offensive again. I chased after him. Pepe grabbed a heavy wooden chair and intended to hit me with it on my head like in WWE. He was weak and miscalculated his energy to lift a wooden chair. When he lifted the chair, he could not propel it downward toward me with his full force. I saw him letting the chair go and having gravity do the work. The chair hit my head but I didn't feel much. My adrenaline was at its maximum. I finally was fighting like a champion. Pepa screamed, "You'll kill each other!"

Pepa's screams were futile. This was between Pepe and me.

I ran away down the stairs toward the front door. I had overestimated Pepe's weakness, there was still some gas in him, and I was running out of steam. Pepe followed me. We took the fight to the street.

"Come on, Pepe. Come outside. Fight me like you always do," I yelled out. I was bluffing. I was tired. I was taking the fight toward the security guard at the gatehouse nearby. There I was hoping for him to break up the fight in case Pepe finally overpowered me. Pepe came out of the house and took a knee. He was bleeding and resting. I stared at him in defiance. He stared back. There was my brother, all bloody and bruised because of me. We stared at each other for what felt like forever. He went back to the house to tend his fresh wounds. Blood kept coming out of his body. A Band-Aid wasn't enough.

I was still outside, catching my breath, with an all-time high on adrenaline. The neighbors had stepped outside to see what all the fuss was about. Pepe came out moments later and looked at me. His eyes told me we were done fighting. This was the end. Then he left through the neighborhood gates toward the hospital. I didn't try to stop him. I stood there on the street in my shorts and bare feet. My breathing was heavy. I felt no remorse. I watched him limp through the streets. I'd finally unleashed the years of abuse in this one battle. It was kill or be killed. I didn't want to be a victim anymore. I'd rather kill or die than continue with this fucked-up life. I kept staring at Pepe's staggering body until my eyes became blurry. I was crying out of rage.

About three hours later Pepe came back to the house with a gauze on his neck, arms, and ribs. He got six stitches on his neck. The doctor told him he was lucky that his jugular wasn't cut; the knife only missed by a few millimeters.

I was still in shock. My brother had gone through a near-death experience. He came back humble. He didn't want to harm me anymore. He asked me for a couple minutes. We both were tired. Enough blows and blood for one day. We sat down at the dining table. My eyes were wet. His eyes were wet. His eyes were more than wet, I saw thick tears coming out of him. He told me:

"We should not do this to one another, we are brothers! I love you."

I'd never heard those words from him before. More tears came down my cheeks. Then his voice choked. We never had a straight talk growing up. We didn't say much to each other that day. We just sat there and looked at the room for the most part. But a lot of things were said without having to speak.

He firmly promised, "I will stop hurting you." He bowed his head and a couple tears touched the table. My hateful eyes just listened. It took a deathmatch for him to know that I was willing and able to kill.

I said: "Now you want peace! You will stop hurting me!" Then a calm moment came to both of us. It was quiet and it was sobering. I told him, "I am sorry! I don't know what I would do if you had died. I would be a criminal who killed his own brother. I'm sorry!" My tears were pouring, this time out of shame. Pepe gave me a hug and kissed my forehead and then went back to his room. I stayed in the dining room, shaking, thinking about how my life would have changed had Pepe died that day.

Hardy

HARDY GREW UP UNDOCUMENTED IN LOS Angeles and is now a professor at Arizona State University. I visited him in his faculty office at ASU on a nice campus full of college students. The largely desert state of Arizona is located in between California and New Mexico, and Hardy has lived in all three states. As a result of this visit, I learned quite a bit about what each of those states is doing about their policies affecting undocumented students.

Hardy was born in Guanajuato, Mexico, and moved with his parents to the US, crossing the border when he was four. His family settled in South Central LA. Hardy recalls the reason his parents had for moving to the US: "For a better life." Yet, as a young boy, he looked out the window and saw the 1992 LA riots that happened as a result of the beating of a black man, Rodney King, by police officers. Three police officers were acquitted despite video footage of the senseless beating. Hardy also saw his neighbors getting caught up with drugs and suffering from violence and police brutality. His parents told Hardy to never talk about his immigration status; otherwise, he could get deported. Hardy learned to keep his mouth shut. Did the parents give him a better life? That is a question he had back then while he watched homes being vandalized, cars destroyed, and stores looted.

Hardy's parents put pressure on him to stick to the "straight and narrow" and he did—mostly! He was bright and worked hard in school.

In high school all his friends were getting driver's licenses and Hardy made excuses as to why he did not get one. All his friends were talking about going out of state for college or going here and there. Hardy felt his choices were much more limited. Fortunately, since 2001, California had a law that allowed undocumented immigrants to pay in-state tuition—and to actually compete for some scholarships. (California was one of the pioneers when it came to investing in students. It does help that California has a lot of money in its budget.) He did not say much to his friends, but he saw the local Cal State, Dominguez Hills, as the only college he could afford. In the meantime, Hardy was fortunate to live with his parents rent free.

Hardy needed money and a job. But he had to work without papers, so he saw the McDonald's a block from campus as his best option. He worked day and night—for years his shift started at 4:00 a.m.—and that was *after* an hour bus ride to get there.

After a few years working at McDonald's, he aspired to get a better job and he applied to the prestigious position as an usher at Universal Studios telling people where to sit—and enabling him to watch concerts for free! He made it through the first rounds of interviews and was about to be hired when Universal did a background check on Hardy and found he did not have papers. That sucked for Hardy. He wanted to cry. He felt doomed to work at McDonald's. The Universal experience was a message from the Universe.

But Hardy did not stop. He said, "Screw this, I'm going to keep going to college and I'll see what happens." He paid tuition with his McDonald's money and continued to live at home with his parents. He continued at Cal State, Dominguez Hills and double majored in history and Chicano studies. He only had money to pay for a few courses at a time. He took the bus back and forth. He did not have much of a love life either, as all he did was work and study.

He did this for eight years.

Many people might have given up and tried selling drugs instead. (Or maybe start doing drugs.) But this dude didn't. He sucked it up.

But deep down, Hardy did not want to graduate—because he did not know what else he could do with a piece of paper that said "college grad!" After accumulating enough credits for one degree, he took more and more classes to continue to get shelter from his reality. *After all, college students are supposed to be broke and have low-paying jobs, right?* It was a self-defense mechanism. Even his family made fun of him for being a perpetual student.

Over the years the McDonald's franchise owner noticed him and asked him to stop flipping burgers and come work at her small office managing her properties and doing paperwork. Now Hardy got a break and had a desk job. He continued in college. He read books. He crunched numbers at work.

He continued riding the bus. Why didn't he buy a car? Because at that time undocumented people could not have a driver's license. California would not pass a law to grant driver's licenses to undocumented people until 2013.

While at Cal, Hardy was also an activist—and while working to establish a campus Latino Heritage Month celebration he met Professor Smith, who changed his life. Professor Smith was the director of the Chicano Studies Department. Hardy began to take the professor's classes and, at her urging, took on a Chicano studies major. Even after Prof. Smith left to chair the Chicano Studies Department at the University of New Mexico in Albuquerque, they stayed in touch—and she encouraged Hardy to go to graduate school. Hardy was flattered that his professor saw him as grad school material, but at first, he didn't think it was realistic.

Prof. Smith continued insisting with a dialog that went something like this:

Prof. Smith: "Hardy, you have to go to grad school, what the hell are you doing? You almost have a second degree."

Hardy: "That is a nice thought and a great challenge, but I like my job and friends."

Prof. Smith: "That is hard to believe…"

Hardy: "Okay, fine, I admire you, and I thank you for everything you have done, but this is not for me." (Hardy looked down with fire in his eyes.)

Prof. Smith: "I know you. Do you even know how capable you are?"

Hardy: "I know what I have and I know I can do much better than others. But I can't!"

Prof. Smith: "Are you scared?"

Hardy: "No, I'm not! You wouldn't understand…"

Prof. Smith: "Try me."

Hardy: "I don't have papers! And there is nothing I can do about it. I wish I could continue researching, studying, and learning, but this is the crappy life that God gave me for some reason." His eyes were wet. Hardy had not disclosed his undocumented status to anyone before this.

Prof. Smith: "Is that it?"

Hardy: "You want more?"

Prof. Smith: "Sit down, you are going to grad school with or without papers!"

Hardy sat down with fire in his watery eyes. As his parents instructed, he'd never talked about this and it was consuming him from the inside. But he admired this professor so much that he was open about it. He trusted her. She understood him well and genuinely wanted the best for him.

Prof. Smith: "There are scholarships and there is a fellowship program at the University of New Mexico. I will help you get it, but you have to be in it 100%. Your tuition and board will be covered, all you have to do is fight with the books the way you know how to do."

Hardy finally had a plan, a plan that gave him something to look forward to.

And he packed his bags for Albuquerque, New Mexico, for a master's in American studies.

While Hardy was in grad school, DACA was approved in 2012 and that helped him get a work permit. As a result, he could join a PhD program in American studies—and, as a PhD student, the university employed Hardy to conduct research.

Now, Hardy is a tenure track professor at Arizona State University. He wrote his first book called *Illegalized*.

■

While I chatted with Hardy in his standard-issue professor office at ASU, he described the differences among New Mexico, California, and Arizona. Like California, New Mexico has a big Latino population and allows undocumented students to pay in-state tuition and even get driver's licenses. They are very progressive like California; however, New Mexico does not have many job opportunities and does not have a big budget. Arizona is bigger and has more jobs than New Mexico, but has a sad history. Hardy told me that Arizona and New Mexico were supposed to be one state but the white population at the time did not want to mix with the Latino population of New Mexico, so they formed two different states.

There is a clear segregationist movement in Arizona. In 2022, Arizona still did not have in-state tuition for undocumented students. I could not believe it; it was 2022 and Arizona was still making the lives of brilliant kids hard. I was pissed. Toward the end of 2022 Arizona finally passed legislation to allow in-state tuition. They were twenty-one years late compared to California.

Knowing there are still states that make it difficult for students to go to college just does not make sense. These kids went to high school, the state paid for the full twelve years of education, but now they stop investing in these folks. Why? To guarantee more workers for McDonald's? They may be undocumented now, but eventually a lot will become US citizens at some point. And they will not forget who held them back while they were undocumented.

ON THE OTHER HAND: I also learned that Texas was the first state allowing in-state tuition to undocumented students—back in

2001! This blew my mind. You mean conservative Texas? Yes. They can seem to have backward policies sometimes, but they are not stupid. There is a high concentration of Latinos there, including lots of people without papers, and they reflect the future of the Texas workforce. I guess some of the folks in power understood that if they don't have enough highly educated and skilled workers, Texas's economic future will suffer. (California became the second state to provide in-state tuition. California wasn't going to let Texas be more progressive.) I don't think Texas will become blue, though.

■

I left Hardy's office with more knowledge. I walked around the ASU campus and saw a few college students on their skateboards. Hardy still has DACA and still does not have a permanent residency. A professor in the US is teaching our students because of DACA.

My last stop in Arizona led me to talk to Bella, a beautiful young woman with a down-to-earth personality. Bella introduced me to her sister Tusk. Together they found a way to make college work in the state of Washington.

7

Welcome to America

If we ever closed the door to new Americans, our leadership in the world would soon be lost.

—President Ronald Reagan

IT WAS SEPTEMBER 2001. I WAS LIVING IN EL SALVADOR in the family home while my parents struggled in the US. One morning my sister Mari suddenly woke me up and told me that planes had crashed into the Twin Towers in New York. I felt a strange energy that made me jump out of bed and go straight to the TV. I saw the planes crashing over and over. I saw humans falling again and again. I saw the collapsing of the huge buildings. Uncertainty came to my head. I was to graduate high school in a couple of months. I didn't know whether I could go to college because my parents were away and they didn't have money to pay for my college. On top of that, the world was coming to an end.

The world underwent a big shift, and the US mobilized its military to the Middle East. I was in the eleventh grade. In El Salvador there are only eleven grades, not twelve grades like in most countries. In 1997, the Salvadoran government came up with the brilliant idea of saving money and the politicians were so creative in cutting costs that they took away education for their youth. It was one of the most incompetent decisions a politician has ever made. It's been more than twenty-eight years and no politician in that country has bothered to fix that.

I'm not going to lie; I enjoyed the freedom I had without my parents. I knew that school was important, but eventually I stopped caring. At the beginning of the year, I was good at math and physics, but the separation of my family stressed me out. That stress carried through my studies. At some point my physics teacher pulled me aside. He told me he was concerned for me and that my grades used to be so good, but it seems like something happened to me. He looked at me with the same pitiful look all teachers give their students when they know something is going on.

He was right. I wasn't okay. I didn't have the stamina to invest in my studies and be good at school. At this point I wanted to hang out with my friends. Who was going to tell me no? I wanted to smoke cigarettes with my friends behind the market. Who was going to tell me no? I hated the smell of smoke but I wanted to look cool. I could go home when I wanted and drink as many beers as my limited budget let me. Who was going to tell me no?

No one would and that's the problem. I had to leave El Salvador or lose myself to oblivion.

My parents eventually called late one night. I asked my dad if I could live with them in the US.

"Can I please come live with you? I really want to learn English and get a good job."

There was a slight pause from my dad. "Graduate high school first and I'll take care of the rest." My confirmed ticket to the United States.

I talked to Mom for a bit before hanging up. Something about Mom's tone didn't sound right. She didn't sound like herself—in fact, it was almost as if she wasn't present.

■

Once I graduated high school, my aunts and uncles threw a celebration for me. I asked my family to provide me with a few dollars if they wanted to give me a gift. *No gifts, cash only* was my policy. Ten dollars here, five dollars there. In all I collected $110. My parents sent me an airplane ticket. I put all my clothes in a heavyweight top-load canvas duffel bag, put my $110 in my pocket, and took off to the US.

On the plane ride, I could see America. A country where there was no racism, no religious fanatics, justice for all, and the legal system works for everyone all the time. A country with no social classes and no nationalistic feelings. I was on my way to the perfect country. So I thought.

I landed at Dulles Airport on a tourist visa. I got out of customs and saw my dad waiting outside with balloons and flowers. I felt weird. I sensed something was wrong. I perceived a strange energy coming from him. I saw his physical appearance with bags under his eyes and a four-day beard shadow. His coat was dirty. This was the beginning of the toughest time in my life. Whatever I suffered thus far was just a prelude. The next couple of years were hard and I had to adapt to a new culture, new language, new social class.

■

I was no doctor, but I diagnosed my father with a mental problem. Between him losing his toe, his business, his country, and his family, the man was bound to go crazy.

Dad and I hugged for a moment and he then shoved the balloons and flowers into my hand. "Give these to your mom when you see her today." He turned around and started walking to the car.

I followed him and got into the car. I turned to look at him strangely. "Why would you bring her flowers? Why isn't she here?"

Dad stared directly at the road. He started to mutter in a low tone how this country conspires to let its people lose their lives, and in between his conspiracy theory, he started talking about how Mom had had multiple affairs with multiple men. The old man was gone.

"I don't think so, Dad, there must be a mistake—"

"You are so naïve! Wake up!" he yelled out. Dad kept staring intensely at the road ahead. I realized I had to walk on eggshells.

Dad was staying in Stafford, Virginia, and that day he drove me to Gaithersburg, Maryland, about an hour and a half away, to go see my mom at my aunt and uncle's house. I got there and Dad told me to knock on the door while he stayed inside the car. My mom opened the door and looked at me with watery eyes. She wrapped her arms around me and kissed me all over my face. I gave her the balloons and flowers. Mom just uttered a small thank-you. Behind Mom was my aunt and uncle. I gave them a friendly smile and said hello to them. Apparently, the seventeen-year-old me didn't know how to read a room. They looked around and gave Mom and me a moment. Mom looked at me. "You should go with your dad, I'm staying here, though."

I was confused. "Why are you even here, Mom? What's happening?"

"I'm sorry, Lito, but this is for the best."

"*What is going on, Mom?*"

She just stared at me with her sweet brown eyes. Her hand glided through my hair to the base of my neck. How she always did when I was little. "Just trust me on this, okay?"

I got no answers that night. After thirty minutes of trying to get an answer, Mom told me to get back to Dad and to take care of myself.

I went back to the car where my dad was waiting. We drove to Virginia. We were driving on I-95 and my dad was rambling on about how he did all of this for the family and Mom. Big trucks and a bunch of cars were on the highway. I really didn't know what was going on, but I let Dad talk. I tried to crack a joke to lighten the mood, but Dad was in no mood for jokes. I tried to say a few words in English to show my progress using a computer course I took. Dad wasn't impressed, and neither was I.

Dad and I got to his place. He'd rented a room in the basement of a suburban house. A room with a bathroom on the side and a closet/kitchen where a fridge with bread and ginger ale waited for me as my dinner. The neighborhood was nice with big houses and big backyards. It was a nice place to live, but the spirit of this man was broken.

Dad said, "Tomorrow we're going to school to enroll you."

That was my goal. I lay in the twin bed next to his double bed and crashed.

Another High School Story

The following morning, I enrolled again in high school even though I'd already graduated in El Salvador. Since El Salvador only had high school for eleven grades, I told the school in Stafford, Virginia, that I did not finish the eleventh grade and that I wanted to finish the eleventh and twelfth grades. They accepted me with open arms.

It was cold in December and there wasn't much going on in Stafford. I remember watching movies about how developed the US was and how pretty things were. In the movies the skyline was full with high-rises and the houses were always built like dollhouses. Well, I was in Stafford. It was freezing and everywhere I looked I saw trees. I thought, *Dad must have taken me to Russia.*

High school in America through Hollywood movies looked rough. I was ready to get into a fight with the bully of the school and gain respect from others quickly. I walked to my classes looking over my shoulder expecting an attack at any moment. Then I went to lunch with my guard up; I thought something was about to happen to me—but nothing yet. In my fourth-period class, nobody wanted to fight me. These kids welcomed me. I thought it was a trick to take my guard down. I saw a few All-American-looking girls that I had never seen in person. I was used to people looking like me when I lived in El Salvador and at that point I saw different people. People around me looked different. It was another dimension and I liked everything new around me. It was a whole new world.

There were three Latino kids in the entire school. I was one of them. By default, I had two new best friends whom I could communicate with. Many kids were children of military parents from the Quantico Marine Corps Base.

I was determined to learn the language as soon as possible. I took refuge from my family drama in my history homework. Back then I had a pocket English/Spanish dictionary and I looked up any word I didn't know.

Family Conflict

Christmas break soon came, and that winter Mom came back to live with Dad and me. I finally saw both Mom and Dad living together with me in America the way I'd envisioned. That day things were more or less fine. What I thought was going to be my first peaceful Christmas with my parents, however, soon turned to shit. That same evening Dad insisted that Mom apologize to him. But Mom held her ground and said she had nothing to apologize for. They argued. Mom went to sleep on the couch outside the room. The tension was building. Dad went outside to argue with Mom. I let them argue, as I never got into their arguments. Then I heard Mom screaming and crying.

I jumped from my bed and headed out my door. "What's going on?" I looked at Mom standing close to my dad facing him with her eyes red. She was shaking. I asked her, "Did he hit you?!"

She immediately denied it and got out of the living room into the bedroom. Mom defused the situation, telling me that nothing really happened. I did not believe her, but she wanted to protect me. She wanted to protect my peace of mind. I looked at Dad and I was ready to take him on like I took on Pepe. *I can take on this forty-six-year-old man.* I probably would not be able to, but that was what I thought.

I called my cousin and asked her if she could give my mom a ride back to her parents' place. My cousin came an hour later and picked up my mom and me. I spent the Christmas break with my aunt and uncle in Gaithersburg, Maryland. I felt powerless. It wasn't the American Dream I had envisioned. Most American Christmas movies showcase a sweet white Christmas. The family gathers around the table with lots of food and they all say how happy they are to be together on Christmas. That was a stark difference from my life right now. Mom was suffering. Dad was suffering. What could I do? There was nothing that I could do to mend what they had broken. I lacked the sophistication and training to help my parents. Dad's mental health would get treated by the only resource he had: time. And it took a lot of it for him to recover. Mom's domestic violence trauma got the same treatment. *Does time really cure it all?* Mom and Dad separated shortly after. That was the end of the road for them. Even years later Mom refused to talk to me about what Dad did to her despite the intense cross-examination techniques I used on her.

Mom returned to El Salvador on New Year's Eve. I said goodbye to her at Dulles Airport. The goodbye wasn't emotional. It was more of a formality. Little did I know it would be years before I saw her again.

I went back to my dad that day and I wanted to have a conversation with him. A straight talk. I suspected he was mistreating Mom.

He tried to diminish his behavior, saying: "I hit her just like a father hits a child to correct her."

That pissed me off. "The problem is that she is not your child."

"I never hit her very hard," he said defensively.

"Well, Dad, I have to tell you that you don't look well mentally. You are not the same man you used to be. I can feel it in the way you talk and the way you act. How about you listen to me and we'll get through this together."

He said: "I don't have to listen to you, you are a child."

"I'm pretty smart, you'd be surprised." Then he started crying at the top of his lungs. I had never seen him like that, and that broke my heart. Here was my father crying before his son. My father was broken in spirit, mind, and body. I was the only one next to him. He alienated my entire family and I took it upon myself to try to be there for him.

It was time for me to face this new world and make my own decisions. One of those decisions made me choose between a rock and a hard place.

PART II

8

Adapting to My New Life

*Your life does not get better by chance; it gets
better by change.*
—Jim Rohn

DESPITE ALL THE CHALLENGES WITH MY dad, he was still my dad and
I saw his suffering. I wanted to figure out how I could help alleviate
his pain.

Dad worked as a cashier at Shoppers Supermarket earning seven
dollars an hour. He didn't make much money, but it was something.
Then he had a second job working at Shoney's restaurant for another
seven dollars an hour. He got a fake green card to work, as many
undocumented workers do. Without some kind of ID, a business
owner would not hire you. There is this form called the I-9 that
employers must fill out, attesting that the new hire has shown documents proving their right to work legally in the US. As long as an
employee gives any of the listed documents, the employer's legal obli-
gations are met. An employer does not have to verify whether the
employee is telling the truth, or that the documents are real. All the
employers want cheap labor and all employees want to work. This
is a win-win.

I saw my dad as the king that lost it all. He lost his business, his
family, and his country. It was a self-defense mechanism to lose his
sense of reality. Reality was too harsh to tolerate. I blamed him for
everything that happened to us. Had he just played it safe and sucked

it up in a nine-to-five job for the rest of his life, we would be just fine. I was seventeen and I did not care about his dreams and aspirations, I cared about my own security. Now I had to go look for a job to be self-sufficient, so I went to work at the local Taco Bell. I came down from an okay social status in El Salvador all the way to the bottom in the US. I became a hardworking undocumented immigrant. I thought to myself, "What would my friends think if they saw me working hard in a fast-food joint? What would my family think?" Later my perspective changed. Little by little I started to care less about what others thought about me.

Now I don't blame my dad for trying to pursue his happiness by taking his risks and trying to open his own business. He took a gamble. Some may say that he gambled the whole family away, but I say he tried to achieve his goals. Not the goals of his peers, not the goals of his family, or the imaginary goals of society. He did not gamble for a boss's goals, no sir, he had his own goals, and he went for them. He tried to achieve his goals and failed. I respect those who try and fail more than those who never even try. You will never have peace of mind if you never try to achieve what you really want to be. The one thing that is scary is to ask yourself, "What if I had tried?"

My Best Friend

I met Francisco in high school. He worked at Taco Bell. He became the only guy I could speak with fluently in Spanish and thus he became my best friend. He's from Mexico, and we spent many days in his house. His mom cooked the spiciest beans in town. It took me some time to get used to the flaming hot beans. Francisco was the guy who would help anyone in need. He wasn't pretentious and didn't care much about fashion. He had a brother, a sister, and both his parents living in a townhouse close to school. The family had the American Dream.

I told Francisco about my lack of immigration status over a couple of beers on top of a hill overlooking the local Walmart. He was cool about it. He knew family and friends who had no papers. He himself lacked papers for some time until his family got green cards.

"I need papers to work."

He said, "Don't worry, let me make a few calls and we'll get you papers."

I said, "Francisco, you're the man, you know everything about this country."

So that weekend, Francisco stole his mom's car and we drove an hour and a half from Stafford to Columbia Road in Washington, DC. He didn't have a license and he forgot his eyeglasses. Without his glasses he was legally unqualified to drive. He could see enough blurs to hit the gas and press the breaks. Francisco asked me multiple times while driving if the car in front of him was near or far. He evaded cars left and right. He almost hit a couple of pedestrians and acted so proud that he didn't hit anyone. I was going along with the ride looking out the window assessing where I would run in case of an accident.

It was February 2002, and it was cold in DC. All the buildings were covered by chipped paint and wrought-iron bars on the windows. This wasn't the vintage part of Georgetown; this was the forgotten zone of DC. I was terrified. The sketchiest type of people stumbled down the road looking cracked out. Francisco put his "bad" face on and I followed with the most "badass" face I could muster. To everyone else we looked like kids with constipation. Just a couple of teenagers walking through the part of town your parents would warn you not to go through. DC crime was high, and all I wanted that day was to come back alive.

We walked to the intersection of Columbia Road and Eighteenth Street and saw a few guys selling fake IDs. They were chanting in a soft voice, "*la mica, la mica*," which means "fake IDs" in Mexican slang. Francisco acted like he knew what he was doing and he randomly selected a dude standing next to a trash can. I grabbed the $110 from my pocket—that was all the capital I had—and I gave it to the dude. The guy told me to go get my picture taken in the business right behind him, and Francisco agreed. I did not ask questions; I did as Francisco told me. He was my sherpa in this part of the world. So, I went to a store right behind me that had a sign in Spanish of "We Sell Passport Pictures." It was a well-organized operation. After I took my picture, I gave it to the dude, and he told us to wait for about forty-five minutes. We went to get something to eat. We walked past a black car with big antennas, which probably was an FBI patrol. I got worried. Now, knowing what I know about the government, I'm pretty sure they were surveilling the whole situation and probably got a kick out of my ordeal. But fortunately, they were not going to bust a dude on the street looking for a fake ID because they were more worried about busting actual terrorists.

Those forty-five minutes turned into two hours, and I started to think that someone just took $110 from me. However, the dude came back with a little envelope. I saw the ID. It was all chopped up. My picture was clearly glued into that plastic and my face was cut rough around the edges. Nobody would believe that shit was real. It was the fakest ID I had ever seen. I gave it to Francisco to inspect it and he placed it on top of a trash can. He looked at it with a serious face and gave his nod of approval. *Really, no comment about how fake it looked.* The dude said bye and told me to come renew it in ten years. Francisco and I looked at each other and we walked away fast without turning back.

We got to the car, and I started screaming, "Dude, what the fuck was that!"

"Did you see the FBI car?" Francisco replied. "Holy shit, we have to get the fuck out of here!"

I said, "Good idea, hit the gas, Frank!"

Francisco quickly drove away. It was getting dark and Francisco remembered that the taillights did not work. That's why his mom didn't let him use the car at night. We were about fifteen minutes from Francisco's house when we saw a cop right in front of us waiting at the light in a lane next to our lane. We had almost made it to home base.

We had to turn left. Francisco got the brilliant idea of hitting the brakes to turn on the taillights while he pressed on the gas so that the cop could see the taillights were working. Instead of a solid taillight, he was doing Morse code with the breaks and gas, plus the car was stopping and going. This immediately got the cop's attention. We turned. I looked back. Nothing. I looked back again, and I saw the flashing red and blue approaching us.

"Damn it, Francisco, what do we do now?"

Francisco calmly replied, "Just be cool."

How the fuck is he calm? "How can I just be cool?"

Francisco started pulling to the side of the road and turned to me. "Just trust me and let me talk. Don't panic."

I started praying.

Mr. Officer looked like the standard-issue white American male portrayed in the movies. Young, clean shaven, and with a pressed uniform. He approached Francisco's side and asked for the standard license and registration in a standard voice. This was the first time I saw an American cop this close. Francisco gave a learner's permit. The cop took it and after a few minutes came back. He said, "You know, this is only a learner's permit, not a driver's license, so you should not be driving this late, plus your taillights are not working."

Francisco said, "I'm sorry, Officer, I was doing some errands for my mom."

The cop said, "I'm not going to arrest you, but make sure you go straight home. I see your friend is not wearing a seatbelt." I took it off as soon as we pulled over. I was assessing where to run. But I froze and did nothing.

Francisco said, "He just took the seatbelt off."

The cop said, "Oh, okay, just buckle up and go home, nowhere else." He was a very nice cop; I did not expect him to be this nice to us.

Francisco drove the car like nothing happened and I was in complete disbelief. "Francisco, how the fuck did you do that? What the fuck do you eat? What happened?" In my mind, Francisco just did a Jedi mind trick on a stormtrooper. He was my Obi Wan.

That was my first encounter with a policeman. At the moment, I thought I was about to get deported. One thing is for sure, from then on Francisco was a friend I would trust. We survived our first battle. Unfortunately, there were going to be many more—way tougher.

SUCCESS FORMULA

FROM NOW ON AT THE END of each personal chapter I will give you a takeaway formula for you to think about. These formulas worked for me and other Fellows. It is a formula; you can change them according to your own needs. Most of the formulas I share are for those who are in survival mode. Although everyone can implement them to have more success, some formulas are extreme and they will resonate more with people who are struggling. Here you go:

1. Take a chance from time to time. The system rewards those who take risks. If you don't take risks, you don't win. If you always play it safe, you will be safe, but no excitement comes to those who live a safe life.
2. Take calculations. Don't risk your well-being for the sake of risking it. If you do, you have a gambling problem. Only take risks if the rewards are needed or worthwhile. Unnecessary risks get you in trouble.

9

Bad Crowd

Tell me what company you keep, and I will
tell you what you are.
—El Quijote

I GOT A JOB AT TACO Bell and went to school. That was my life. I worked like I had never worked before. That is because I had never worked before. I was excited. I was always doing something. I cleaned the line, swept the floor, cooked, washed dishes, and even operated the register with my broken English. Some friends from high school stopped by and made fun of me because I charged money using my faulty English. I would laugh at their jokes and tell them in my broken English, "I give you food but first, you give me my money." We laughed at that. I remember when I got my first paycheck. It was $155.00. I could not believe it. I looked at it again to make sure the number didn't change. I'd worked hard for the previous two weeks and I did not think much of it. My bosses were excited to have such a hardworking guy, unlike the other high schoolers.

The following weekend Francisco's mom took us to church. Francisco told me that church was a good place to get good girls. At that point I was blindly following Francisco, so the thing about good girls had to be true. I didn't meet any of them, but it was a nice try.

On our way back home, we stopped by the drive-through of the bank and his mom cashed the check for me. She gave me an envelope with $155 cash. I looked at the cash, I looked at my hands. I had never had $155 cash in my hands! I was rich, and if I continued working, that meant that more money was coming in the future. That day I grew a few inches taller. I felt like a man.

Francisco introduced me to his friends. I saw a bunch of bums. High school dropouts who spoke broken Spanish. Some were pot smokers who looked like they never showered and always smelled like pot. Others were the tough gangster wannabes who spoke like they were in the prison yard in their macho man voice. They were not my crowd and I did not want to be there, but they were the only support system I had, so I'd better be nice to them in case I needed their help. I made them laugh with a few dirty jokes, so they welcomed me.

Have a Backbone

Living with Dad was a routine. I came home late and soon I went to bed. The following morning, I usually woke up and went to school while Dad was still sleeping. We were roommates. I did my thing and he did his. Father and son living together, surviving together. I said hi every other day when our schedules matched.

Everything was okay until one morning when my dad, unusually, was up. I could see in his eyes that he hadn't gotten much sleep. He'd been calling Mom, who had gone back to El Salvador to live with my siblings. Dad begged her to come back and be with him. He used so much money in calling cards. Mom would not come back to him. She was safe in El Salvador and she liked it that way. She did not have much money but she had peace. The calling card did not have any more minutes and the dial tone went off. That's when he went on a rant.

"You are old enough to find your own place. I don't have to support you anymore, go be a man now. You have a job; you can take care of yourself. Go away! This is my room, go find your own place. At your age I was already independent."

I looked at him with a dead serious face. That face that condemns a poor bastard with just the eyes. I told him with the same confrontational spirit, "It is also not easy for me to live with you in these conditions, but that is all we have. You are my father and I am a minor. It is the law for you to provide for me. If you do not want to do it, that is fine. I've seen the sheriff's car up the street. I will go up there and knock on his door. I will ask him to come down here and explain to you the law. Maybe he should take you away because you are a shitty dad."

Dad got quiet, and I saw fear in his eyes. He felt a dark force coming from me. We kept living the way we had for the rest of my junior year.

In Bad Company

Hanging out with the Stafford crowd I had a few beers here and there. I saw them smoke marijuana and they offered. I always declined. *I wanted more out of life*. I respected them but I wasn't one of them. I felt like a prince who got dethroned, like Prince Vegeta from Dragon Ball. I wanted to be stronger so I could finally conquer the world. They would crack a few jokes at my expense for being a wuss who did not smoke, but that meant there was more pot for them. I wanted to protect my brain, as that was the only thing that separated me from them. Inside, I felt alone.

I took shelter in books. Whenever I got mad at something, I hit the books. I started reading and learning. I would tell myself that the more I read, the stronger I could be. When somebody at work pissed me off, I got home and read books thinking that one day I would be rich, and I would buy the whole company and fire that asshole I had as a boss. If some dudes in school made fun of me, I would hit the books thinking that one day I would hire these guys and then I would fire them. I was a power-hungry dude. I had the eye of the tiger. I descended into a dark place.

With the Stafford crowd, we organized what in our minds was a mastermind plot for shoplifting. We thought we were Ocean's Eleven. There was Dan, the white dude who hung out with the Hispanic kids, who used to work the cash register at the Ross clothing store. Some of us used to go there pretending to be customers, and Dan, our inside man, would take away the security devices of the garments and we would walk away with the merchandise. We then moved to Circuit City, the electronics store where Dan had a second job. Dan was a hard worker but he also liked the finest things in the store for himself. His seven-dollar-an-hour wage would not let him buy a high-capacity memory card for his computer, so he joined the plot.

It was a Make-a-Wish Foundation Day. We saw the stores and we could pick anything we wanted. Francisco went for the nice jeans; I went for the nice shoes. Dan preordered the high-capacity memory card. We were with this guy, Bobby, who got video games and a PlayStation console. It all was a game for us and we had a bond of camaraderie. We got to Francisco's house safe and sound and shared the loot like it was Christmas. "I got this nice shirt," said Francisco. "I got this nice winter hat," Bobby said. We played the latest video games until late in the evening and it was time to go home. Francisco gave us a ride home in the same car without taillights. This time he used the back roads.

On our way back, Bobby showed me a few knives he had hidden in his pocket and told me, "Yo, yo, you know...I had these babies with me." Showing the brilliant blades. "Next time I should bring a gun in case something goes wrong. You know. Yo. Just to scare people in case we have to. We don't have to use it. We should have guns just in case something goes wrong." That was a big red flag for me. If something goes wrong, a gun is not the solution. If something goes wrong with a gun, a person dies. If something goes wrong, we are talking about hard-core criminality. What was this guy thinking, "if something goes wrong"? Shoplifting a shirt and a pair of jeans was one thing, but pointing a gun at someone was a completely different thing. I had to dissociate myself from this dude. I said many times that I had to work or I had homework for school and couldn't hang out. They did not mind; they saw one less guy they had to share the loot with.

A Quarrel with a Friend

Francisco and I met from time to time at the hill overlooking the Walmart to drink a few beers he bought from this Indian guy who worked at the 7-Eleven. He complained to me that his father was comparing him to me. He said, "My dad called me lazy today. He was going at it saying, 'Look at Jose, he doesn't even have papers but he does more in a day than you do in a week. He works, he studies, and he even has a car.'" Francisco had just dropped out of school and quit Taco Bell. I had just bought my first car for $1,000, a 1987 Pontiac Grand Am with red interior.

"You must admit, Frank, your dad has a point. You should be better since you have a green card."

"Oh, so you think you're better than me."

"I am." I said that arrogantly. "If you want something, Frank, you work for it. You have it all. You have a green card, a home, and a mom who cooks for you. But you dropped out of school? For what? To be a bum?"

"You don't understand, Jose."

"I don't understand you, but I do understand what needs to be done."

We started to part ways.

It was me, myself, and I again. I avoided the crowd and worked as much as I could to make as much money as I could. This work ethic meant I was at Taco Bell for many hours. Because of this, I experienced an incident that almost took my life.

SUCCESS FORMULA

1. Believe that you are destined to greater things in life. Others' opinions do not matter. You can always be better and you will go far. Keep believing and do not succumb to peer pressure.

2. Do not do drugs. Protect your brain. Your brain is the only thing you actually have in life. Anything else can be taken away. Addiction is real. Pot during high school will diminish your intellect. Your brain keeps developing until the age of thirty.

3. Bonus points if you can stay away from alcohol (I didn't, but you could be better than me). There is a balancing test between socialization and being a drunk. If you find yourself drinking alone, you have a problem.

4. Stop hanging out with losers and criminals. Being alone is better than associating with bad decision makers. Your associations will define who you are. The decisions of people around you will also impact your life. Find friends who add value to your life.

5. Learn. Read in order to learn. Practice what you learn. Expand your vocabulary. Use words that others don't use. Knowledge is power. Never stop learning.

10

Work-Life Imbalance

Let's face it. No kid in high school feels
as though they fit in.
—Stephen King

MY LIFE CONSISTED OF WAKING UP at 5:30 a.m., catching the school bus, and surviving class. By the third period I was so exhausted that I succumbed to putting my head down on my desk. I just could not keep my eyes open. At 2:30 p.m. I took the bus back home. I took a forty-minute power nap and then I started work at 5:00 p.m. until we closed shop at midnight. Then I went back home to do homework until 2:00 a.m., just in time to sleep for three and a half hours. Then the freaking alarm buzzed at 5:30 a.m. to start all over again. I repeated this Monday to Friday. Somehow, I managed to keep up with homework and the readings. During the weekends I slept from 3:00 a.m. until 4:00 p.m. I hibernated to make up for the hours I did not sleep during the week.

It was May 2002. As usual, I was working hard until closing at midnight at Taco Bell. It was Tiffany, another girl working with me, the manager Angie, and I. Tiffany wasn't supposed to close that day but they were short on staff and she felt generous to help. We finished as usual and I fixed my typical burrito and a cup of soda to eat at home that night.

We exited the store, and Angie intended to drive us home. Angie and Tiffany got inside the car quickly. Then I noticed a dude running toward us from the bushes. I said with a friendly tone, "Hi, how are you, I think I know you." I don't know why, but I thought it was a friendly guy. Then he got closer and closer. That's when I noticed he was wearing a black mask. I was in deep shit. He was wearing plastic gloves and had a gun pointing at me.

Angie saw him and locked the doors of her car. The masked guy yelled, "Get out of the car!" They did nothing. Then he saw me and said to them, "If you don't get out of the car, I'll shoot him," pointing the gun closer at me. I was quiet. I took a sip of my soda. Then Angie got out of the car with Tiffany. The guy escorted us to the walk-in fridge. He took Angie to the safe to get the cash. Angie was quiet. She tried opening the safe the first time but her nerves didn't let her key in the right code. The guy was yelling, "Bitch, open that shit or I'll shoot you." Angie replied, "If you keep pointing that gun at me, I'll keep getting nervous and it is not helping." She tried a second time and it worked. "Hurry up, bitch," I could hear repeatedly. She put all the cash in a plastic bag. Then the guy took Angie to the walk-in fridge with us.

Tiffany was panicking. She was crying, telling me she wasn't supposed to work until closing that day. "Why did I choose to stay?" she said. I was thinking to myself, *What a crappy life I lived. Now I'm going to die here. Man, I did not do much in this world.* Angie got back inside the fridge. The guy looked at us and told us, "Don't call the police!" Then he closed the fridge and ran away through the back door. Angie got out of the fridge five seconds later. Thank God the walk-in refrigerator did not lock from the outside. Angie peeked outside the back door to make sure the robber had left. Dude was gone. We called the police.

A few cops came and did the whole investigation. They questioned me and I told them what I could. "The dude was a black guy, with a gun that looked like a revolver with a round barrel..." Dogs came in and we stayed until 3:00 a.m. answering questions. The robber was never found. He took a $5,000 prize. Angie and Tiffany did not show up for a week. I came to work the following day. I wasn't going to miss my hours; that was money on the table. I wasn't going to leave if I didn't have to. I didn't care, I wanted to get paid.

This robbery became the foundation for one of the worst ideas a dude from the Stafford crowd had. That crazy idea would almost land me in prison.

Living on Your Own

The summer going into my senior year, I worked so hard. One time I clocked in 104 hours in a two-week period.

Toward the middle of the summer my dad moved to Wheaton, Maryland. I had my doubts about moving with him. I wanted to remain in Stafford and finish high school. I did not want to move yet again and make new half-friends. I moved for a few weeks with Dad to try it out. I told Taco Bell that I was quitting. I professionally gave my two weeks' notice and headed to Maryland.

We were looking for new schools, and Wheaton High School was in my district. We went to talk to an admin. She asked me: "What was your highest level of schooling in El Salvador?" I felt like telling the truth and said I graduated already—in part because I did not want to be with Dad, and in part because I wanted to go back to Stafford. When the administrator heard that, she said that high school in Wheaton was not an option, that I had to go to college if I wanted to continue studying.

Based on this rejection, I told Dad I was going back to Stafford on my own. He looked disappointed. This was a time when my father was going to be completely alone. I was about to turn eighteen in September, so I saw the writing on the wall if I stayed with Dad. He tried kicking me out once and he couldn't because of the law, but once I turned eighteen, he could easily get rid of me. I would rather be prepared than be thrown out, especially during winter. So, I moved back to Stafford to rent a room with the same man who gave us a room. I went back to Taco Bell and talked to the general manager. I told her that I was moving back. She was so happy to see me as she needed hard workers, so she gave me my job back. I was happy to use my fakest green card to get this high executive job back. I finished my summer, working long hours, closing at 2:00 a.m. and getting home to get some sleep. That was all I lived for that summer.

Senior Year

Whether in Maryland or Virginia, none of the high schools ever asked me for papers. That's because there is a Supreme Court ruling giving a constitutional right to every child to attend school in the US regardless of their immigration status. That said, it was 2002 and I learned to keep my lack of papers to myself. Francisco was the only one who really knew who I was outside of my extended family in the area. I didn't try to go live with the aunt I had in Stafford because I was really not her responsibility. Plus, my dad and my extended family had a falling-out. In reality I had nobody to talk to about my issues. That took a toll on my emotions. I decided to do the best I could.

In my senior year I decided not to take ESL classes because the school's ESL program was small and I wanted to have a normal life. Stafford at the time did not have many international students. There were about nine of us in the entire school. Some had different English levels. One dude did not speak any English whatsoever and a girl from Cameroon was almost fluent. In the past six months I'd learned enough English, I thought, so I told my counselor to let me out of that class, that I wanted a challenge. Supporting his theory of full assimilation, my counselor let me do it. Or maybe he didn't care—either way I was taking normal classes like everyone else.

I cut communication with everyone in my family. I was on my own. Maybe Mom called a few times here and there, but it was a short conversation of less than two minutes. I probably checked on my dad every three months for another two-minute conversation just to see if he was still alive. I was in survival mode. My feelings and emotions were no longer a priority. I felt the need to be isolated from everyone. Everyone from El Salvador, everyone from my family—it was a true desert. In part because I thought being alone would be good for me instead of being in a corrupt environment, and in part because I felt like everyone abandoned me. I felt like the youngest member of the family was left to his own devices. If that was how things were going to be, then I would show everyone that I could make it on my own.

At Taco Bell there was a manager who wanted to look good before the general manager and save money on labor. He would clock the employees out by midnight, even though the work wasn't done. I had to do the work without pay. I told another manager what was happening and she told me, "If you don't like it, you can go home, but you won't have a job tomorrow." I took it just like that. I needed the job. I didn't want to keep using my fake ID in order to get another job. On my way home I shed a tear out of fury. I read until 4:00 a.m. that night and I still caught the bus at 5:55 a.m. This is for Mr. Manager Jason—if you are reading this, go fuck yourself!

This was my life between my school, family, and work. Neither was great to me but all I could do was my best. One day at a time. While in survival mode, there wasn't much work-life balance.

Try Serving Your Country

During lunch in school one day, I saw an Army recruiter. *This is my way out of poverty.* I wanted to join. I'd heard about the French Foreign Legion. France gives French citizenship to undocumented people willing to serve three years in the Legion fighting for France. The key to getting papers in France through the Legion is that people have to remain alive for those three years.

I thought the US must have something similar. I was excited. We talked about them paying for college and sending me all over the world. I would have weapons training, housing, and a salary. I thought that was a good deal. *Sign me up!* I completed the Selective Service form and they gave me a number. Every male in the US between the ages of eighteen and twenty-six has to fill this out by law regardless of their immigration status. *Alright, I'm in! I have a military ID.* A few more conversations happened and one day the recruiter told me I had done everything and a final interviewer would call soon.

I finally figured it out! In my mind I was going to have a military career in the most powerful nation in the world. I didn't give myself a chance to consider the downsides. I didn't realize I would be putting myself in the middle of a battlefield and having to end another life on the other side. I was a boy who watched too many movies. I imagined this romanticized idea about the military that I had in my head.

A few months later I got a call from Sergeant Connor. I was amazed. I could see the movie in my head: *This is not a drill! I have to save the world against the machines! The Terminators are coming! Sergeant Connor needs me!* I picked up the phone immediately. "Hi, yeah… this is Sergeant Connor…, can I speak to…Jose Campos."

I quickly said, "Yes sir, this is him, sir!"

"Yeah, um, hey, listen, we don't have a copy of your green card. I need you to provide that to us."

I confidently said, "I understand, but I am still willing to join and make the sacrifice for this country. I am confident I can be a great soldier."

Connor said, "Hmmm, yeah, in order to join the Army, you have to be a US citizen or a legal permanent resident."

I said, "Yes, I know, I don't have a green card but I wondered if you could help me get a green card. Trust me, I'll join."

Then I got a mechanized voice back from Connor: "You must be a US citizen or a legal permanent resident. When that happens, you can join." Then the call ended. I didn't understand what happened. I had a plan. My life was figured out. I was going to turn into Rambo. Then there was silence on the other end of the line.

Looking back at this episode in my life I still don't know why the US doesn't have a military program like the French Legion. There are a lot of undocumented kids in dire situations who wouldn't think twice about joining the Army, Marines, or Navy. Now I think it probably was good that I didn't join. There's a high chance I would have died in battle in Iraq or Afghanistan.

A Typical Day in Class

High school kept going and I was running on autopilot. Did I mention that I slept very little? Let me repeat it: I worked, went to school, and caught four hours of sleep when I was lucky. I existed. I lived by myself and paid my own rent in a basement room. No girlfriend, no friends, no family, no money, no future to look forward to. I became an automaton.

Toward the end of high school, I started to understand my classmates. It was magic. A classmate misspelled the word "Tomorrow," writing "Tomarrow" on the chalkboard. I went up to him and told him, "Man, even I know how to spell *tomorrow*." The guy started laughing. That was a great feeling. It had been a while since I made someone laugh.

During my Global Issues class, I was randomly selected to debate about gay marriage. I got picked to debate in favor of it. I came from a homophobic culture. Then I remembered the philosophical debates I used to have with Dad as a child. I decided to advocate for the good of humanity. My classmates were not expecting much from the quiet kid. I prepped my arguments.

I looked at the future and said in a dead serious voice in 2002, "I'm in favor of gay marriage. This is the evolution of society. Not long ago blacks and whites could not be in the same classroom, and look at you now. You even enjoy each other's company. They said similar things about black people. However, integration turned out to make this country even stronger. I don't see gay people as a threat; if they can adopt a human being in need and provide a good quality home, we all should welcome it." It was 2002 and gay rights were not common in America.

A kid told me that was the smartest thing he heard. Thirteen years later the US Supreme Court struck down all the bans on same-sex marriage. I was ahead of my time.

I graduated that year. Graduating was one of the most significant accomplishments of my life. It doesn't matter all the other degrees I acquired later. Having this high school diploma meant a lot because I was a kid hustling, working, and facing multiple circumstances that could have easily derailed my life. A lot of kids drop out of school, as they don't see the point of continuing with their education. If you are a kid in a tough spot, please continue fighting. You will succeed eventually, do not give up.

Graduation

It was my high school graduation day. Following societal protocols, I invited my dad to the ceremony. Dad wanted to see me on this special day. I picked him up from the Franconia-Springfield Metro station and drove to Stafford. I only had a learner's permit, but thankfully, I avoided being pulled over by a cop. We kept our words to the essentials—*Hi, how are you? I'm good, and you? Good. That is good.* I was a proud young man, I wanted to tell him that I did not need him. My silence showed it.

Toward the end of high school, my English skills had gotten better. I was no longer the quiet kid. Keiko, a Japanese exchange student, cheered for me when I marched with my graduation gown. Every day during my senior year, we had lunch together in school. On our last lunch, I told her this was probably the last time I would see her and that our time together had been very nice. She smiled but a few seconds later she started crying. I felt moved. I had no real bonds in high school other than a few of the international students I shared lunch with—they were probably the closest thing I had to real friends.

After the graduation ceremony, Dad took me out to celebrate. His budget took us all the way to the McDonald's in Alexandria. I had a sundae, and he had a burger. We ate in silence and just sat in the booth for a bit. Dad had this look on his face. Pride and sadness radiated in his eyes. "I'm sorry for everything, Lito. No matter what came your way, you always handled it."

I could see a tear well up in the corner of his eye. I wasn't used to seeing him this vulnerable. For some reason, I couldn't bring myself to share the same emotions. I was proud and insensitive. My skin had gotten too tough to allow myself to feel emotions. I stared at my sundae and kept eating it without making any comments.

Dad asked, "What are you going to do now?"

I said, "I don't know."

"Come join me in Maryland. A fresh start would be good for you. Living closer to DC could give you more job opportunities."

Indeed, I knew I had to leave Stafford. But as an eighteen-year-old adult, I was too proud to accept his support.

"No, thanks, I'll do my own thing."

That was the end of that conversation. I dropped Dad off at the Metro station and drove myself home. Memories of the past year started to flood my mind. I worked, I paid rent, and I studied on my own. I got no favors from my teachers either. I took classes like everyone else and earned the grades I earned. I was no longer the quiet kid.

I felt tears rolling down my cheek on my long drive back to Stafford.

SUCCESS FORMULA

1. Work is your priority. Money is a tool that you need in every decision. Without money you can't decide well. Prioritize anything that gives you an income. If you are working, you are not out there spending money.

2. Don't burn bridges. You never know when someone you meet will be able to help you in the future. Don't be a douche to random people. Maybe right now some are in a bad place, but maybe tomorrow they are in a higher place. Be friendly and kind to random folks and they will remember you when they get to higher places.

3. Be known as the person who gets things done and works hard. Your reputation will follow you everywhere. People like those who accomplish things because people like to be with those who add value.

4. Always find the positive out of any negative situation. You may not see it right away but you will see that the toughest times are the ones that shape your character. In times of adversity a person shows their true character. Embrace adversity because it provides moments of growth.

Bella and Tusk

SISTERS BELLA AND TUSK COULDN'T BE more different. Tusk is reserved, while Bella is outgoing. However, they are both smart and resourceful, and both had their fate shaped in a dramatic way by their parents. At the respective ages of three and seven, Bella and Tusk came to the US in the early '90s. They recall the trip crossing the US border with their mother, father, three other sisters, and a brother. The journey started by being thrown into the back of a covered pickup truck. Before they knew it, a helicopter was flying overhead while everyone hid in the bushes. Bella's job was to stay quiet. Mom prayed. It worked.

The family moved to Mattawa, Washington, to work in the fields. Mom and Dad picked pears, cherries, apples, and asparagus. They lived in a trailer park for farmworkers. In the winter, the ceiling of their home would sink low as snow piled higher and higher on the roof. Everyone in the trailer park had similar conditions. Mom and Dad could provide what was needed, but nothing extra. The family ate generic cereal brands and no junk food. That was too expensive. There were no presents at birthdays—having another year of life was a blessing already. Bella wrote to Santa every Christmas but the dude never came with presents. Mom and Dad told her that Santa got really busy at the North Pole. Dude didn't even have time to bring coal.

The entire village worked from sunrise to sunset in the fields picking the crops. Working conditions were difficult. Hard work was expected, even with 100-degree temperatures, dirty bathrooms, and

no drinking water. There were senior people working hard, giving everything to the job, including their bodies. These people would not get a 401(k) for retirement. Mom and Dad brought their children to labor all day in the fields, but Bella and Tusk were the weak links. Everyone complained that these two girls were terrible field-workers.

Tusk wanted more for herself. She knew her skills did not match her environment. Tusk did not want to be a senior citizen working in the fields like many of the village workers. She believed there had to be another way to live life and that getting an education was key.

Tusk found power in school. She believed that she was as smart as any kid. The teacher would ask, "Who would like to go to college?" and all the white kids would raise their hands along with a few Latino kids. Tusk realized that she was as good as any kid, with or without papers, so she raised her hand too.

Tusk excelled in high school and her little sister followed her lead. Bella took challenging Advanced Placement (AP) courses and became a cheerleader. Both girls had a pretty normal life as teenagers, including getting a driver's license, thanks to a Washington state law passed in 1993 that allowed undocumented immigrants to get a driver's license. Then, a new law in 2003 offered in-state college tuition to undocumented students going to college. The dream of an education was now a real possibility, because of where the girls lived.

Tusk graduated high school in 2005 and applied for college. Tusk's goal was to improve the working conditions of people in the fields. She saw the treatment workers received, as if they were inferior human beings. On top of that, the news on TV would describe "illegals" as criminals. The narrative on TV portrayed undocumented immigrants as stealing jobs, money, your family, everything. Tusk saw this injustice and wanted to do something about it. But what could a young girl do? She realized: nothing! But what could an educated woman do about it? Everything!

The plan was to turn herself into a powerful educated woman working for the rights of others. Tusk was lucky to have a mentor who worked in her high school and helped her with college applications. This mentor was like a counselor without an official title. The mentor revised her college essays and asked her: "What do you like fighting for?" Tusk said: "I want to fight for farmworkers." The mentor said: "Write about that."

The mentor helped Tusk compile a list of college scholarships that did not require a Social Security number, and Tusk applied to all of them. She was awarded $10,000, enough to pay for her first year of college!

Tusk got $5,000 in her second year of college, and $3,000 in her third year. She had to work different jobs in order to pay her way through college. She rolled up her sleeves and worked at Taco Bell. Did I mention that great minds are forged at Taco Bell? She also went to work in a call center. She had no papers, but she had to eat and she had to study. You should never apologize for working or studying. Tusk used a fake ID to work, so what? This is a basic necessity; thus, it is a defense.

■

Tusk being the elder of the two siblings was the pioneer when it came to going to college. Bella, four years younger, watched Tusk's example. Bella looked up to Tusk. She wanted to be like her older sister, and she even attended the same college, Eastern Washington. However, Bella began to forge her own path. She participated in the school pageant competing to become the next homecoming queen. Bella told a very personal story during the interview phase. She talked about her friend Frank, who had to drop out of college because he was undocumented and did not qualify for federal financial aid. She told the judges how she organized a fundraiser selling Krispy Kreme doughnuts and raised $3,000 for Frank. That was her platform to win the hearts of the pageant judges. Bella gave a tearful pageant speech about how Frank deserved to be in college. Through her sobbing,

Bella said: "Even if I don't win this pageant, I am still going to help Frank and I will fundraise for him and that is why I wanted to become Miss Eastern." Bella had a flashcard memorized for the speech but she threw it away, she spoke from the heart. With tears in her eyes, she won the pageant and became homecoming queen.

■

College was hard on Tusk. Sometimes she felt alone, pushing hard, swimming upstream. She felt that she was sentenced to live a life in the shadows. She was sentenced without committing a crime. She did not ask for this life.

Instead of pouting, Tusk decided to do something liberating. She became vocal about her undocumented status. She would go up on campus stages and share her story. I asked her why she would do such a thing and expose herself. I never had the balls to do such a thing. She said:

> To me, I could sit in my room and cry all day. Or I could be part of the solution. I wanted to tell myself that I did everything I could to change things, to improve things. I also felt that I hadn't done anything wrong and I needed to tell people that. That I'm just as human as they are. I wanted to put a face to those that are undocumented. I wanted to say, "Hey, talk to me, I am here, you can look at me," while I spoke with people at a church and to other students. I wanted these people to call their senators, their representatives and say, "I know Tusk and I wonder if you can help her situation."

Bella also spoke publicly about her undocumented status. She recalled one day participating in an on-campus stage presentation at 11:00 a.m., publicly sharing her story of being undocumented. This brought her to tears in front of everyone. Afterward, she had to put herself together before her 12:00 p.m. class.

Despite allowing themselves to be vulnerable, both girls had an iron will to graduate—and they did. Tusk graduated with a double major in political science and international affairs in 2010. She was a smart, college-educated woman, so now what? She felt the feeling of emptiness again. Could she get a better job using fake papers? She decided to continue studying and get a master's in public administration in order to kill time. There had been talks about immigration reform since the early 2000s, so maybe by the time she graduated with her master's degree in 2013, her immigration status would change. (I have news for you: it is 2025 and immigration reform has not happened.) But DACA happened in 2012, which changed things for some people. Tusk was able to get a work permit, which gave her a big break while she was studying for her master's. Now she had the confidence to go get whatever job she wanted. She got a better job that paid more. She graduated in December 2013 with a master's degree. Tusk continued despite her situation, and she did not give up. You never know when life is going to give you a big break, so you'd better be ready when that happens.

■

To this day their mother continues to work in the fields at the age of sixty-three. Dad works taking a crew of people from place to place and also drives a tractor. Tusk would like to see them not working so much, but it gives them a sense of empowerment to be productive and work in a beautiful field. Tusk tells me that Mom and Dad enjoy the work. They feel useful. Maybe there is something to staying active; according to *The Blue Zones*, by Dan Buettner, the world's healthiest and oldest people live an active life. Tusk and Bella's parents have Blue Zones traits of getting physically active, working long hours, and walking for long periods in the open air. Now Mom and Dad are green card holders and can take an annual three-month vacation to Mexico, which also helps.

Now, talking to Tusk, I perceive a very bright mind. She turned into a powerful, educated woman and she is fighting for others. Tusk successfully advocated for student loans for undocumented students. The state of Washington is so progressive that they now provide loans! Instead of FAFSA (Free Application for Federal Student Aid), they have WASFA (Washington Application for State Financial Aid), for people who can't file a federal financial aid package. Even though Tusk did not get student loans, she wanted to improve conditions for the next generation of students. Just like the generation before Tusk advocated to win in-state tuition.

I asked Tusk when she was going to go to law school. Her mood changed as if fantasizing about the idea. Then her look came back to what it was and she told me she wanted to start a family and debt at her age would not be fun. She wants to be financially secure. I nodded. I do think she would be a fine lawyer fighting the good fight. Tusk is risk-averse now and I get it. Humans should not have to constantly fight battles. Peace is a natural desire.

■

During my last stop in Arizona, I spoke to Bella in the middle of the desert and dry heat provided by Tucson. While driving between Phoenix and Tucson, I recalled making that same trek ten years before. Crossing the desert and red rocks of beautiful Arizona gave me memories of the times I spent there while I was still undocumented. I enjoyed talking to Bella over dinner in a not-so-authentic Mexican restaurant. I didn't know you could get unauthentic Mexican food in Arizona; I thought that only happened on the East Coast. She is definitely an all-American girl. Bella is about to buy her first house. She goes out to colleges to give motivational speeches about her story, and she gets a nice fee for it. She misses her family in Washington. At the time of this writing Bella had a green card and was applying for US citizenship. She is pursuing a PhD degree in higher education. She wants to help other students pursue their education. She married a US citizen and received her permanent residency. Bella's husband was deployed to Afghanistan and he came home with PTSD. It was Bella's husband who introduced her to therapy. Bella's therapy helped her heal her undocumented wounds.

Talking about what I was doing with this book Bella told me: "What you are doing is something that only white people would do." I was in shock *How?... What!!?... You? Why is this chick saying such a thing?* She said: "You know, only white people would leave their jobs to travel around the country getting stories." I still did not get it. I said: "OK... I take that as a compliment?" Then she explained, "Not everyone has the privilege of just taking off whenever they want to do whatever they want." Then I understood. Yes, I was in a position of privilege, and I understood that she was only used to meeting privileged people who were white. I see a more notorious segregation on the West Coast than on the East Coast, which is why the work being done by people like Tusk and Bella is so needed.

Next, I will tell you about Fresh. She can tell you what it's like to grow up as black and undocumented in America. She told me that the black community does not talk much about their undocumented status. She said she camouflaged her undocumented status with her blackness. She tells me that this camouflage is not treated as a privilege, they get the same discrimination that comes with being black plus the double whammy of being undocumented.

11

A Much-Needed Change

*Life is like riding a bicycle. To keep your
balance, you must keep moving.*
—Albert Einstein

*To improve is to change, so to be perfect is to
have changed often.*
—Winston Churchill

THAT SUMMER AFTER HIGH SCHOOL, TACO Bell's district manager told
me that she received a no-match letter and asked for my paperwork.
A no-match letter is sent by the Social Security Administration to
notify employers that there is something wrong with the employee's
Social Security number. The district manager was nice, but she didn't
know about my immigration situation.

I told her, "That's weird, I'm not sure what happened. Let me
check and see what's going on. I'll bring my paperwork tomorrow."

*Damn, they found out; I can't work here anymore. Is anyone
coming to arrest me?*

The store manager knew about my situation and she said to the
district manager that she did not know what was going on. She kept
my secret.

Every two weeks, the district manager would ask for my paperwork. I kept on coming up with excuses.

"Oh man, I forgot, I'll give you that tomorrow."

"Oh snap, I knew I forgot something today when I got out of the house."

"Do you really need that? I'm sure it's a mistake."

She kept insisting on my paperwork, and when I ran out of excuses, I told her I was quitting in two weeks. She insisted that I was a valuable employee and that I should stay. She begged me to work something out with my store manager. She wanted me to become a manager after graduation. After all, I knew how to do everything in the store. But I didn't want to be a Taco Bell manager. There was a fire in me that said, *you must aspire to something more.* So, in a very professional manner, I gave her my two weeks' notice. Deep down, I wanted to do something else. I worked at Taco Bell for a year and a half, and I was burned out. I just wanted to sleep more, read a book, watch a movie, run a little, and live life.

Plotting a Crime

Right after I gave my two weeks' notice, Francisco returned to work at Taco Bell after he quit for the fourth time. He used to quit out of the blue, but the managers kept on hiring him because he was such a good worker. We were hanging out again. We had so much fun working together. We challenged ourselves and played the who-works-the-hardest game. The managers loved it. They saw a couple Latino guys moving up and down nonstop. Very different from the other high school kids. We were immigrants and had something to prove.

Francisco's brother, Chepe, was a couple of years older. He heard the complete story about how a guy robbed the Taco Bell a year ago, and he thought he could do it too. Francisco liked that idea. When I heard them talk about it, I thought they were joking—they were not. Their plan was to rob Taco Bell again. Chepe was to come and sneak inside the store from the back door while Francisco and I were dumping the trash in the dumpsters. I would leave the back door slightly open so Chepe could go in. He would bring a gun, gloves, and a mask and get a $5,000 payday.

When I realized they were serious, I understood I was in the middle of a plot to commit a crime. I didn't know what to do. I turned to Francisco and said, "This is the craziest thing you'll do in your entire life. Either you do it with everything you got, or don't do it at all."

Francisco said, "Yeah, man, we'll do it with everything we've got."

I felt scared. Francisco continued, "Besides, you're quitting, you're entitled to a severance package. Taco Bell owes so much to you." I wanted to disagree with Francisco, but he made a lot of sense on that one.

The night of the crime came. I looked at Francisco and asked, "Are we really doing this?" He was dead serious. He saw me being nervous and he told me that everything was going to be fine. I didn't believe him. I believed Francisco many times, but this time I didn't. I made sure I was the last person to exit to take the trash out.

We took out the trash as usual during closing time. Chepe was hiding in the dumpsters. He was wearing a mask and carrying a gun. Francisco and I dropped the trash and walked back to the restaurant. Chepe got to the back door. He tried to open it, but it was locked.

Francisco looked at me. "Did you forget to leave the back door open?"

I said, "Sorry, I forgot. I guess I closed it too hard and it shut all the way."

Chepe took off his mask and exclaimed, "Dammit, Jose, you screwed everything up. We aren't doing this anymore." He put the gun inside his pants and walked away.

I truncated their stupid plan. I "forgot" to leave the door open on purpose. I stopped them from messing up. A crime like this would have taken us to prison and the next stop would have been deportation. There are so many kids out there who need guidance. Instead of doing productive things, they make up stupid plans to "get rich quick" without thinking too much about the consequences.

This was it. I needed to leave Stafford or I would become a criminal. There wasn't much going on here and I wasn't hanging out with the good guys.

I quit Taco Bell and I spent the remainder of the summer in Stafford chilling for a few weeks. I didn't know what to do with myself. So, I decided that a few weeks of no work, no school, just "me" time was proper. I visited the library to check out books and movies. I ran regularly and did push-ups. My Taco Bell days gave me a few extra pounds that I needed to let go. I ate well and slept even better. I got a little taste of what a beautiful life was. It was a much-needed break; and now, I was getting ready for a much-needed change.

Three weeks of full rest and recovery went by and then I found myself idle. These no-work days were getting boring. How much could I rest? My dad's offer was all I had. So, I decided to move to Montgomery County, in Maryland. How about I try my luck close to the big city of Washington, DC? I called Dad and said with a monotonic voice, "Do you have a place for me to join you in your basement?" He said, "Yeah, come over." I could hear excitement in his voice.

Now our relationship had to improve. It wasn't the best father-son relationship—but it was a start.

SUCCESS FORMULA

1. Take a break from time to time. If all you do is work, you burn out. Even the Lord rested on the seventh day. Are you saying you are better than God? You probably can push through a couple of years working nonstop when you are in your early twenties. But later your body will shut down if you don't give it enough rest. Take that trip with someone or on your own. Unplug a little so that you can reconnect and give it all later.

2. Express yourself by working. Work is your creation. Don't do the stupid thing of joining a strike to improve the working conditions so that your boss notices your absence. Your boss will find someone else. If you want your boss's attention, work so hard that they realize they can't do without you. Make yourself so valuable to your boss that they will hurt without your hard work.

3. Crime is not the answer. Your conscience will suffer first and then your freedom. Despite how tough things may be, crime can only bring negativity toward you. Whatever short-term gain you may have with it, it will exponentially take a toll on you. Petty theft for food and clothing is something most people can understand; committing a violent crime will get you no sympathy.

12

Maryland

Education is the most powerful weapon
which you can use to change the world.
—Nelson Mandela

I JOINED MY DAD IN THE summer of 2003. We lived in a small basement in Wheaton, Maryland. It was dark, cold, and humid. I put a bed next to the space adjacent to a kitchenette and the fridge. My dad had a small room with a door and a three-foot-square bathroom. For the first month I was a tourist. Wheaton is conveniently three Metro stops away from DC on the red line. I would take the Metro to the monuments at the National Mall and see all the different Smithsonian museums. I got to see the Air and Space Museum with all its original space capsules. The American History Museum had artifacts from the American Revolution. The Natural History Museum had its big mammoth that I encountered right as I entered. I strolled through the DC streets like a tourist.

A full month passed, and I was finally getting bored. I picked up a few history books that I kept from high school. I read them until 3:00 a.m. I became a friend of the library as that was the only source of internet I had.

I used to send a few emails back to my family in El Salvador. Dad had stopped sending money back to El Salvador and Mom didn't work. My siblings had to assume the responsibility quickly to pay the mortgage. My brother had the nerve to ask me for money.

"If you send us one hundred dollars a month, we could make it," he would write to me.

"Bro, I have no interest in that house. You have to deal with it. That's not my problem, I have my own problems," I would respond.

In Latin America, a lot of people think that life in America is easy. That anyone can get rich quick. We might have more opportunities, but success is not an overnight event. My savings were going down. I was unemployed and I had to start looking for work. I told my brother to find another way.

Job Hunt

I bought a day pass to ride the Metro to start looking for a job in the DC area. Instead of the fast-food chain place I was used to, I was looking for a job with higher pay. I began targeting hotels. I couldn't tell you how many hotels I applied to that day. Every stop on the Metro I was getting out and handing in my resume. One called the day after asking for an interview as a front desk clerk. It was the Holiday Inn in Friendship Heights on Wisconsin Avenue. I was excited. It was my first interview in this big city. I met the front desk manager a few days later. She liked what she saw, so she took me to the general manager, Ross. Ross saw me and immediately began his interview. He also liked what he saw. I was playing the part of the big executive, making myself sound as serious as possible. When it came to the salary part, I said I wanted $8 per hour. I was used to $6.75 per hour at Taco Bell. Ross was an arrogant middle-aged man from Romania. He looked like a shady guy who would nickel and dime whatever he could. I heard rumors that he used to take the food and drinks for his own house parties at the expense of the hotel owner.

"How would you react to an angry guest?" asked Ross.

I had no experience in being a front desk clerk at a hotel. All I could do was make up a response from my experience working the cash register at Taco Bell.

"I would respond like this: 'I'm sorry to hear that, Mr. Guest, but let me do an investigation and I'll see what I can do for you.'" I had a smile on my face.

I continued, "If I can't find the answer right away, I will ask my supervisor for guidance."

Ross liked that answer. *Shit, I liked that answer too.* Ross smiled, I smiled. The Romanians and Salvadorians were getting along.

"When can you start?" he asked.

"I can start tomorrow. What time should I come tomorrow?" I said.

Ross smirked, "I haven't offered you the job yet."

His smug smile taunted me. He leaned over the desk and looked me up and down. "I'm willing to take a chance with you. I can start you at $7.50 an hour. You really don't have any experience. What do you say?"

What a crappy wage. I squeezed my face up when I heard $7.50. Ross must have taken notice because he continued.

"In three months if you turn out to be right, I'll give you a dollar more," he said.

It wasn't much but it was a job. I got to wear a suit and tie all the time. Here I was at the age of eighteen thinking I had a big executive job. I borrowed a suit from my dad that was noticeably too big for me but I still used it every day.

I was excited to work in a *fancy place.* It was nice to me, but it was no Ritz-Carlton. I was chilling at the Holiday Inn. I got to work the first day and the human resources manager asked me for my papers, so I gave her the fake ID I got in DC a while back. They didn't ask many questions.

I oversaw the checkouts early in the morning. Rush hour was 8:00 a.m. to 10:00 a.m. Tourists, diplomats, and businesspeople were the typical guests. My job was to check them out as fast as possible. I mostly explained to them that if they got a bill in the middle of the night underneath their door and nothing has changed, they can drop the room keys in the box next to me and they can be on their way.

That was the Express Checkout. Some people were old-fashioned and wanted a final printout of their receipt and I printed it quickly for them.

A secret evaluator gave me a high score in my customer service and Ross was impressed. Ross personally came down to speak to Anthony, the front desk manager, and said to him that I was a "good man" and to give me a raise. I was excited. I liked the environment; I was supporting myself. Things were getting better for me.

Even things with Dad were getting normal. Dad worked in a furniture store selling furniture and from time to time we had the weekend together. For the Fourth of July that year we planned to go see the fireworks. A big kid and his dad being a couple of tourists in DC. One weekend we even went bike shopping at the local Kmart. We took bike trips to downtown DC to ride all over the Capital Crescent Trail together. Dad was happy. I guess he was happy to have company and to be a provider once again. He paid most of the rent and we both had a job to talk about. Each of us was the only thing that the other one had. We both made an effort to regain the relationship that circumstances took away from us.

I made a few friends in the hotel. Most of the housekeeping personnel were Latinos. We used to hang out and I found out that most of them didn't have papers either. That hotel was profiting from our cheap labor. From an outside perspective, some would think we were being exploited for our low wages. But in reality, I think the majority of us were thankful that the hotel still hired us despite our lack of documentation. We were thankful that we could bring home an income to support our families. This hotel is certainly not the best, but it saved many of us from working on the streets.

At the hotel I was able to meet professional guests. Doctors and lawyers would stay at the hotel for conferences. I was impressed by their ability to express themselves. I would sneak into their presentations just to sit and listen. They were able to carry themselves so confidently and talked with fluidity. They had spent years learning about their craft, and these presentations showcased their skills. I wanted to be like them. I remember talking to my coworkers about some of the doctors. The coworker told me, "Doctors take years to study and practice their craft before they become certified."

That struck a chord with me. *Studying.* My whole purpose in coming to the States was to study and learn English. I learned a bit of English from high school and my work experience, but I wasn't at the level of these doctors and lawyers.

I kept on thinking, walking down the street on a cold day, *I have to go to college.* But how? I had no papers, and the little money I made was to pay for rent, my gym membership, and a couple beers. Colleges charged undocumented people like me out-of-state tuition. That is three times the regular in-state tuition. I did the math. I saw my budget. I made some cuts. I came up with the answer. I could pay for four classes a semester in the local community college and still have twenty dollars left for emergencies. The following January, I took the plunge and dumped all my savings into one semester of college.

College

I talked to my manager Anthony and explained to him that I needed Tuesdays and Thursdays off to go to school. I'd work the weekend shift, but I also needed to take Monday and Wednesday nights off. Anthony didn't like to have restrictions on my schedule, but he helped me out. "You want to go to college? Alright, but you owe me."

I'd registered for four classes at the community college because I wanted to have a normal college experience. It wasn't a full load of five courses, as my budget only allowed four classes, but it would be a lot of work when combined with the hotel shifts. I could have taken two classes to start and not work so hard, but that would've postponed my graduation by three extra years and I would not be a "real" college student. That wasn't what I wanted.

I took the bus and read on my rides everywhere. I used to come to work with little sleep. I was no longer the happy guy checking people out. I was tired and grumpy. My face showed a burned-out old man.

I was twenty years old with the face of a thirty-nine-year-old on a hangover. The hotel accountant would walk by and ask me, "Why are you so serious all the time? You're young, you're supposed to be full of life. At your age I was having the time of my life." *If I had papers then maybe, just maybe, I'd understand what you're talking about.* I took the criticism from the accountant but I really didn't pay more attention to him.

The hotel job went from the best job of my life to the crappiest job. At the time, I needed the job to pay for my college, and every six months my bank account drained completely. I had no life. I worked and studied. That was my life. My will to succeed was strong but it took a toll. At the time I could only find a way to pay for it at the expense of my health and happiness. I was young and healthy, so I had extra energy to spare. During the summer months I would work two jobs to afford my next semester of college.

■

More time passed by, and I saved as much as I could. I was on a mission to keep paying for my college tuition. After working the front desk sometimes, I would pick up extra shifts as a banquet server in the hotel during special events. The hotel would host New Year's parties and that would give me extra work too, which was good for me. The extra money was good.

I bought a car with this money. My previous car broke long ago. I saved enough to buy a Kia Sephia 2000 with standard transmission. I had taken a couple of lessons from my brother back in El Salvador on how to drive a stick shift. My brother was impressed that I made the car go on my first try. The first day I drove the Kia I was super scared. I almost got into five car crashes. I used all my brainpower to pilot that stick shift. After a week of the stick shift, I had begun getting the gist of it. That car took me to work and school. It did save me time and I could sense my sanity improving, even if I was driving without a license. Maryland at that time did not give driver's licenses to undocumented people. When the law changed a few years later, I quickly got my driver's license. The little plastic card made me feel like my life was a little normal.

That summer of 2004 I was lonely. I didn't have many friends. On my days off, I would grab a book from the library and go to campus to read on one of the picnic tables until I got tired. Sometimes, I'd take a twenty-minute nap on the bench. I'd wake up and start reading a little more. I had no money, no friends, no love, and no family—except for Dad. I used to come home late and couldn't talk much to him. I had no life.

I enjoyed my Tuesdays and Thursdays, my college days. I spent the whole day at Montgomery College. I would start my day by going to the Olympic-size pool on campus and swim. I practiced swimming three times a week. At the beginning, I was bad, but I watched other swimmers to see how they did it. By the end of my two years in college, I learned how to swim butterfly style decently.

After swimming I spent hours and hours reading my textbooks and dissecting my economics lessons. I chose to follow a business program because I wanted money, because I knew what the lack of money does to your life. I even took calculus even though it wasn't required for my business program. My rationale was that I was going to make the best curriculum I could. Going to college certainly was costing me a lot of money, so I wanted to get my money's worth. Hours of reading and working math problems would help me years later when I had to spend hours and hours reading law books and understanding case law.

On the weekends I used to go to this small Latin club in Rockville. I even got a few beers while the bouncer wasn't watching, as I wasn't twenty-one yet. Those were the fun nights. I would still have to clock into work early, at 7:00 a.m., on Saturdays and Sundays. There were times when I went straight from the club to sleep in the hotel meeting room underneath a table and woke up at 6:45 a.m. to start working at 7:00 a.m. I would wake up, shower at the hotel gym, and head back to the lobby to start my day. I was so young and full of energy.

I could do stunts like that and still be okay.

I still hadn't registered my new Kia with the Motor Vehicle Administration. It had been a few months and I was procrastinating. I used old license plates to go out clubbing with my friend Josue, the housekeeper. That night I wasn't drinking. I was being responsible, until Josue grabbed a beer and literally put it in my mouth. *I guess I could have this one beer.* I was still under twenty-one and one beer was all I had. After spending a few hours at the club, dancing a few salsa songs, it was time to head out. I was driving with Josue to the hotel to crash underneath the same table as usual when I saw a cop in the rearview mirror. I kept on driving. I kept my cool. Five miles later the cop turned on his emergency lights and stopped me in downtown Bethesda. The cop approached the window and tapped it for me to lower it. He leaned down to my eyesight. "License and registration."

I gave him my license but no registration. My car wasn't insured either. He asked me, "Have you been drinking?"

I said, "Um, not exactly. A friend put a beer in my mouth."

That was the wrong answer. Just admitting to one sip of beer is reason enough for a cop to ask you to step out of the car and suspect you of drunk driving. The cop conducted a full sobriety test on the streets. People were looking at me and I didn't like the feeling.

"Alright, sir. I understand your reason, but you should go catch the real criminals." The cop did not like that.

His partner came over with a Breathalyzer and made me blow on it. Both cops looked at the results. Both of their smug smiles were wiped away in a second with a frown. They couldn't arrest me. The Breathalyzer read "0." I ended the night with a couple of tickets and a must-appear-in-court citation for not having insurance.

"What happened to the Breathalyzer?" I asked.

"You're lucky, it's zero," The cop replied. But they towed my car because it wasn't registered. Josue and I took a cab the rest of the way to the hotel. Normally I slept underneath the ballroom tables, but Josue had keys to the housekeeping closet where they stored rollaway beds, so we crashed there.

All I could think during that night was: *I can't believe I'm immune to Breathalyzers.*

In a few weeks I had to go to court. The judge at court scared me by telling me that not having insurance in a car was a jailable offense and that I could go to jail for sixty days if I did not have a lawyer next time. I didn't think it was a big deal to drive an uninsured car, but apparently the law thought otherwise. I hired a lawyer, and he told me to register the car and insure it, so I did that. Ultimately, the prosecutor dropped the case.

Thinking about this cop interaction in Bethesda, Maryland, it could have been bad had I been in another part of the United States. The truth was that the officers were polite to me. I wonder what would have happened had I been in Alabama. From that moment on, I tried to stay out of trouble.

SUCCESS FORMULA

1. Advocate always for your best interest. You are the number one person you should care for. You can't save others if you yourself do not have the basics. Save yourself first, then you can save others.

2. Have a goal and never forget it. Never stop thinking about your goal. Day and night ask yourself: What is one thing I can do to get me closer to my goal? Have goals that you don't know if they are possible to achieve because you will always try to figure it out. Who knows, you might achieve it.

3. Smile often and smile to everyone genuinely. People like friendly faces. A serious face is an obstacle for others to interact with you. The more people interact with you the more opportunities you create.

4. Success is not easy. If your goal is giving you a hard time, that is a sign that you are onto something worthwhile.

5. If you want to learn something, go to the places where people with knowledge go. If you want to learn Spanish, go to Spanish restaurants and clubs. Even go to another country. If you want to learn medicine, hang around the local clinic and hospital; you will meet a doctor who can tell you where to go next.

6. Be polite to people in power (cops, judges, etc.). If they want to make your life miserable, they can. Most people in power are nice and do their jobs. But if you encounter a bad one, don't give them a reason to hurt you.

Fresh

I TRAVELED TO WEALTHY THOUSAND OAKS, a city next to Los Angeles. Big houses with nice cars full of rich people. I met Fresh in a local Del Taco under the umbrellas of the outside patio to enjoy the beautiful California weather.

Fresh was born and raised in a small town in the countryside of Jamaica. She is the second to last of five siblings. Her mother had different baby daddies and was in trouble with the Jamaican law. Her mom was incarcerated for selling stolen goods when Fresh was three months old, leaving Fresh to be raised by her grandmother. Fresh's grandmother was very strict. Grandma forced Fresh to go to church every single day. Bible reading was mandatory. House chores were a must. She had to clean here and clean there. Carry water from the river to cook. Bathe in the river while doing laundry. Fresh lived in a house made out of zinc. They collected rainwater to drink and went to the bathroom in a hole outside the house. Fresh was living the Jamaican Cinderella story without the Prince Charming part.

Her mother got out of prison when Fresh was twelve years old but did not claim Fresh from her grandmother right away. Instead, Fresh's mother hid away on a boat to America. Fresh's older brother had plans to move to America and join their mother. This brother was so excited to go to the US that he bragged to everyone in town about his plans. A jealous guy thought he was being pretentious and started a quarrel. The dude stabbed the brother to death. Just like

that. People don't mess around in Jamaica. The next in line to go to America was Fresh's next older brother. They told him to keep his mouth shut until he arrived in the US. After seeing the older brother's fate, this brother kept quiet. Each sibling went to America one by one soon after.

Eventually it was Fresh's turn to go to America. She was twelve. Fresh's family introduced her to a "friend" who was in charge of taking her on a plane from Jamaica to the US. She never met this woman before, but Fresh was used to doing what she was told. It was a capital offense to question her grandmother. This "friend" had passports for her. What kind of passports? The fake ones. Fresh wasn't going to check the validity of her legal papers. All she knew was that she had to take an airplane to go see her mother. She had never been on a plane before. She hopped into a big tube made out of steel and flew to Inglewood, California, where her mother was waiting. She literally met her mother for the first time in her life when she got off the plane. There was no more Grandma there whom Fresh was familiar with. Now there was this strange woman who claimed to be her mom. To Fresh's surprise, Mom wasn't as strict as Grandma. Mom did not check homework. Mom did not check grades. Fresh was no longer living in a strict military barracks with Grandma; now it was up to Fresh to control herself. Grandma gave her a good foundation that kept Fresh accountable, that is all that Grandma could do. That was the best thing that Grandma did for Fresh. Fresh felt from time to time that she was slacking in school. In the back of her head, she could hear Grandma's voice screaming at her: "Fresh, go read another chapter for school! Fresh, now read your Bible chapter! Fresh this! … Fresh that! Freshhh, Freshhh, Freshhh!"

Fresh was surprised to see the luxury items she found in the poor apartment in Inglewood. She saw a toilet with running water, a kitchen with a refrigerator. Only super rich people in Jamaica had luxuries like that. She thought her apartment was in a great neighborhood. However, she soon learned that she lived in the hood controlled by the

Bloods or Crips. She learned that she could not wear blue or red while walking down the street. Those colors belonged to the gangs. If she had the wrong colors in front of the wrong gang member, she risked getting hurt. She learned not to buy any clothing with red or blue.

Fresh only met her father one time in her entire life, when she was fifteen years old. Dad was in California and came down to meet his child. After that one visit Fresh kept in touch by phone with him for about six months. Then Dad disappeared. It turned out Dad went to jail and got deported back to Jamaica. Dad is dead now.

Fresh's two older siblings also got deported. Her older sister was traveling and got caught with fake papers at an immigration checkpoint. Her siblings used fake IDs in order to work because no employer would hire them without any kind of papers. When I say any kind, I mean any kind. Some employers know that the papers are fake, but they cover their rears by pretending that they don't know. In case the government does an I-9 audit, the employer can claim ignorance and say they didn't know they hired undocumented immigrants. It was a win-win for the employer and the sister, until she got caught. The older brother was at a party and someone was talking trash about him. The brother, pretending to be an alpha male, put that dude in his place and beat the shit out of him. He got arrested, which means he also got fingerprinted, and the immigration officers put the brother in his place too. He got his one-way ticket to Jamaica.

Fresh's mother had another baby that was born in America. Her mother was living in an abusive relationship with a deadbeat guy. It was a rough situation for Fresh. She was poor, from a dysfunctional family, in a bad neighborhood, and black. Being undocumented and black was a double whammy. She could camouflage her undocumentedness because most people think that the only undocumented folks are Mexican. However, Fresh suffered discrimination. Fresh was tired of living in a rough place. She was desperate. Her family went through a lot of traumas and it was a matter of time before it was her turn to suffer. What comes next was a big break for her.

Fresh found comfort in church. The very same thing that Fresh was forced to do in Jamaica was what gave Fresh a break. She attended church regularly, and her pastor noticed her. The pastor saw a smart, dedicated girl. He saw a good heart, hard work, and consistency in Fresh. Her pastor won over Fresh's trust and she felt accepted. There were many counseling sessions at church, and during one of those sessions Fresh opened up about her situation at home and asked her pastor if she could come live with him and his family while she finished high school. The pastor welcomed her into his home. Fresh left to live with the pastor in a good part of town. Her mom did not object. Her mom could actually see that it was the best for Fresh. In this new home Fresh could focus on schoolwork, free from oppressions, free from intrafamily violence, free from gang threats. She focused her energy on her studies and she did very well.

Fresh worked hard in middle school and high school. She knew that her way out of poverty was education. There was a counselor in high school who worked with Fresh to apply for scholarships. Fresh told Mr. Counselor about her struggles and her undocumented situation, and Mr. Counselor told her to keep going, that he would find a way for her to go to college. All that Fresh had to do was to keep her grades up. Fresh believed in her counselor and she did her part. At the time, most scholarships for undocumented students targeted Latino students; there were not many scholarships targeting black undocumented immigrants. But the counselor made Fresh apply to over fifty scholarships. She got a full-ride scholarship to California Lutheran University in the rich area of Thousand Oaks. Now she had to figure out how she would pay for her living expenses.

The counselor kept on helping her and made the connection with the Ritzes. The Ritzes were this upper-class Anglo-Republican family. They believed in doing good deeds. Mr. Counselor talked to the Ritzes about this poor girl who was super smart, he'd never seen someone with this kind of success spirit. The Ritzes were intrigued. They invited Fresh to come down to their home in Thousand Oaks for an in-person meeting. That was one hour away from LA. Now Fresh had to think how to get there.

Fresh asked her pastor for a ride, and he took her to meet the Ritzes. She arrived at this huge house with a long driveway and fancy cars parked in the garage. The door to this house was so enormous that an elephant could enter. When she and the pastor entered, she saw the tallest ceiling she had ever seen with fancy chandeliers hanging from it. Fresh was approached by a maid, who directed her and the pastor to come in and wait in the living room while the maid announced them to Mr. Ritz. Nice carpets on the floors and art on the walls decorated the living room. All of those items looked very expensive.

Mr. Ritz appeared in the living room with his German shepherd and wanted to talk to Fresh by himself. The pastor excused himself and left Fresh alone. There she was in Thousand Oaks with this rich white man. It was the first time Fresh was alone with a white man. She was scared. She was also scared of the dog. Mr. Ritz said, "The dog is a good dog and it won't bite." They shared lunch and Mr. Ritz inquired about Fresh's story. This was Fresh's moment; she was there at the advice of her counselor to come share her story with this man who could help her if he heard a good story. Fresh shared with Mr. Ritz things that she had never shared with anyone else. Here she was with an unknown man and Fresh was telling him everything about poor Jamaica, gangs in LA, lack of papers, discrimination, and schoolwork. Mr. Ritz liked what he heard. He said, "I never met an *illegal* before. But I'm very impressed with your story." He said, "My family likes to help people and I think we can make a difference in your life. If you let me, I will pay for your college expenses." Fresh was shocked. She'd found her fairy godmother.

The Ritzes gave Fresh the option to live in the luxury house with them or live in a dorm in college. Fresh did not want them to spend money on her, even though the Ritzes had plenty of it. Fresh felt bad for "wasting" money when she could live in a perfectly good house and she just had to ride her bike to classes. Fresh stayed in the big house with a pool. The Ritzes even paid for Fresh's swimming lessons. The Ritzes gave her cash for her to spend. To be transparent, Mr. Ritz sat down with Fresh at the end of the year and disclosed to her in a very delicate way how much they had spent, showing her an expense report. "Here is what college costs, here is what we spent, you can pay us back when you can." Fresh's shy face dropped to the floor. "I'm joking. We are doing this for you, no need to pay us back." Fresh had her eyes wide open with a smile. "Although I would not mind if you pay me back when you make it big." Fresh nodded her head with a bigger smile along with Mr. Ritz. She started to get his sense of humor.

After college Fresh actually got accepted to law school but she decided to pursue a master's in public policy. The Ritzes had paid for college and she felt inappropriate asking them to pay for grad school. Luckily, by the time she had to go to grad school it was 2013 and DACA gave her the opportunity to get a work permit. Fresh worked for a living and paid for her own master's degree.

Fresh's family did not understand the concept of graduate school. They did not understand why people went to school after finishing school. Fresh also told them about some internships or service opportunities that were unpaid. That flipped the family as well. How can someone work for no money! She explained it was experience, knowledge, etc. The family wasn't happy with her explanation. How could Fresh explain to her family about helping people and the concept of giving back without expecting anything in return? Her family in Jamaica and in Inglewood were struggling to survive. The concept of volunteering was foreign. But Fresh learned from the Ritzes that you can make a difference by helping others in need. She was blessed by the Ritzes. Now it was her time to pay it forward.

■

When I met her in Thousand Oaks, Fresh was struggling with her religious beliefs. She grew up in a religious environment and she had recently broken up with her same-sex partner of four years. The ex was a white woman from Iowa. Fresh was a black woman from Jamaica. Both of them had sexual shame as communicated down to them by their religious dogma. The stress they felt led them to split. It was a mix of racial, religious, cultural, and family differences. The father of Fresh's ex is a pastor. Fresh was grateful for the shelter that church provided her while she was in survival mode. But she was conflicted with the way the Church ostracizes the LGBTQ community.

Whatever life brings to Fresh, she is a success and she will continue thriving. She now has a PhD in higher education administration and is working as a director of undergraduate admission for California Lutheran University. She also is the founder of Embracing Undocumented, a platform to serve undocumented people. You can read her book *Amplifying Black Undocumented Student Voices in Higher Education*. She tells her own story there.

While I'm on the subject of black undocumented folks, let me tell you the story of Magnet. She went to the US Congress and changed the law, giving thousands of people permanent legal status. How many people can say they were undocumented at some point and later they went to the US Congress to change the law?

13

Working Hard

Success is often achieved by those who don't
know that failure is inevitable.
—Coco Chanel

Do the best you can until you know better.
Then when you know better, do better.
—Maya Angelou

ON A RANDOM MONDAY, A MAN dressed in business attire walked into the hotel. His eyes wandered for a moment before they landed on me. I was working the front desk. The man started walking in my direction with a smirk on his face. "We're hiring at the luxury condo, Somerset One, next door. You should apply."

He wrote down his phone number and walked back out. *Why not, let me apply, I have nothing to lose.* I walked to the condo, and they gave me an application. The application asked for a bunch of information, including references. I had no idea who could be my reference, so I wrote down that the man in the suit was my longtime friend. They called me for an interview the next day and I went during my lunch break. The manager, Mrs. Garfinkel, a Jewish lady in her upper sixties, was inquisitive of me. After a good thirty seconds of inspecting me and my voice, she liked me. I was a good-looking young man, sharp, with a good demeanor—I did learn a few hospitality tricks at the hotel after all.

My couple of years of experience in hospitality made me an ideal candidate. I could see it in Mrs. Garfinkel's eyes that she wanted me to work for her.

"How much are you making at the hotel?" she asked.

"Ten dollars an hour," I lied.

Mrs. Garfinkel spoke straight to the point in a loud way to make herself understood. She wrote something down. We talked a bit more and she kept asking me questions. By the end of the interview, the lady told me that they will let me know within forty-eight hours if I got the job. I thought it went well but then the feeling of starting a new job came back to haunt me. *I have a job in a hotel—what if I quit the steady paycheck at the hotel to go to this condo building and the new place finds out that I don't have papers?*

The following day, I got a call from the assistant to the general manager. "The job's yours! Come ready and we'll be happy to bring you in. The pay is ten dollars an hour." Many would have probably jumped at the chance of a bigger wage. I was insecure.

"Thank you for the offer but I already make ten dollars where I work now. I don't want to leave this nice job to go to a new one that pays me the same."

The assistant was quiet, there wasn't much to say. He couldn't believe I rejected the job. I was afraid of going to a new job and having to go through the hiring process again and telling them that I had papers when I didn't.

A week later Mrs. Garfinkel called me and asked me to come see her. I was surprised. I went down to her office during my lunch break. She was sitting at her desk working on her computer. When she heard me walk in, she stopped what she was doing and smiled at me. "I think you should come work for us, but $11.00 an hour is outside our budget."

"I understand, ma'am, but this probably won't work anyways because I need Tuesdays and Thursdays off because I need those days to go to college."

Mrs. Garfinkel's eyes widened at that statement. "How lovely, you're a college student! I love workers that go out of their way and want to advance their education. Jose, I think you'd make a great asset here. The only way you can get $11.00 an hour is if you're a supervisor. If you accept my offer as a weekend supervisor, you can get $11.00 an hour plus tips."

I got a promotion without having started. On the inside, I was laughing my ass off. The more you act like you don't want a job, the more they want you. In my most posh accent, I said, "Very well, Mrs. Garfinkel, I do accept those conditions and I will be delighted to join the team."

I was ecstatic, I was laughing on my way back to work. The bluff actually worked. The job was even easier. But it hit me, I must quit my current job and take a chance on this new job. I had to answer the papers question again. Most undocumented people would agree that there is anxiety when it comes to applying for a new job. Will they give me a job? Will they find out that I don't have papers? Will they call immigration if they find out? What if I try to get a new job but then I lose both jobs?

I gave my two weeks' notice and decided to leave my hotel job. However, the front desk manager told me that I couldn't quit. "No, you can't quit now, Jose. You can't do this to me."

"Alright, Anthony, I won't, but they're offering me $11.00 an hour. Can you match that? You guys are only paying me $8.50 an hour."

"That can't happen, but I'll see what I can do."

"By the way, Anthony, I have to start in a week and a half, so I won't be able to make it to the last day of the schedule."

"You're coming to work, you put your resignation in writing. If you don't come to work that day, I will tell your new manager that you are a quitter and are not leaving this place in good condition."

I said, "You can do what you think is proper, I cannot stop you from doing what you want to do." Then I went back to the front desk. I finished working in the hotel except for the last day. That day I called in sick but in fact I went to work in the new place.

I started in the building and it was very nice. The rich residents were nice people and one by one introduced themselves to me. The phone rang and I picked up every call with a cheerful greeting. I said hi to each new person that came my way. I was happy again. My smile returned to my face. Then the phone rang.

I picked up. "Somerset One, good morning, Jose speaking."

"Is this Jose?"

"Yes sir! How can I help you?"

"So, you are not sick?"

"Absolutely not, sir, I am full of energy!"

"But you called in sick." That was Anthony on the line. *"You aren't leaving this job on good terms. I will tell your current manager that you aren't to be trusted."*

"Again, Anthony, I said to you before that you could do what you think is proper. I wish you the best and I thank you for the opportunity. That is all I can do. Now excuse me, I have work to do."

A few months later I heard that Anthony complained to Mrs. Garfinkel like a little bitch and Mrs. Garfinkel defended me, telling him that she heard nothing but wonderful things about me.

This job didn't ask me for much documentation. The assistant working at the manager's office asked me to fill out the paperwork and I did. This time I gave her a fake paper receipt coming from the government indicating that my green card renewal was accepted. It wasn't a fake ID this time, just a photocopy of correspondence from the Immigration Service where I added my name. I could tell the lady was a bit shocked, but she didn't pay much attention since I worked in the hotel next door. I started working without problems. I was relieved. I didn't even have to show her a fake green card.

I was excited and full of energy. I emanated such a positive vibe that people loved me. The weekday employees liked me, the residents loved me, and the visitors were gracious. Until I met the weekend employees. I was twenty. I couldn't even legally drink yet. The people I was supervising were significantly older than I was. They ranged from their thirties to fifties.

Not just that, but they were black. Not just black, they were Africans. Here I was, a young Latino kid being the supervisor of these grown men and women. That was a slap in their faces. I didn't think much of it at the time, but now I understand. It was 2005, the white residents had black people serving them. This time they were not in the plantations. I want to believe that Mrs. Garfinkel decided to hire me instead of promoting one of them because I was in college. Now that I think back, she may have decided to promote anyone that wasn't black. I tried to be the cool supervisor, but that backfired. All I could do was my best. For my first managerial job, I did okay. It was hard to win their respect. I mean, I was just twenty, I didn't know much about leadership back then.

When the guys at the valet parking were busy, I went there to help park cars and bring packages to the units. They welcomed my help, and the service was prompt. Little by little the weekend staff appreciated the hard work during busy hours. The residents tipped me regularly. I was uncomfortable getting tips at first but my supervisor told me, "Don't be ashamed to get the tips, it's part of your work." I rarely got tips at the hotel. After a while I got used to getting a few dollars here and there. My beer money was growing. Money is money after all. If they wanted to give me money, I could only help them by taking it.

Moving Up

Once in class, my literature professor made an announcement. "Hello, class, a good friend of mine wants an intern, and the job pays eleven dollars an hour. He owns an English-to-Spanish translation firm in downtown DC. If you are interested, please let me know after class." I was interested—it was a professional job, an office job in downtown DC. That's where the action happens. I approached my professor after class. She gave me the contact info.

I called the number and a tough voice on the other line said quickly, "Send your resume to that email." I did. A week later I got a call, and the tough voice asked me quickly, "Can you come tomorrow for an interview?" I did.

I got off at Metro Center Station between G and Thirteenth Streets. It was a busy weekday, people rushing to their destinations. I walked past the Macy's store and went into a nice downtown building. *Real business is conducted there,* I thought to myself. Just walking inside was intimidating. I went to the reception desk and said I was there for an interview. They sent me to the tenth floor. I checked in with the receptionist on the tenth floor and the tough voice called me inside.

"Come over!"

I met this older man in his seventies. He was a Cuban American with a thick Cuban accent. He had a super serious face. We chatted, I told him about what I've done, and he said that my literature professor was his friend.

He said, "Let me give you a test. Come to this computer and write in five minutes in English and in Spanish why I should hire you." I did. I came back with a printed write-up of three paragraphs and he read it.

He said, "Your Spanish is very good. And so is your English… Well, kid, when can you start?"

I went with the standard two weeks' notice. I had to notify my current employer. I was excited again; I was moving up in the world. I wasn't making much money but I was in an office in downtown DC. I was where business was done. You never know, next time I could be working in Congress.

■

I went back to work at the luxury condo building and I was excited. I didn't tell them I was quitting. I just wanted to enjoy for a day the fact that I had a future waiting for me. I was taking a pay cut because the new job required fewer hours, but I did not care because I was going to an office job with a cubicle like in the movies. That meant I would have more time to study in college and more sleeping time. I cut my expenses too. These were the days when I ate cereal for breakfast, lunch, and dinner. I was broke but I didn't mind; I was working in downtown DC.

I was actually fired from the luxury condo job one week before I started the translation job. I ripped a page from the log book trying to hide the inefficiency of my weekend team from the manager. I owned my mistake and the manager told me that I had to go. It wasn't Mrs. Garfinkel this time—she was let go without severance after a new property management group took over. The new manager needed political points in front of the other employees, so she fired me. It was a nice ride and I owned my mistake. I did not mind much, so I took the rest of the week to rest before I started a new job.

■

The new firm was small with three workers: Jack, my boss, Richard, my second boss, and me. I was third in command. My job was to do anything that Jack wanted. From getting coffee to translating a few documents to going to the local pharmacy to get his Viagra. Jack had worked for the Clinton administration and he was well connected. He had even been the vice president of the Democratic Party way back in the 1980s. In his later years he kept busy translating manuals from English to Spanish for unions and other businesses.

Whenever there was a computer freeze on Jack's screen, he would yell profanities, and everyone would hear them. You could hear Jack from his office shouting, "Motherfucker... Piece of shit... Bitch... Fuck." In that order and for no reason. He was at the point in his life that he didn't care much about what people thought of him. Jack would call me into his office to fix his computer. I used my computer skills of "Control, Alt, Delete" to unfreeze his screen. I would put Jack back on track. I became Jack's go-to man for all things.

A month into this job, Jack asked me to make copies of my immigration papers and put them into a file. I gladly made a copy of "my papers" and gave him the file. Jack didn't even look at it. He could look like an ogre sometimes, but that was a façade to his kind heart.

I was scared of him, but little by little I started to get him. Thanks to this job I could pay for college and still have time to study.

The office in the building provided free milk and apples. I ate what I could for free and saved my money to pay for my out-of-state college tuition I had to pay as an undocumented student. It sucked—I was jealous of others who had to pay less—but I made it a point to continue with my education. Resentment built up in my heart. I won't deny that.

Then You Meet a Girl

During an ice cream social at the office, I met this beautiful twenty-one-year-old mid-Atlantic girl. Her name was Christy. She had green eyes, and I felt her energy. She worked right next to my cubicle. I'd see her in the hallway and I'd say hi. I'd see her at the kitchenette and I'd say hi. I'd see her on the elevator and I'd say hi. We smiled at each other a lot. She was a temporary worker. Christy was on a probation period. Then three months passed. She came to my cubicle suddenly to tell me, "Just wanted to let you know that my probation period ended and I'm not staying here. My last day is in a week."

"That sucks, they don't know what they are doing."

She nodded and left for her cubicle. Later that afternoon I kept thinking, *It's now or never*. I walked up to her cubicle acting calm, cool, and collected. I propped my arms over the side of her cubicle and she immediately took notice. "How about we go for a beer tonight to celebrate your freedom?"

She looked up at me and smiled. I took that as a yes. I quickly said, "Okay, write your number down and I'll call you." She did. I grabbed the number instantaneously and walked back to my cubicle as fast as I could. I felt like The Man. *I got a girl's number!*

We went out that night to a couple of bars in downtown Silver Spring. We had a few drinks and walked around. We started talking about how China was the most capitalist country on earth despite them being communists. Christy studied international relations and spent a semester at Oxford during college. She was a bright girl. I walked her to her apartment building. A nice relationship started.

We went out every weekend after that. She met my dad. I spent Christmas with her family in Delaware. We were in New York City for New Year's Eve. We did everything together. This was my first love.

Trying It Out as a Waiter

The summer of 2007 I got a second job as a waiter in an Italian restaurant in downtown Bethesda. I needed more money. Besides paying for college I had a girlfriend to take on dates. Christy didn't like the fact that I had to work every weekend. In the end, you can't make them happy—you work weekends so you can take your girlfriend out, but then you don't have much time to take her out.

I wasn't a good waiter. I mixed up orders and couldn't pay attention to the customer's details. Their constant chatter, always complaining and telling me what they wanted. The chef of this restaurant was a stressed-out old creep who was cranky. He straight up yelled at me many times. This was definitely not my vocation. The restaurant promised me $15 an hour. It was decent money. But on my second paycheck they only paid me $10 an hour. I talked to my manager and pointed out the mistake. He told me he was going to correct it in the next paycheck. My third paycheck came back to $15 an hour, but it didn't include the money owed to me from my second paycheck. When I went to confront the manager about the missing money, he told me he was letting me go. I wasn't the best waiter out there and I acknowledged it. I told the manager that it was fine to fire me, but they had to pay what they promised.

I was furious. They said $15 an hour. I called them many times, but they never answered my calls. They blew me off. Something had to be done about it. I went to my local courthouse and learned how to sue somebody in small claims court. They owed me $150. That was a lot of money to me. I sent multiple letters to the restaurant demanding my money. I made multiple calls to different managers.

I asked one manager her name and she said, "Hey, man, I just work here, I have nothing to do with giving you the money, it is up to the owner." It took me three months, but I gathered all the documents I needed to file a lawsuit in court. I was in full litigation mode. I didn't care that I had no papers; I was taking them to court. I got to the courthouse and went up to the clerk. The clerk told me that I was missing a piece of paper.

"Can you make a copy for me, please?"

She said, "It will be $1.00."

One dollar for one copy! That's outrageous.

"No, that's fine, I have a copy machine at home." I went home to make that one copy so I could come back to the courthouse. As I was walking into my house, I checked the mail. I saw a letter from the restaurant. I opened the envelope and found a check with the money owed to me. I was pissed! I did not want them to pay me. I wanted my day in court. I really wanted it to be my first litigation experience. I wanted my fight and this motherfucker chickened out. Funny enough, the restaurant went out of business a couple years later.

Next, I'll tell you how I really got to pay for the rest of my schooling. Without this move I would not have been able to go to law school.

SUCCESS FORMULA

1. Always think about your growth. If you know your destination, people will get out of your way to let you reach your goal. Some will even help you.

2. Eventually you will meet people who will present obstacles. You cannot control what they do, all you can do is your best. Eventually most people will see who you really are due to your hard work and good intentions.

3. Don't undercut your value. Believe that you are worth the money you are seeking. It is called earning a paycheck. You are not working for free. Your job is lucky to have you. Believe in yourself. If they don't want to give you the money you want, they cannot afford your quality to begin with, so move on and be in the place that deserves you.

4. You are bound to make mistakes. Have a second plan in the event that a mistake appears. Most people will accept you to rectify your mistakes, but be ready to move on when they don't.

14

An Unusual Mentor

*My job is not to be easy on people. My job
is to take these great people we have and to
push them and make them even better.*
—Steve Jobs

IT WAS THE SPRING OF 2006. My last semester of community college.
I had to figure out how to continue my education. To get a bachelor's
degree, I would have to attend a four-year institution. But a four-year
university program costs a lot more money than community college.
I had a job, but the math didn't work out. Even with two jobs, I
could not pay out-of-state tuition at the University of Maryland. It
wasn't until 2011 that University of Maryland would allow in-state
tuition for undocumented students. *What could I do?* I thought about
selling drugs. I heard cocaine was a lucrative business—probably
good enough to pay for college. *Yeah, that's a great plan.* And even
if it wasn't, what did I have to lose? Then I thought about guns and
prison. I tabled that plan. Then something else hit me.

Because I used to work at a luxury condo, I'd met a lot of rich
people. What if I started a scholarship campaign fund asking them
for donations? In my business classes, I learned that direct mailing
was one of the best ways to get customers. I decided to send a letter
to all the rich residents of the building. If each one of them donated
$1,000, I would have plenty of money to pay for my next two years
of college. I could even rent a decent apartment. The man who told

me about the job at the condo still worked there. I went to him for help gathering all the names of the residents and their unit numbers. I addressed each letter by name and apartment number. *Even if I have a 10% success rate, in a building with fifty units, I would receive $5,000.*

The letter said something like this:

> *Dear Mr. Wallet,*
> *I hope you remember me! I worked here, for you, for the past two years and I've enjoyed the friendship I have made with you. I'm on my way to a four-year university and would love your support in the form of a donation! I am smart, kind, and good-looking wanting to expand my education. With your help, success is around the corner.*

At the end of the letter, I included a picture of myself working at the front desk. It seemed like a good plan. I sent the fifty letters, then I waited. Nothing the first week. During the second week, I received a letter from one of the residents. *I hit the jackpot.* I opened the envelope and saw a $100 check. This must be a mistake. I read the written portion of the check and it said ONE HUNDRED DOLLARS. There was a note,

> *I commend you for your effort. Look into government grants and financial aid from the government.*

Thanks… I would have done that sooner, but people like me aren't accepted by FAFSA. Then I got another envelope with a $50 check and another one with $100. That was all I got from my fundraising campaign. *What was I supposed to do with $250?* I deposited the money in my account and continued thinking about ways to pay for college. I did some research on scholarships; however, all of them required immigration papers. No scholarship at the time said, "It's okay if you don't have papers, we encourage you to apply. You'll get it on the merits." Then I was back to the drug dealing plan. But not really, I was too scared to do that.

A few weeks later, I got a call from Lenny, one of the residents in the building. Lenny was in his late sixties. He lived alone and wasn't popular among the residents. A few years before, he brought home some suspicious people. That night he got shot in the head by one of them. It was a miracle he was still alive. Lenny was Jewish and gay. He had lived in the closet all his life growing up in the Jewish community back in the 1950s. He was even engaged to marry a woman, but the woman canceled the wedding. Back in his day, they wouldn't have accepted Lenny for who he was. Lenny asked me if I could come to his place and talk about the letter. I decided to go and see what he could offer.

I'm not going to lie; Lenny gave me the vibe of a creepy old guy with bad intentions. I came into his apartment and the place smelled weird, like old people do. He opened the door and looked at me with a fantasy smile and staring eyes. I shook his hand and he shook mine with both hands, taking an extra seven seconds. Lenny took me to his living room and started to subliminally talk about beds and getting comfortable.

"Would you like to take your shoes off?" he said.

I looked at him with a weird face. "No, I came here because I thought you had a donation for me."

"If you behave well toward me, I can give you money afterward," he said.

I was getting annoyed; I just wanted a check and to get away from this creepy guy. "What do you need?" I said.

"How about something sexual?"

Fuck no! I thought. *How the hell do I get out of here?* I was getting pissed and my face showed it.

Lenny saw my pissed-off face and said, "Don't get like that, I was just joking." He continued, "I thought you were gay. You write in your letter that you were a good-looking man. I thought you were offering your services."

I intended to be funny but this guy did not get my joke, he wanted to get some. I was disappointed that another donation attempt to the Jose Campos College Fund was failing. I stood up and politely spoke to Lenny, waving goodbye.

"Thanks for the talk, sir."

"Call me Lenny."

"Thanks for listening and offering to help, Lenny. I guess you can't help me and I can't help you. If you want to hang out some other time, as friends, let me know."

"How are you with computers?" he asked.

"I'm pretty good," I said while looking at the door and possible escape routes.

"My assistant just left me, and I need someone to help me on the weekends to do some bookkeeping work."

"I just finished my Accounting II class, so I can help. I'm really good at accounting. I love accounting." That was a bad lie, but Lenny didn't care.

"Okay, good. Come next weekend and I'll train you. I'll teach you what you really need to know. All the things you are learning in your accounting classes are good, but you'll know what really matters. Is $15 an hour okay?" he asked.

"Yes, that's good," I said with a calm tone. I was happy to get $15 an hour!

After that, I started working for Lenny for a few hours during the weekends. That was extra cash I needed. I didn't mind Lenny's creepy presence. A job is a job. Lenny eventually understood that I was straight and stopped the harassment.

Over time, Lenny and I developed a friendship. Every Saturday I would work hard early in the morning to work on spreadsheets and matching the bank accounts to his profit-and-loss statements to make sure tenants paid rent to Lenny. I would make sure his balance sheet was in order, checking that his investment funds deposited dividends accurately. I worked all Saturday until late at night.

During lunch we would talk about accounting principles and business laws over pizza, salad, and minestrone soup at Ledo's Pizza. Lenny would tell me about taxes and how much money he has to save in order to pay his quarterly taxes. This was real-life business exposure.

After the long hours of my Saturday workday, Lenny took me to dinner at Chadwick's, a local place on Wisconsin Avenue where we kept talking about rental incomes, stocks, and mutual funds while I had all the beers I wanted. It was open season for beers. When you are broke and a college student, you take all the free beer you can get. Lenny always picked up the tabs. I took advantage of the job perk.

He owned a flooring company, and we talked about employees and customers. His business knowledge was amazing. Lenny went to George Washington University Law School for one semester while he opened his business, but the business took off and he couldn't handle law school at the same time.

Everything I was reading in my college books; Lenny had done in real life. I worked hard for Lenny to keep his books well. Lenny also liked to have a decent conversation about business with a smart kid like me. I would tell him what I was learning in college and Lenny would give me a real-life example. From time to time, we would go to a comedy show to watch local stand-up comedians. Beer was on Lenny. The truth was that Lenny was lonely. He didn't have a family and didn't have smart friends with whom he could talk. I liked his business knowledge and beer.

He became close family for me too. All I did was work and go to school. I did not have money to go out on Friday or Saturday nights. Christy got into a PhD program in California and she took the weekends to go to Delaware and prepare to move there, so she wasn't around with me much. Eventually she moved and we did the long-distance thing.

Lenny liked when I cracked a joke from time to time. Over the years, we developed a great friendship. We even went to Broadway shows in New York City. At that time Broadway was way out of my budget, but Lenny did not mind taking me during the summer. He did stay in the Econolodge out in New Jersey instead of Manhattan. Lenny had millions of dollars, but he was cheap as hell. But he did not like going to shows by himself, so he took me. The direct mailing fundraising campaign did not get me much money, but it opened a friendship with Lenny, which turned out to be more valuable.

Lenny was an unusual boss. His personal finance knowledge is one aspect of him that I try to emulate to this date. He gave me the advice to invest in a Roth IRA as early in my life as I could. I started investing in it even when I was broke. Thanks to his advice, this retirement account has grown significantly over time.

Lenny would be key for me going to law school. I liked talking about my business law class with Lenny and he liked it too. Lenny knew that law school was hard, but he said that if I really wanted it, I should try it. He told me I had a chance, not a great one but maybe I could handle it.

In the back of my mind I thought, "You have to be really sick to go to law school."

SUCCESS FORMULA

1. If you see an opportunity, take it. Even if your first endeavor does not work, one opportunity leads to another. Even if you fail, you will encounter benefits in your journey.
2. Don't spend money that you don't have. Restaurants and bars are for those who don't know what to do with their money. If you can, let someone else pay the tab.
3. Start saving for retirement. If your employer offers a 401(k), max it! Don't expect the government to fund your retirement. It is your responsibility to fund your retirement. Plus, when you want to buy real estate, your retirement account looks good to creditors.

Magnet

I MET MAGNET FOR COFFEE in the local Starbucks in Irvine, California. Then we went for crafted tacos at a joint called Taquiero Mucho.

Magnet was born in Botswana to Liberian parents. Because of that she has Liberian citizenship. In 1997, when she was six, she came to the United States with her mother. Her mother fled Botswana because Magnet's father used to beat her up badly. Her mother eventually said "enough is enough" and took Magnet to the US. Magnet's father stayed in Liberia. Magnet was raised by her mother and stepfather in the state of Georgia. In middle school she moved to Maryland. When Magnet was in high school, she moved to Delaware. Staying in one place was not in Magnet's destiny.

Magnet's journey was marked by a particular immigration status called Temporary Protected Status (TPS). TPS is given by the US government to citizens of countries in dire conditions to allow them to stay in the US while the conditions in that country improve. TPS is evaluated every eighteen months by the federal government (a.k.a. the US president) and they decide whether to renew TPS protections or end it. Let me give you a quick history about this "temporary" immigration status for Liberians.

Liberia was a rare American colony founded in 1821 when the US Navy invaded African territory in order to obtain land so that blacks from America could resettle back to Africa. President Monroe saw a "black problem" and did not like the idea of free blacks living among

167

whites. In 1847 Liberia declared independence and it became the second republic run by former slaves in the world (after Haiti). The powers of the world did not like Liberia and isolated it economically. From the beginning, Liberia was in trouble.

Fast-forward to 1991, President George H. W. Bush announced that approximately 10,000 Liberians would receive TPS because there was a civil war in Liberia. This ensured that Liberians with TPS would not be deported. In fact, they would get a work permit. The rebels won the civil war in 1997 and peace came back to Liberia. President Clinton decided to end TPS in 1999. Instead of TPS, Clinton created a program called Deferred Enforcement Departure (DED). DED is similar to TPS in that it gives a work permit and saves people from deportation. Like the name says, the United States does not deport anyone who is granted DED. It's like the United States is saying: "Hey, I want to deport you, but not now." President Clinton said that TPS wasn't needed anymore because there was no civil war in Liberia. However, the economy and democracy of Liberia were still fragile, so he kept some protection for Liberians.

In 2002, civil war broke out again in Liberia and President George W. Bush designated a new TPS program for all Liberians in the US. This enabled Magnet to get TPS immigration protection when she was eleven years old. She did not understand much about immigration law, but her mother applied for her. The second civil war ended in 2003, and Bush kept extending TPS every eighteen months until 2009. When President Obama came to office, he said that TPS was no longer needed, and ended it, putting in place DED protections for Liberians. They were saying: "We don't think that the country is a mess anymore and we want to deport you again, but not right this second."

In 2014, Obama granted TPS again for Liberians because of the Ebola virus outbreak in West Africa. Obama kept the TPS program for Liberia for the rest of his presidency due to dire economic conditions in Liberia, and he gave them TPS right before he left office until

2018. When President Trump came into office, he decided to let TPS expire in 2018 and then gave Liberians one more year to have DED status. Trump said to Liberians: "Enough, guys, you have to go to your sh**hole country."

While in high school, Magnet wanted a job. She applied to the local Bob Evans restaurant, but she did not get the job because she did not have a work permit. Magnet did not realize she needed a work permit and cried when she was told by the Bob Evans manager that he could not hire her without one. Although she had TPS status, she did not have a work permit card because her mother did not want to pay the fee to the US government. Eventually Magnet gathered the money working odd jobs and then she paid for her work permit so she could work at Bob Evans.

In 2012, Magnet got a bachelor's degree magna cum laude in history from Delaware State University. She babysat children during the summers, got a second job at Toys R Us during the Christmas holidays, and worked at Macy's during the rest of the year. She saved her money and paid for her education. Magnet did not qualify for federal student aid because she wasn't a green card holder or US citizen, so she had to work and save money to pay for tuition out of her pocket. To supplement her expenses, Magnet got a private loan and conned her aunt into cosigning for private student loans at a 14% interest rate. That is a *high* interest rate. Magnet's parents also paid for her first two years of community college.

With a bachelor's degree in history, Magnet did not know what else to do. What can you really do with a bachelor's degree in history anyways? She thought she had to go to law school, but she saw the price tags of most law schools and instead she went for a PhD program at UCLA. PhD programs pay their students to teach or do research. With her work permit she could apply to PhD programs and get paid. So, what kind of PhD did she get? You guessed it, she got a PhD in history from UCLA. It actually turned out to be okay for Magnet.

In 2019 she was the DED/TPS poster child for Liberians. A PhD historian from UCLA. She went to the US Congress and testified before House members advocating for the Liberian Refugee Immigration Fairness Act. This act passed Congress and gave Liberians who had lived in the US since November 2014 a green card. This was a mini-immigration reform for Liberians only. Magnet became a rock star in her Liberian community. She did not go to law school but she changed the law.

It took Magnet twenty-five years to return to Liberia and see her father again. Magnet met her stepmother and two half-siblings. Twenty-five years of lost time. Magnet's relationship with her father wasn't strong, to say the least. She had many questions to ask him, such as: Why did you treat my mother the way you did? Why didn't you come to the US with us? These questions were too painful for Magnet. She decided not to ask them. Maybe she will have this conversation in the future, but for now she is burying her pain from the past twenty-five years.

Magnet is now a US citizen. She is an associate professor at UC Irvine. She is no longer in survival mode. She no longer has to be the perfect poster child. She can relax now. We laughed under the umbrellas of the taco joint enjoying sunny California. She can dress casually and meet friends for lunch. She can travel abroad and enjoy the freedoms that education and money gave her. Magnet has done well, and she is thinking about starting a family with her partner of ten years.

Now let me tell you about Sister. She had a green card but she lost it. Sex, drugs and rock & roll took her down a shaky path. She got in trouble with the law and did time in jail. She had a rough time in Iowa. What she revealed to me shocked me.

15

College Days

*Life is what happens when you're busy
making other plans.*
—John Lennon

IT WAS 2006 AND THERE WERE talks of immigration reform. I figured that by May 2008 this reform would happen, and I'd have papers just in time for graduation from community college. Then, I would be able to go to a four-year college with no problem. Still today, at the time of this writing, I am still waiting on that immigration reform. So, my plan didn't quite work out.

I applied to the University of Maryland originally to become an economist. However, I heard that they had a more prestigious business program compared to the economics program, so I applied to both. Just in case I didn't get accepted into one, I might have a shot with the other.

As I was filling out my application, I was sure they were going to ask me about my papers. But to my surprise they never asked about my immigration status. The closest they came to that was, "Are you a permanent resident living in Maryland?" I quickly marked the "Yes" box and moved on. If the question was "Are you a legal permanent resident according to the Immigration and Naturalization Act?" I would have to answer no. That's a completely different question than what was asked. Did you know that you could be a legal permanent resident according to the Internal Revenue Code and not one according to the Immigration and Nationality Act? I answered to the best of my knowledge and belief.

A month later I was in limbo. I didn't know what to expect out of life. I was keeping tabs on the postal service to see when my letter would come in. This letter would decide the next few years of my life. Would I be able to continue my education? Would I have to work and never be able to continue my schooling? I didn't feel like I had many options. I had finally reached the end of the road.

A month and a few days later, I saw a letter from the University of Maryland in the mail. At that point, I couldn't see how Maryland would accept me. In my head, the University of Maryland had access to the United States Citizenship and Immigration Services database and would reject me because I didn't have legal papers. It was nerve-racking opening that letter. My hands were slightly sweatier than usual and all the street noise was drowned out by my heart thumping. I tore open the envelope and opened the letter. "Congratulations.... you have been accepted to the Robert H. Smith School of Business..."

That was it. I did it! I could continue with my college career and pay in-state tuition. This meant the cost of college would be covered by the income I earned with my office job, with enough left over to cover $500 rent, gas, and some food. Occasionally, I could even afford to take out Christy, maybe grab a beer, but the money for this would be very tight. Christy was low maintenance and that helped me financially. I came to understand the power of a dollar. Money is very important. You can do great things with it, and you can be unhappy without it. It is not a source of happiness, but it sure helps attract happy people.

I had a life to look forward to. I was still a college student. Another broke-ass dude existing in this universe. It was okay for me to be broke. "Hey, I'm just a college student with no money" was my typical response. My plan was to graduate from college in 2008 and then the real immigration reform would come. Again, that wasn't much of a plan.

Before deciding to attend the University of Maryland, I wanted to have at least one more option at a college where the name was well known. I applied to George Washington University in downtown DC after taking a tour there. I was aiming high, so I also toured Georgetown University. A girl attending that school mocked me when I told her I was thinking about transferring there coming from Montgomery College. She scoffed, "This is a really good school, they don't take people from Montgomery College." Georgetown was an impressive campus that offered an equally impressive degree; but all I needed was the knowledge. I heard the application process was so competitive that some applicants would get private classes for coding, math, and foreign languages—none of which I did. What I lacked in resources I overcompensated for in grit. Grit, my friends, is the number one indication of success; scientifically proven, by Angela Duckworth in her book *Grit*.

I did not apply to Georgetown; I could not afford to pay the application fee. George Washington sent me a rejection letter. I couldn't pay for either school anyway. They wanted $40,000 every year in tuition. I was intrigued, though, so I called the admissions office and asked them what I needed to do to get into GW. A nice lady from the George Washington Registrar's Office said, "Your grades are not enough. You also have to give us a letter of recommendation from two professors." Applying for college was a whole task in and of itself, but here I was, a young guy figuring out how to go to college on my own.

Who could I get a recommendation from? I did well in both history and communications classes, so that was a possibility. European history in college was hard but I enjoyed the class. I didn't know how to ask for a recommendation, so I started by simply asking.

My history professor responded by asking me to write a page about myself so that he could "know who I was." I think a much better way for the professor to know me would have been for me to do volunteer work for that professor. Then, I could have asked for a recommendation based on my time working with that professor. While I did not have much time to work more while taking college courses, this hurt my chances of getting a good recommendation. The idea behind a letter of recommendation is to get written thoughts from someone who knows you well and cares about your future success, like a mentor. So, my advice to anyone reading: When seeking a mentor, get involved with that mentor. Back then I just approached my professor after class and out of the blue asked for a recommendation. This was at least something, but if you are reading this book, you should know that getting a recommendation from someone requires more effort.

My communications professor wasn't as thoughtful as the history professor. She completed a recommendation ten minutes before I picked it up. At least I asked, but I sure could have done better. If you don't have someone to give you advice with the admissions process, throw yourself into the lake, you will eventually learn how to swim. But just don't sit still—do something.

University of Maryland: A Night Out

Having been accepted to one school meant my option was very clear. So, Maryland it was. People come from all over the world to attend this well-respected school. I still have friends from college to this date.

Most of the students in the business program were smart and dedicated to their studies. I perceived a higher level of brainpower from my classmates. I spoke to people from countries I didn't even know existed. At the University of Maryland, the workload was higher and I felt like a real college student. It was a big difference from community college, where people don't really stick around to make friends. The University of Maryland shaped my mind to understand finance, marketing, and cultural interactions. I spent lots of time at the library shaping my mind.

One time at the library I was doing some homework. I had spent hours at the library already. I didn't have breakfast, lunch, or dinner. A friend came by and asked me if I wanted to go to a bar with him in Baltimore. All I needed was $20 to get into the bar and they'll give me all the drinks I could swallow. It was a great deal. I had $20 in my emergency fund and this was an emergency.

Around 7:00 p.m. we went to Baltimore. The club was so loud, people had to yell at each other in order to talk. Nice girls in sexy dresses. Drunk people being sloppy in the background. I started off with a few whiskey sours. After that I switched to gin and tonic. My friend started rounds of tequila shots that I could not say no to. (I still didn't dare touch a vodka Sprite). I was hanging out with my friend, and it was a good two hours of poisoning my body while I cracked jokes with other drunken college kids. It was closing time and I wanted my last drink. The bartender wasn't giving drinks unless people would tip him first. I pulled out a green fake bill that I got somewhere and put it on the bar. It was a phony bill with George Bush's face on it. It looked like a real bill with all the club lights. I got my drink and moved out quickly. When the bartender noticed the bill, he got mad and threw ice at me, but my jacket shielded his subzero attack. With drink in hand, I looked back and made a toast at him.

I may have won the battle, but I lost the war. On my way out the alcohol hit me. My friend was driving. I warned him so he could stop the car. There I was, on the street throwing up on an empty stomach. I learned the term "being wasted." My friend took me to his home and I crashed on his couch. In the middle of the night, I was a mess. I had to go to work for Jack in downtown DC early the following morning. I took the Metro from the Wheaton Station near where my friend lived and was on my way to Metro Center. It was about ten stops away and I decided to snooze a little in order to be fresh at work. When I woke up, I was at the Friendship Heights Station on my way toward Metro Center. I had gone to the end of the red line and was on my way back in the same seat. I was exhausted. I was certain I wouldn't miss my next stop, so I decided to shut my eyes for a little more. This time I woke up at the Takoma Park Station on my way toward Metro Center. I had gone again to the end of the line and back. My eyes were bloodshot red. My pants were dotted with dried-up vomit I splashed on them the night before. I got to work two hours late. I went to the bathroom at work and washed my face and pants. Coming on the elevator I saw the IT guy next to me a little sleepy and he told me he'd had a rough night. "Tell me about it." I walked outside the elevator. My boss Richard was there. He saw my face and didn't say much.

I'm not drinking ever again.

Cross-Country Trip

Christy and I hung out a lot during my college days. She was a smart cookie, the simple-looking kind of girl. She was not the typical girl. She did not wear sexy skirts, did not have her nails done or wear any makeup. I liked her simplicity. While I was in college, she was applying to PhD programs, and one day she told me she got accepted into a program in Santa Cruz, California. She was scared to do the long-distance relationship.

"Don't worry, things will be fine, but you must go. You have to reach your potential," I said to her.

She knew everything about me. I told her I didn't have papers early in the relationship. She was supportive. She cast a spell on me by the mere fact of accepting me for who I was. We made an agreement before she left for California. I'll come visit her and she'll come visit me. She had to drive her car to Santa Cruz, so we decided to make a cross-country road trip.

Summer of 2007, we packed her brand-new Honda Civic Hybrid and drove from DC to Santa Cruz. It was an awesome seven-day trip. We took the southern route along I-81, which connects to I-40. We stopped in Nashville on a Friday night. Lots of music on every corner. Stopped in Memphis and visited the Martin Luther King Museum. We camped in Lake Sylvia, Arkansas, where I went swimming to the middle of the lake and back. My boss Richard told me he had a friend in Oklahoma City, so we crashed with her for a night after we visited downtown Oklahoma City. We stayed in a cheap motel in New Mexico after we visited Old Town Albuquerque. We camped at the Grand Canyon and I hiked to Plateau Point and back. Christy stayed behind as she wasn't as athletically inclined as I was. I liked physical challenges and she didn't. Plus, I thought, *When is the next time I will be at the Grand Canyon?* I had to make the most of it. It was a good physical challenge where I experienced the cold and hot weather on the same route.

From there we visited Las Vegas and gambled a little. I was amazed to see people drink beer on the streets. We were on our way to Los Angeles to crash with Christy's cousin, but the cousin forgot that we were coming. We immediately diverted to Monterey to stay with other relatives of Christy's. Then we went to see San Francisco for a day and I got lost in Chinatown. I asked people for directions on how to leave Chinatown, but nobody spoke English. We just kept walking toward the center of the city and eventually hit a place that spoke English.

That was the best road trip I have ever had in my life. I had a spreadsheet with a complete itinerary with miles traveled, approximate times of arrivals, and places we were staying. Once Christy settled, I took a one-way flight back to DC. I miss the eight-hour drives to go from one place to another.

Christy visited me a couple of times in Maryland and I visited her in Santa Cruz. We had a long-distance relationship for a year. Phone sex helped. You didn't need to know that. But I'm glad you do. I feel more comfortable telling my story now. It was May 2008, and I was about to graduate from the University of Maryland. By this time, I had given up on expecting immigration reform. Congress wasn't going to help me with my immigration problem and give me a fresh start, but maybe Christy would. I really loved her, and this long-distance thing was not ideal. I was ready to move to California and try my luck there after college. I made a plan and off I went to see Christy.

In Santa Cruz, we got into a few fights from time to time. Something wasn't right, but I didn't pay much attention. I had the bad habit of making her angry. I don't remember what I said, but it was something along the lines of communism is bad for the world. We were in Santa Cruz after all and she hated capitalism, so she got mad, which fueled me to agitate her even more. I'm not proud of it, but I was an unhealthy partner at the time. Regardless, I did want to be with her. I guess I didn't consider much of what she wanted.

We hung out with a few friends from her program and she introduced me as her lovely boyfriend who visited from Washington, DC. We went to a couple bars with her PhD colleagues, and a couple excused themselves early that night. Another girl also excused herself, as she also did not enjoy my anti-communist jokes. This girl said she wasn't feeling well; she looked like she wasn't having a good time with me in particular. Christy and I continued having a couple more beers.

On a day trip to visit San Francisco, we talked about our long-term plans. We toured the Golden Gate Bridge on this beautiful sunny California day. The water was blue and tourists were walking along the bridge. I was young and foolish at the age of twenty-three. We walked along the bridge and I stopped to look at Alcatraz, the famous prison where people spent their last days alive (how romantic).

"Hey, my situation sucks, I don't have money but I know I can make it big. We are doing this long-distance thing and I want to try it with you. Do you want to marry me?" There, this was my actual proposal to her.

I saw her face, she was excited, she saw me with love, but then reality hit her face. I felt like crap that I was proposing to her without a ring, money, or anything. There was a long pause. She didn't answer. I looked again at the prison island. I shed a tear of embarrassment.

"I have to think about it," she said.

"I'm sorry—"

"It's fine, Jose. Everything will be fine."

I went back to the East Coast and a week later she called. Her voice was broken. She said, "I want you to be fine, and I know that you will not be fine. But I want you to be all you can be. I believe in you, and you're an amazing person. I've cried myself to sleep for the past few days...I...I...I can't marry you."

I was broken. Silence governed the next forty-five seconds.

"What is going to happen now with us?" she asked.

"I guess this is it," I managed to reply.

"I guess this is it," she confirmed, sobbing.

I hung up the phone and sat there. I could feel this pressure squeezing inside of me where my heart was supposed to be. It hurt. My vision was getting blurry, and the tears started falling into my lap. I cried a couple of times alone. I cried a couple of times in my car. This heartbreak was a new phenomenon.

For the next few months, I was heartbroken. I'd broken up with my first love. Six months later Christy changed her Facebook status to "married." I was in shock. I didn't believe it. I felt anger with the fact that she married someone else in such a short time after breaking up with me. Then I bargained with myself, telling myself many times that there must be a mistake with Facebook, maybe she clicked the wrong button. So, I called her over and over in the middle of the night, but she never picked up. I left weird voice messages asking her to call me back. I drunk-texted her demanding an explanation and there was never a reply. After being ignored I felt depressed thinking about how I could be so stupid as to ask a person I loved to marry me. Eventually I accepted it. But before I accepted it, I wanted to know who this new guy was. I Facebook-stalked Christy and her status still said "Married to Cassidy." I knew it, I knew there was another guy. That son of a bitch. I bet I met him there. They had an affair all this time while I waited for Christy in this long-distance relationship. That motherfucker will see who I am. I bet I can kick his ass. His name was Cassidy. What a funny name for a bastard.

I saw Cassidy's picture on Facebook and it was not a "he." Cassidy was a girl.

SUCCESS FORMULA

1. If you don't have money, DON'T SPEND it. Spend less than what your income is. First cover your necessities. Rent and food. Transportation is not a necessity. Walk if you can. If you can walk to a place within one hour, then walk. You can save a lot of money walking, plus you get exercise to keep you healthy.

2. If you need help from someone, ask for help. You will be surprised by how much people are willing to help you succeed. If you don't ask for it, you will not get it.

3. Don't be afraid of love. You may get hurt and you may fail. But who has fallen in love who has not gotten their heart broken? In order to feel love, you have to try it, even if you fail. A heartbreak is a sign that you are a living human.

16

Birth of a Salesman

Growth and comfort do not coexist.
—Ginni Rometty

Our greatest weakness lies in giving up.
The most certain way to succeed
is always to try just one more time.
—Thomas Edison

IT WAS THE SPRING OF 2008 and I had just graduated with my business degree. My father was proud of me. My family came to visit from El Salvador. I hadn't seen my mom in person since 2001. Yet I wasn't in the most celebratory of moods. I had my degree but felt lost. Like Dustin Hoffman in *The Graduate*, I didn't know which step I needed to take next.

Dad wanted to throw a party but he did not want to see my mom. I told him that I didn't care who came to my graduation. I said, "I did everything on my own. I paid for my degree without anyone's help. If you want to go, you can go—graduation is an event open to the public and anyone can go."

He said, "The landlord told me we could use her house, I want to celebrate."

I said, "Then celebrate, I'll be here."

I realized graduation isn't a success just for you, it's a success for the people around you as well. The people in your life who have supported you feel that success and pride from your accomplishments. They have this small feeling that your graduation was because of them. From the ones who gave you that one meal the time you were hungry, the ones who gave you that ride when you needed it or offered help when you needed it most. In your success, everyone wants to be with you. Take your time to celebrate with those who want to celebrate. Life can't always be work and no fun. Let your close ones be happy. What's a better blessing than to be the cause of happiness to others? I was able to reunite my family for a moment. All gathered to have a big party for my graduation.

I was twenty-four. I felt like I was at a point in my life where I needed to break away from my dad. He wasn't my patriarch at that point, but merely a roommate. I didn't need him around anymore. I had this growing resentment of things I hadn't told him. How he made me feel, how I saw him, how all his choices were my consequences.

It was Saturday evening at the landlord's house nearby the Rockville Metro station. The Coronas and Modelos were displayed all over. Latin beats could be heard down the block. I got to the party after the graduation ceremony. I started off with a few beers in the house, talking to the different guests, then moved outside to enjoy some alone time. I sat down on one of the lawn chairs and stared at the night sky for a bit. The bass from the music could still be heard, but focusing on the moon made the music drown out.

Dad came a bit later to check on me. He sat in the lawn chair next to mine, placing his beer on the ground. I didn't want him there, I wanted to be alone. I was enjoying my time alone and he came around without asking. Maybe I was drunk or maybe I was feeling some liquid courage. I kept looking at the moon when I felt my mouth start moving.

"Look at the moon, Dad. I once heard from a movie that everyone sees the same moon. When you left us in El Salvador, I stared at the moon all the time and you were probably watching the same one. Have you heard about your son Pepe? I heard he is a complete loser. He has no job and he dropped out of college. What about your daughter Pepa? I heard she's struggling. And Mari? She's in no good place. You were the one who failed your kids. You raised them to lose in life. But for some reason, I didn't do the same thing. I saw how you treated them. I saw how your advice only led them to a shorter end. You never went to college, you have no money, no family, not even a country. But hey, we both share the same moon. We both lived under this same moon, yet I'm making it farther in my twenty-four years of life than you have in your fifty-three years."

I could hear him sniffling, but I couldn't stop. I inserted a knife in Dad's soul, I might as well twist it.

"Remember those times you hit me as a kid? I remember each one. Did you know as my dad you weren't supposed to do that. Also, how could a father not protect his son from broken bones? I can't blame you that much, you barely knew what a book was. You were my dad, but now you're just some roommate I share rent with. Isn't that sad?"

He sat there silently taking every single word in. I could hear him whimpering at every sentence. I couldn't care less. It was finally my time for payback. For all the suffering he caused my mom, my siblings, and me. He deserved every second of it. For every time he struck me with a belt because I was a "bad kid."

I was drunk, but not from the beer. I was in charge now, not him. All the repressed feelings came out that night. That African proverb was true, "The child who is not embraced by the village will burn it down to feel its warmth." I was burning my progenitor. Then finally I saw his eyes and I no longer wanted him to feel bad, I'd had enough. My rampage on Dad was over and I took one more look at the moon.

"I'll go back to the party; I need another beer." I stood up from my lawn chair and left my dad behind. I had let go of all my repressions, hidden feelings, and negativity. Now I understand that Dad did not have it good either. My grandpa was a real son of a bitch. He was an abuser and borderline criminal. A complete womanizer and deadbeat drunk. I'm not proud of what I did that night to Dad. I had an unhealed wound. I needed to cut open deeper, extirpate rotten flesh, cauterize and sew it back up. Time passed and it was no longer necessary to cause pain to Dad. I no longer wanted him to suffer. It was enough. That night I forgave.

I moved out of the house and went to live with a friend. Dad moved away too. Our relationship started to heal from the distance. I had a 1998 Chevy Cavalier made in Mexico. I was still working for Jack at the translation firm. He called me into the office one day and told me I had to start looking for another job, and I deserved it since I was a college graduate. As much as I believed that was true, I pointed out that no one was hiring due to the recent 2008 market crash. Jack agreed but he was already set on closing his business since contracts were lacking. With that warning I went job hunting.

My Dream Job

I applied to a few jobs using the college career office at the University of Maryland. I saw a great stock analyst job at Stifel Nicolaus, a big brokerage firm with offices in downtown Baltimore. I applied and all I could do was dream. They called me for an interview, and I went. I put my suit on that hot summer day. I interviewed with seven people all over. One of the managers took me to lunch at the Capital Grille and I thought it was a fancy lunch. I ordered the same thing he ordered. Everyone was so nice. I felt like a million bucks. At the end of the day, I went back to the manager, and he liked what he saw. He took me to their human resources department. The lady gave me a packet and told me to return everything to her within two days. I thanked everyone and left the building. I couldn't believe it. I saw my dream job. I always wanted to be a stockbroker and make millions of dollars. I wanted to be one of those "Wolves of Wall Street."

At the top of the packet, it said in black bold letters, "You need to be a US citizen to apply to this job." They didn't even ask me for a green card. They wanted United States citizenship. I was baffled. I got in my car and the big deception inundated my spirit. I never returned the job application and I didn't receive a call back from the investment firm. Had they asked for a green card I would have given my fake green card like Julissa Arce did when she went to work for Goldman Sachs. Julissa tells her story in her book *My (Underground) American Dream*. She used a fake green card to work on Wall Street and made lots of money. But that was her story, not mine.

■

One sunny day, I went running at the National Mall after work. I ran around the Smithsonian campus, through the Museum of American History, the Museum of Natural History, the Air and Space Museum. I headed toward the Washington Monument and passed the fountains of the World War II Memorial. I headed to go see Lincoln, who was seated on his big chair. I went up the stairs and admired the forty-four-foot-tall marble columns around the big Greek-like temple of the Lincoln Memorial. I looked at Lincoln. I read he was a great man, saved the union, freed the slaves, and all that. I leaned on one pillar after my run. I was tired. I was looking at the reflecting pool straight to the Washington Monument. I could see the Capitol hiding behind the big obelisk. Then I went to the last column of the Lincoln Memorial to get a better view of Congress. I thought, *if these guys would only pass a law that would give me one shot, I would eat the world*. Then it hit me. These motherfuckers are not going to help me. I've been waiting for them to do something to help people like me for a long time, they are never going to do that. That was when I decided to take the law into my own hands. *I'm not waiting for anyone anymore; I am tired of surviving the law, I will take the law and make the law if I have to*. Right there I promised Lincoln that I would become a lawyer, just like him. I decided to go to law school. I did not know how, but I knew I was going to. That was a supernatural feeling that I could not describe, and I still don't know exactly how to explain on paper what I felt.

Selling Dreams

I applied to a few jobs. Dish Network was hiring salespeople to go business to business selling their satellite TV channels so that people could watch them. It was a remote job. No office to go to. I would go to the customers. I met Steve, the sales team leader, at a Starbucks. He gave a questionnaire to do right there on a laptop with a wireless internet card. I thought that was high tech. I completed the aptitude test, and he told me that the next step was for me to go for training at the office in Baltimore. Steve explained to me that they needed a man like me to go sell the product to all the Latino businesses in the area. I knew nothing about selling but I needed a job.

I showed up to the office in Baltimore. We got some sensitivity bullshit training on how not to hurt people's feelings. Then they said to the entire group: "Now we must fill out the paperwork in front of you. You will see your I-9, W-4, etc." *Snap, okay, I'll fill this out and pretend everything is fine.* Then a manager stopped by each new hire to complete the part of the I-9 to verify the papers. I pulled my ID out. I gave her my driver's license with *la chueca*[1] underneath. She had to go check the documents of thirty people in the room. She was on cruise control, so she wrote down her part in the I-9 and returned the documents back to me. I put the IDs away quickly and acted cool looking at the Kumbaya video they were playing on screen. My heart was pumping. The lights were dimmed in the room. At the end, the lady in the front of the room yelled out, "Alright, people, welcome to the team, let's go to work!"

I thanked God for this job. Selling is a skill that everyone needs in life. It doesn't matter who you are, you need to sell something. In order to have a business you need to sell. If you don't sell yourself, you have no money and with no money your life is not so great. You get the idea.

---

1   Fake green card

When I first started in this new sales job, I wrote a script to recite to potential clients. It was like a commercial with a lot of statistics and information that I repeated like a robot. People got lost and bored pretending to listen to me. They heard me for ten seconds and then told me they were too busy for me. I didn't know what I was doing wrong. I gave them facts and data that would be good for their business. I lacked the feeling part. I was an automaton; I was efficient in numbers and processes. I needed to connect with the customers.

One day I was giving the script to every business. Business after business. Rejection after rejection. I was making people angry. They yelled at me many times telling me to read the No Soliciting sign. Some people threatened to call the police. Security guards chased after me. "This is a free country; I can be on the sidewalk," I'd yell at them. One of those guards seemed to be an ex-military guy from an African nation and he got infuriated. I did not want to find out what a pissed-off ex-soldier from Africa could do. I left quickly, I wanted to keep both my arms.

Three days later, Steve came to shadow me. I showed him what I did. It was a rejection again. Then he told me to watch what he did.

Steve walks into a restaurant like he is a customer, says hi to a worker, and smiles almost like he is flirting with the girl. The restaurant is empty. He inspects the room and walks toward the person that seems to be in charge. "You must be killing it today?" The manager smiles.

"I just wanted to give you some information on what we do. I work for Dish Network and I see you could use a TV here for the customers. Check this flier."

Steve hands the manager a flier with all the prices and packages. "Do you want to talk about it?" he asks.

The manager is hesitant.

"I'll tell you what, you're in the middle of rush hour. Keep this flier and call me later." Steve smiles again. He says goodbye to the first employee he met and then we leave.

Outside the business Steve looked over at me. "You have to act naturally with people. Don't act like all you want from them is money. Gain their confidence and then they'll ask you for help. Once they ask you questions, you make your move. Now, I want you to come tomorrow and follow up with this business to see what they think. Most businesses will want you to visit them more than one time."

Freaking Steve was right. I showed up the next day. I acted cool. I smiled at the same employee and went to the manager.

"Hey! Business seems to be really picking up!" The same joke on an empty business. The manager smiled. "I'm on my way somewhere so I can't stay much, I'm just stopping by quickly to check on you as we talked to you yesterday. Is TV something that people like to watch while they eat?"

"Oh, yes! I talked to the boss, and I told him that was something we needed. Come at 3:00 p.m., he'll be here," she replied.

"Alright! I'll check back then."

I left quickly and called Steve. He did not pick up. I left a voicemail.

"Steve, call me back please." He called me right back.

"Steve, they told me to come back at three to speak to the owner of the restaurant. What should I do?"

"Go meet him! What else can you do?"

"But what do I say to the owner?"

"Flirting is over, now you must go for the kill. Now it's all business—you know what to do, you're good at the business part. The business owners want to talk numbers and whether it will help the business. I know you know the business part, all you needed was help with the emotional connection part. Now go get the sale."

I went to the restaurant at 3:00 p.m. I asked the person at the counter if I could speak to the manager. She went to the back and in a few moments a man with a mustache came in.

"Hi, I'm Jose. I'm with Dish Network."

"Yes, we talked about it, give me a minute. Go have a seat, I'll be right there."

I did just that. Mr. Mustache went to say a few things to the employees and came back.

"Tell me, what do you have?"

"Very quickly, these are the three packages we have. Some people like to watch the news, others like to watch sports depending on the time. At the very least, something should be playing on a flatscreen TV. Everyone likes it. It's just $29.99 a month, a customer in one meal pays for this."

"Okay, let's do it," he said.

"But for $49.99 you get more channels..." I continued. "...And for $69.99 we can get even more channels."

Mr. Mustache made a gesture of confusion. That's when I realized I'd made a mistake. The man was ready to buy but instead I kept on talking. When a client wants to buy, don't do anything to stop him from buying. Have him buy first and once the deal is completed then you can sell some more. Mr. Mustache got even more confused with the different options. The prices were starting to increase.

"Do I have to get into a contract?"

"It's a two-year contract, but—"

"Stop! I don't want to do it!"

The two-year contract wasn't a big deal, and I'm sure the business could pay even $100 per month. My number one mistake was that I made the client hesitate. Had I remained quiet, I would have made the sale. When a customer tells you he wants to buy, shut the hell up and let him buy.

The sale did not go through. However, I noticed my mistake. I failed but I learned where I went wrong. I wasn't going to repeat that mistake again. I now was ready to go hunting for more business out there.

I went to a completely different area. I created a different persona. I was cooler, I was smoother. I talked to people around and I even started to believe the things I was saying. I went into barbershops, restaurants, tax preparers, law offices, doctor's offices, pet stores, anyplace that had a business. I walked in like a customer. I looked around and studied the scene, then I identified the prey. Sometimes the business helped me by having a TV off. To which I said, "Hey, can you turn on the TV? We need to know what the stock market is doing." Or "Is the game playing? Turn it on to watch the score."

To which I would get the usual response from a business manager. "We don't have cable and I don't have time to call these people, but we're working on it." That was music to my ears.

"Let me help you, you don't have to do anything, I work directly for Dish Network. Check this out, for $29.99 my crew will come with free installation. That's exactly what I do. Headquarters identified this area as an underserved area, and we just want to help people."

"Really! You guys are great. Here's my credit card."

I made the sale. After that it was sale after sale. I got good at that. I met my quota to remain alive month after month. I got a base salary plus a commission if I exceeded my quota. Which I did. If you don't make your numbers, you find yourself without a job in this business. But if you made above a threshold, you made commissions. People in sales make a lot of money if they are good at what they do. My salary was decent at the time. After a year I saved good money in the bank.

■

I walked all over the DC metropolitan area for my sales job. Some days I was lucky and sold, other days at the very least I met business owners and chatted with them. I had a smile on my face most of the time. I saw places I'd never seen before. I was free.

But I still remembered my day at the Lincoln Memorial and the promise I made. I remembered Mel Gibson giving a speech in his *Braveheart* film. I imagined myself riding that horse with a face painted blue and white telling people that "I will be on my deathbed ... wishing to have one chance to go back in time and trade all my days for just ONE chance to apply to law school ... I will see regret in my face for not having done it ... They won't give me papers, but they'll never take my FREEDOMMMM!"

It was time to implement my plan. Plans without action are like they never existed. I did not know how to even start my quest to go to law school. I was a lonely soul driving from one place to another.

Then I googled, "How to go to law school?"

SUCCESS FORMULA

1. Celebrate your successes, whether they are big or small. People like to be with winners. Be a winner and people will energize you even more.

2. Heal your childhood traumas. Some of us have more than others, but all of us have pain. Embrace and accept that pain. We all go through pain. Pain is constant in life. Life is too short to resent people. If your pain is too deep, seek professional help. There are virtual professional therapists in other countries who will work with you for $25 an hour.

3. Learn how to sell. This is the number one rule in business. If you know how to sell, you will be valuable to any business. Learn to connect with others and others will trust you with their money. Try and fail. Failure is not bad. To the contrary, try as much as you can until you fail, then fail some more, because in order to get success you must fail. If you are not failing, you are not trying your best. What is the point of living life if you always play it safe and never try to achieve your utmost capacity? Go fail and fail some more, but always pick yourself back up, for that is true grit that will give you success.

Sister

WHILE I WAS IN IRVINE, CALIFORNIA, I decided to stop by Anaheim about forty-five minutes away. My time in LA showed me that this city is a big neighborhood. I can't tell you where Anaheim starts and where Irvine begins. You see miles and miles of houses. Pretty houses with a front and back yard right next to each other. By the way, those houses are not cheap. It costs you a pretty penny to live in this place if you want seventy-degree weather all year round. While I was there, I went for a walk around Huntington Beach. It doesn't get any more California than Huntington Beach. Bikinis, surfing, and beach bums. Then I drove to Fullerton to meet Sister at a coffee shop called Philz Coffee. She opened her heart, mind, and guts.

Sister was born in Manta, Ecuador. She came to Ames, Iowa, at the age of ten with a green card in the early 2000s because her mother married a US citizen. Growing up she was raised by her single mother. Sister's biological father was not in the picture. The bio father knocked mom up and decided to marry another woman who was a US citizen. This other woman was his ticket to come to the US. Sister's bio father joined the Marines and had two children in the US. He didn't have time for Sister.

Sister was a troublemaker. She was doing drugs with the wrong crowd and having fun. At the age of nineteen she got busted for possession of marijuana in Iowa. Nothing much happened to her in 2013 when she got the charges. After all, it was marijuana, so no jail

time for her, yet. The following year, Sister decided to take a quick vacation to Ecuador. She had a great time partying in Ecuador where your dollars go a long way. Upon her return to the US, an officer saw that Sister was charged with possession of a controlled substance in the past. That made her inadmissible to the US. This officer believed that the US needed to be saved from this twenty-year-old pothead, so he detained Sister. After all, it was the officer's job and the law still said that marijuana was illegal in the federal books. They detained Sister, took her green card away, and placed her in deportation proceedings. Suddenly, Sister's world changed. Sister liked Ecuador, but she liked it to party, not to live there permanently.

Sister was in the slam for two weeks. Her deportation officer checked into Sister's family and found that her biological father had been a Marine. By then, her bio father had passed away; he died in a car accident while on vacation in Ecuador. The immigration officer was in the Marines too. Because of this the officer gave mercy to Sister. He decided to let Sister out of the detention center on her own recognizance. Sister got out but still had to face an immigration judge to fight for her life in the US. Immigration and Customs Enforcement (ICE) wanted to deport Sister.

Back when Sister was defending her marijuana charge in court, the defense lawyer told her to plead guilty. He said: "Nothing will happen to you. It's just a marijuana charge. You won't go to jail for this, you will be fine." Unfortunately, this lawyer did not understand immigration law and did not know that this guilty plea would trigger something called "inadmissibility" if Sister went out of the country and came back. That little detail.

Eventually Sister hired a good lawyer to help her with immigration court. This lawyer worked with Sister for four years fighting for her life. For those four years Sister had no papers.

■

Before I continue with her story, let me tell you about Sister's high school. It was tough for her. Can you imagine being the only Latina in Iowa? She didn't feel like she belonged anywhere. Sister skipped class multiple times. She wanted to fit in like the rest. Sister shaved her arms, fixed her thick eyebrows, and straightened her hair to fit in with the other white girls. That was a lot of work to fit in. It was easier for Sister to skip school.

On top of all that, Sister's mother did not make her marriage last with the US citizen that brought them to the US. When Sister was twelve, Sister's stepfather was deployed to Afghanistan with the Army. Sister's mother got lonely and she found company soon. She got pregnant from another man, which led to a divorce from the army man. The other dude did not stick around either. Sister got the short end of the stick from this deal. Now it was Sister's job to babysit her little brother while Mom went out to work. Babysitting the brother was another reason for Sister to skip school. At some point, Mom decided to ship Sister's little brother to Ecuador as it would be cheaper for the grandparents to care for him.

With her little brother in Ecuador, Sister had her freedom back. She went wild. She was seventeen. Boys were on the horizon. She started to drink a lot and smoke a lot of pot. She got a fake ID to get into bars. She went to college parties and engaged in risky sexual behavior. Who needs a condom when things are hot and heavy? Sister managed to meet the one other Latino boy in town and they gravitated toward each other. So, you guessed it, Sister got pregnant at the age of seventeen. Her life was over, she didn't know what to do. Sister saw her mother struggle giving birth. What the hell would she do?

It is not like she could get an abortion right away. In Iowa at the time, she had to wait until the age of eighteen in order to get an abortion on her own without the consent of her mother. A couple days after her eighteenth birthday, Sister went to the clinic. She did not tell anyone about the abortion—not her mother, not her boyfriend. Her mother would have kicked her out of the house. She did this on her own. Sister paid $500 cash. She saved that money from her newspaper route job. Five years later, Sister told her cousin about the procedure. Ten years later she told her mother. Fifteen years later she told me.

■

Going back to losing her green card in the middle of college. How did Sister pay for college? She had a great scholarship that required a green card and had great financial aid from FAFSA. So, what did Sister do without a green card? She did nothing. She told nobody that she had lost the green card and that she was in deportation court. Her college admissions office had a copy of her green card on file and that is all they needed in order to keep giving Sister the best education in Iowa.

Sister was at Iowa State University studying psychology. In her sophomore year she joined a Latina sorority. Her sorority required her to apply herself academically and to party less. Sister got clean and got her act together. It was this positive sisterhood that saved her life. She surrounded herself with positive women, and that helped her succeed. Sister graduated from undergrad without papers but nobody needed to know that.

Sister kept pushing to go to grad school. She needed a copy of her green card. Sister had a sorority sister who worked in the admissions office and this sister made a copy of the copy of the green card. She used that to apply to grad school. Without this green card Sister would have had to pay out-of-state tuition for grad school. She now was enrolled in a master of education program in student affairs.

Sister did not have financial aid or scholarships for grad school. She did have an assistantship in the office of admissions, and that paid a stipend, which Sister used to pay for her grad school. She lived with her mother while in grad school and that saved her a lot of money.

Sister told me that psychology helped her understand the way she was. This taught her that previous challenges forged who she was.

She also tells me that therapy helped her to overcome the hard life she lived growing up.

While sipping crafted coffee with Sister, she told me she was bisexual. That explained the LGBT environment of the coffee shop I was in. She always was attracted to women but her town in Iowa was very conservative, making it hard for her to date women. She tells me that now she prefers to date only women. She doesn't see marriage or children in her future and that is a choice she made.

After coffee, she took me to her office at California State University at Fullerton, where she works in the Latinx[2] Community Resource Office. She showed me the LGBTQ Community Resource Office and taught me about the different flags there are for lesbians, transgender, asexual, and pansexual. At that point, I thought that only the rainbow flag existed, but I learned that each letter has a flag. I learned something new. I did more research and found out that there even is a straight flag. I'll let you google the flags.

Sister came out as bisexual to her mother two years ago. Her mother did not like the idea of her dating a woman. But now her mother is more supportive, as her son also came out to her as bisexual. Mom still has a hard time accepting that, but she loves her kids.

Sister does not like to visit Iowa—too many memories come to her while there. She still visits because her mother and brother live there. It is painful for her to relive her traumas. Troubles with the police, immigration, relationships, fitting in, etc. She is still struggling with her wounds from the past, but she sees the light at the end of the tunnel.

Sister eventually won her deportation case and now she is a US citizen and is happily living in Fullerton, California.

Next, I want to tell you about Matter. This guy has an inspiring story. He was so good at science that he convinced the federal government to grant him access to a top security clearance government lab despite his undocumented status.

---

2   I dislike the word *Latinx*. Somehow this got popular. It is not English; it is not Spanish. It is a made-up word. I'm no grammar police but this is too much.

PART III

17

Law School

Acceptance is as powerful as crack.
—Kevin Hart

I KNEW LAW SCHOOL WAS EXPENSIVE. I didn't even think I could go. But I wanted to see how far in the process I could get. *It's okay if I fail, but I'll fail on my own terms. At least I would be able to tell my grandchildren that I tried.*

I needed to take the LSAT, a standardized test that measures how fast you solve logic puzzles and how fast you read paragraphs. There are courses to train you for this test. But these courses can range from $600 to $1,500. I was broke, so I checked out a few books from the public library and got myself busy with them. I woke up early on Saturdays and Sundays to do exercises from the books. I did this for about two months. Then, I scheduled the test. I was applying to law school bare bones without mentoring or money. I learned there are now scholarships to pay for LSAT training. But, when you're in survival mode, you go to war with what you have, not with what you want.

I took the LSAT. My score was low. I don't remember my exact score, but I remember it was slightly above the minimum to get into law school. Law schools have this disclaimer that the LSAT alone isn't a factor to disqualify you, but that's bullshit. They do.

I sent my application to ten law schools. I got rejected from the top schools, my medium-level schools, and a safe school. I was accepted to a couple of Florida law schools. One was a for-profit law school that accepted anyone willing to pay their tuition. The other was a conservative Catholic school, but I was done with Catholic teachers. The last school I was accepted to was the University of the District of Columbia (UDC). Their mission was to help the poor (a.k.a. me) and to pay it forward to others by doing pro bono and public interest work. *Public interest? Screw that. I want to make all the money I can.* The expectation from the law school was that you would do eight hundred pro bono hours—i.e., working for free—in their clinical programs.

UDC never asked me about my immigration status, and it was the cheapest law school I saw. Tuition was even cheaper than my undergraduate tuition at Maryland. I worked for a year in sales and saved as much money as possible. I started to plan my budget and realized I had the money to pay the tuition for the first year of law school. However, my housing was not included in the budget.

I enrolled in school and paid my tuition not caring about paying for rent. Before the school year began, I found a course to take over the summer from a nonprofit called the Council on Legal Education Opportunity (CLEO). CLEO helps minorities get into law school. They paid for my hotel in Atlanta so I could attend the course. They scared the heck out of me. To sum up the entire conference, they told me that law school is super hard and that if you go there to mess around, you won't make it. They weren't joking. This was exactly what I needed to hear.

I had the motivation for law school but I still lacked a place to live near the school. I spoke to my longtime friend Marcos, whom I met while working at the hotel job. He had a studio apartment in Friendship Heights near UDC, so I asked him if I could crash on his couch for free while I went to school. He let me stay over with him in the past and gave me a little speech on being able to count on him for whatever I needed.

A day before law school started, I packed all my stuff from the place I was renting and was on my way to Marco's apartment. It was about 10:00 a.m. when I started calling him. I got no answer.

I left a voicemail telling him I was on my way, but an hour passed and nothing. I texted him I was on my way again. Thirty minutes passed and I texted again. By this point I began thinking something happened to him. But by 8:00 p.m. when I still had heard nothing, I realized he'd done this same thing before.

Marcos once told me he would give me some tickets for a show, but he kept telling me that he was busy. I kept asking him for the tickets and he said, wait a few minutes, I'm busy at work. I couldn't understand why he didn't just say, "No, man, I'm not giving you the tickets." In my mind, if he said he would give me the tickets I expected him to give me the freaking tickets. In the end, I did not get the tickets. Now, the same friend promised me a place to crash in his apartment for free, and I believed him! I wish he would have said: "Hey, man, you can't crash here because I got girls I bring over."

A few blocks away from my friend's place was where Lenny lived. He lived in a huge condominium by himself, and he had a guest room that nobody used. I decided to go over to Lenny's and see if he could help me out. I asked Lenny if I could stay at his place for two weeks while I figured out where I could stay. Lenny didn't say anything to me but nodded his head. On the bright side, I would be able to work for Lenny while also attending law school. Lenny understood that law school was a big commitment.

Lenny proposed another idea. He had rental apartments in DC and some of them never rented because they were in a rough part of town. He proposed a pretty good deal. I could stay in one of his empty apartments for as long as I wanted, and I just had to pay the utility bills.

I went to the DC apartment and it was dark. Spiderman's apartment was nicer. When I called the property manager, he told me, "Are you really sure that you want this place?" He said, "You don't sound like the typical person who rents this kind of apartment. I can tell just by hearing your voice."

Then I asked him, "What is the typical person that rents this apartment?"

"Black people and I'm guessing you are not black."

"How do you know I'm not black?" I said it with my thick Spanish accent.

He didn't like the joke and said, "OK, my man, I will do the paperwork. If you want it, it's yours."

I stayed in that rough apartment. It was dark, small, and old. It smelled like rotten wood. The bathroom at the 7-Eleven was much better and the shower made a squeaky noise when I opened it. It was also scary to be there. I don't know whether I heard gunshots or I imagined them.

I crashed in the DC apartment, but from time to time I crashed with Lenny in his luxury condo with the excuse that it was closer to my law school and I could come do work late at night for his bookkeeping. During the winters, Lenny would travel to Florida for six months and I would "house sit" for him. I couldn't complain about that.

Law School

My first day of law school was an out-of-body experience just like it is for anyone. I was surrounded by a lot of smart students and I was this kid who couldn't speak or read at a high level. I woke up that morning and walked my usual forty-five minutes to school through a nice area in Northwest DC. I walked everywhere to save money on the bus or Metro fare. It was hot and I felt the sweat drops on my forehead, but I was determined to be called a law student. I quit my sales job, moved out, put all my eggs into the law school basket. There was no turning back now.

The first week was orientation week. On the first day the professor gave us a bunch of cases that we had to read that night. It was our welcome present from the professor: no sleeping tonight. I saw a bunch of people staying up until 2:00 a.m. in the library and I was next to them. In the morning, I saw a lot of faces showing little sleep.

What are these words that I'm reading! It seemed crazy for someone like me to try to pull this off, but that sensation of craziness made me feel alive. I barely understood what these law books said. I read words I had never heard or seen before. I looked around the library and I saw others reading. My English was okay for a college graduate, but it was horrible for a law school student.

I was learning a new language. I did it once before, so I could do it again. Every time I saw an odd word, I looked it up online with the power of Google. That is what I did for the first semester. I had no life, I disconnected myself from the world. I disconnected from all my family. I barely spoke to my mom or dad. I watched no TV. Instead, I immersed myself in this monastery.

My routine was to go to class in the morning, then find which student organization had a free lunch event so that I could eat for free.[3] After lunch I hit the books like I never did in my life. I worked twelve-hour days every day. No weekend or holiday breaks. I read more during my first semester in law school than I ever read in my entire college years. My classmates saw me at the library and felt sorry for me. They heard my thick accent and admired my tenacity or were in shock by my craziness. I hear that a lot of minority students feel the "impostor's syndrome," meaning that they don't think they fit into the group as they are different from everyone else. I'm not going to lie. I thought many times, *What the hell am I doing here? I don't have the English level and I don't even have papers.* But I was on a mission and liked the thrill of doing something crazy.

During my first year I felt I was behind everyone in my class. However, the test results came and I made it to the Dean's List! Say what? The Dean's List meant that I would get a scholarship to help pay for my tuition. I was shocked. This meant that I would need less money to pay for my second year of law school.

One hundred classmates started together in 2009. Eighty of us

---

3   When the Black Law Society had a lunch event, I gladly was a brother. When the Women's Reproductive Justice Society had a free lunch, I supported their bodies, their choices. *Pass the pizza, please.* When the Latino Student Association had an event, I was the first one there asking for tacos. It turned out that my universe expanded with these lunches. I learned the struggles of different groups and that enriched me.

graduated in 2012. I enjoyed my classmates. We spent literally every day together for three years. It was a statistical probability that some of us would click and some of us would rub each other the wrong way. Our class was diverse ethnically, socially, economically, and age wise.

I gravitated toward the younger crowd in their twenties. There weren't many of us. I talked to this one girl during happy hour. The first time I saw her, she didn't catch my eye. However, the following semester I was coming out of my library cave, and I saw the same girl. She was well put together and her image changed dramatically. It showed that she worked out a lot and her body looked different. Her hair had a different style. I gravitated toward her during our next happy hour.

"My name is Kylie."

"Hi! My name is Jose." Blah, blah, blah. I cracked a few jokes, she laughed. I smiled and she smiled back. Things seemed to be going well.

During the Halloween season, the law fraternity I joined threw a Halloween party. Halloween was my favorite holiday. You can be whoever you want to be, and every odd, weird, abnormal person is suddenly normal during Halloween. My kind of holiday for my misfit life.

Kylie was at the party, and I approached her. We talked, we drank, we danced, we laughed. After the party, we went to the bar next door with the crowd. She told me she felt bad because some dude had just kissed her without her expecting it.

"You should kiss someone. That will make you feel better," I said jokingly.

"Who should I kiss, Jose? Should I kiss you?" slurring her speech.

"Yeah, that's not a bad idea, you should kiss me."

From then on, we started dating. I felt butterflies in my stomach again. We did everything together after school. Nobody at school knew we were together. That was our secret. While we crossed paths at the library or in the hallways, all we did was make eye contact to keep our secret. We said a lot to each other without speaking.

Kylie was from upstate New York. It's not for me to tell her story, but she felt distressed at the time. She told me her story and I cried for her. It took me several weeks to trust her with my story. But eventually, I grabbed the courage to tell her I didn't have papers. "Everything I'm doing is pretending to be a law student. I don't know why or what I'm doing." I shed my tears in her bed. She looked at me and kissed me. I felt accepted. I was fully disarmed by her acceptance. I fell in love. I was accepted by a woman, and I accepted her.

The following morning, I woke up with fireworks in my head. Triumphant orchestras played in my head, and I put on my sunglasses. There I was, walking down the street feeling like *The Man*. I was in law school. I didn't need money; law students are supposed to be broke. And I had the girl. I felt successful.

Law school was like the high school I never had. I was the funny guy who everyone wanted to hang out with at the bar. I did well in class, and I was involved in student organizations. I became president of my law fraternity. I helped transform the fraternity into the biggest student organization with the biggest budget in school. I learned to give credit to my board members and to ask for their opinions often. Life was good.

As president of the fraternity, I worked the hardest and my board saw all the time and enthusiasm I invested, so they were also motivated to help me. They saw the growth of the fraternity and the popularity of the events. They saw the increase in our budget and how we could do more events that would help more students. We had a solid organization. UDC is one of the Historically Black Colleges and Universities (HBCU), and some administrators did not like the fact that the Black Law Student Association was no longer the number one student organization, as it always had been. But I learned to play the game of attending budget meetings to pressure the student government to ensure they gave the fraternity the money we wanted. I saw the fraternity as an extension of myself and I was determined to make it as big as possible.

For the first time in a very long time, I was living a very normal life, instead of feeling sorry for myself because of my lack of papers. I had everything I needed: good friends, good schooling, a good girl, and a free slice of pizza for lunch.

I survived my 1L year. If you can make it in law school for one year, you can make it anywhere. Now the question was, how was I going to pay for my 2L year? My savings were gone. I worked a few hours for Lenny but that income wasn't much. I had the Dean's List scholarship but I still needed money to take me over the finish line with my tuition.

I became involved with the DC Hispanic Bar because they offered mentoring to law students and events where I could attend and get a few free glasses of wine. I went to many of their events and signed up to their newsletter. That is how I learned to apply for one of their fellowships. The requirements were to go work in a nonprofit organization helping the Latino community and to need financial help (a.k.a. being broke like me). I interned at CASA de Maryland during the summer and helped the underserved Latino population. I was walking down the National Mall when a committee member called me and said: "We selected you to be one of our fellows…" Adrenaline rushed through my brain. I started running like a crazy person in the middle of the Smithsonian. With this fellowship and the Dean's List scholarship I could afford another semester of law school.

My purpose in going to law school was to figure out how I could get papers, and thus far I had taken the typical first-year courses. I did not learn much immigration law until I worked at CASA. Once there, I read and read about the ways undocumented people could get papers, but I still couldn't find a way to qualify for anything. It doesn't matter how smart you are, how long you've been in this country, or how much money you have. If you don't qualify for a particular law, there is no way you can get papers, and a lot of people just don't qualify.

There's Money in the Books

It was the end of the year, and the library did a cleanup. They were giving away old law books to make space for new ones. I saw a pile of law books placed on the library tables with a sign: "FREE." I immediately remembered how expensive my law books were when I went to pay for them in my Amazon account. I saw money on the table. I grabbed one book after another. Arms full of books, I went to one of the library desks, signed up as a third-party seller on Amazon, and posted the books, selling them for one penny less than my competing seller.

Some books sold for $0.99 but others went for $150 with just a few clicks. The library was throwing money away! I spent the whole day at the library selling the books I got for free. Forget homework. When you are in hunger mode you think about every way to make a buck. Online sale after online sale, I walked to the post office with a bunch of books to ship. I was so happy to see an email showing the nice message, "You have a New Order!" and then another. Business was good. I had a pile of twenty books on my desk ready to sell. There were so many books that I discarded the cheap ones and kept the expensive ones. I was there all day and there were still more books to process. I even hid some books underneath the table fearing that some other student would take that book away from me. There were so many books that I could not finish that day.

The following day I was the first guy to come back to the library. I chose a free book, then typed the ISBN into Amazon, and Amazon would tell me the value of that book in their New, Like New, Used, Very Good, Good, or Acceptable version. I worked two days straight selling those books until they ran out. I saw a need in the market and I provided a service distributing the books all over America. I made $2,000 in two days! I had enough money to pay tuition for my second year of law school. I could worry about my third year later—for now, everything was perfect.

Then, my heart was broken.

SUCCESS FORMULA

1. Risk everything for your dreams. The sooner you risk it all, the easier it is. If you wait too long it will hurt to even think about the possibility of losing everything.

2. Your optimism can blind you from the flaws of your friends. Know that even your friends will disappoint you at some point or another. Don't hold a grudge for a few disappointing incidents; your friends also will help you other times.

3. Surround yourself with capable people. Listen to them and seek their opinions. Smart people will only speak if you seek their advice. Fools will be happy to give you advice 24/7.

Matter

I MET MATTER IN A RESTAURANT not far from the University of Chicago. One interesting thing about Chicago is that certain ethnic groups have very well-defined neighborhoods—Ukrainian Village, Greektown, and Chinatown. Blacks, Mexicans, Puerto Ricans—they all have a piece of Chicago. Humans everywhere tend to gravitate toward similar humans and Chicago shows that.

Matter came to the US from South Korea at the age of eleven in 2002. His father had a shoe store in Korea and they decided to move to the US because Korea was in the midst of a financial crisis where people were losing jobs and businesses were closing. Matter's parents did not have the heart to tell him that he was leaving his whole life behind, so they lied. They said, "We are going on 'vacation' to America, so get ready for some fun!" Matter was excited.

The entire family moved to Koreatown in New Jersey, right outside of New York City. Matter's dad and mom worked many jobs. They worked in dry cleaning and nail salons, delivered fish, were janitors, worked with leather, and drove a cab. The whole family—husband, wife, two children (then ages eleven and six), and grandma—lived in a one-bedroom apartment. Grandma babysat the children while Mom and Dad went to work at 8:00 a.m. until they came back at 9:00 p.m.

Matter did very well in middle school and went to a magnet high school. When he was a senior, Matter wanted to get a driver's license and the typical high school undocumented story happened: Matter found out he did not have papers. At first, Matter did not understand

213

what was happening. He spoke to his father, who, breathing heavily, told him: "Hmmm… hmmm… Matter, you don't have papers." That's all he said, period. Then the father walked away.

Matter could not believe it! Did he not pledge allegiance to the flag of the United States of America every day! Matter cried. He felt like his very existence was negated. He had been sure he was bound to go to college and do great things, but now it turned out he could not apply to all the colleges he wanted because he would need financial aid. Matter felt resentment toward his parents. He felt powerless. He was frustrated. In his clouded mind, he felt anger toward the people closest to him.

Back in 2008, telling people you had no papers was taboo. In his nice high school, with all the rich American-born kids, Matter didn't talk about his immigration status. Even in Koreatown, people in the Korean community did not speak much about that subject either. And Matter's high school counselor was no help—he had no idea what to do with students like Matter.

Fortunately, Matter found out that the City University of New York gave scholarships to any admitted student. Matter, a top student in high school, was admitted and set out to major in chemistry.

But, of course, there's more to paying for college than tuition. To help pay for room and board, Matter enrolled in a New York City program in which he could do community service in exchange for a stipend of $5,000 per semester. He used that money to pay $400 rent for a room. Matter's mom sent him food so he had something to eat. Chemistry and books were the one thing that provided comfort to him. He was in a low place, full of uncertainty. He wanted to prove to the world that he was more than an undocumented person. Matter focused on his studies.

Matter's dedication made him the valedictorian of the City University of New York (CUNY) Chemistry Department when he graduated from college in 2013. Because DACA came to him in 2012, he was ready to enroll in a PhD program at the University of Chicago. With a work permit, he was eligible to be employed by the university to do research as a PhD candidate.

US Senator Dick Durbin of Illinois presented Matter's story on the Senate floor, describing how successful Matter was in science and what a great addition to America he represented.

Matter got a lot of publicity. But, with that publicity came the hate mail. He got nasty comments online from people saying: "Kick him out of America, he is not an American." "If he is so smart, why doesn't he go back to his country and help his country?" "If people like him are close to my house, he'd better not come near, otherwise he'll see my shotgun." Comments like that scared Matter. He did not open his social media for a while.

As part of the chemistry PhD program in Chicago, Matter's research required the use of the National Laboratory run by the federal government. That lab, however, was a secured area that required security clearance. The feds rejected Matter's request to use the equipment because he only had DACA, which is not a real immigration status. Technically he had no legal status. But he needed state-of-the-art facilities to conduct special studies. He needed access to the accelerator that shoots protons at the speed of light and the X-ray sensors to calculate some … stuff that sounds like it comes out of a sci-fi movie. We are talking about high-tech stuff; this was not a regular lab with a couple test tubes and a flame.

Matter went to speak to the university dean and Senator Durbin himself. He called many times and visited their offices in person. Matter kept asking and asking until both the school dean and the US Senator intervened on his behalf before the federal government. With this help Matter got special security clearance to access the lab! Thanks to their intervention, but most importantly to the cutting-edge work that Matter was doing, Matter became the first DACA recipient given security clearance to a federal lab. And, in the process, Matter created the precedent for other DACA researchers to access high-tech labs.

Matter's story illustrates how hard it is to be a PhD student without a work permit, as they must be employed by their university in order to conduct research. It makes me think about what to say to the new generation of undocumented students who want to get a PhD. "Sorry, you can't be a scientist or a medical doctor, but you can be a lawyer or a psychologist?" (How about we get more scientists to help cure cancer rather than more lawyers to sue McDonald's for serving hot coffee?)

Sadly, his undocumented status took a toll. Matter told me that his grandma got dementia and it was difficult for the family to take care of her. They decided to send her back to Korea to live her remaining years within her culture and with the support of a more affordable healthcare system. This broke Matter's heart. Granny raised Matter. Granny had always been part of his life. Now Granny was not fully there, physically or mentally. Matter could not go with her to Korea because he did not have papers.

Granny died five years after she left the US, and Matter could not even go to her funeral because, although he had DACA and could get a special travel permit, she died in the middle of the COVID pandemic when traveling restrictions were in place. Matter told me that he normally does not dream, but the night when Granny died, he dreamed about her. He saw Granny come to his room. She sat on his bed and looked at him with a sad face. It was Granny saying goodbye wishing to spend more time, wanting to see Matter come back to Korea as a hero.

Granny did not get to see it, but eventually Matter turned into a superhero.

Matter lost his grandma but he won a wife right after that. They met while working as activists in a nonprofit helping immigrant refugees. Their mutual passion for helping others and their Korean connection intensified the attraction. Matter's wife is a US citizen and she petitioned for him. Now Matter has a green card.

Matter is kicking ass. He is not keeping a low profile. He has a great job working with intellectual property and technology to protect patents for inventors.

Matter's father owns a cab company and he is doing well. The whole family has green cards now. Matter believes that the pain he experienced while undocumented helped him be more empathetic toward others.

The pain is now gone, but it has made him stronger.

My next adventure took me to San Francisco to meet a beautiful doctor with unhealed wounds. This encounter was full of emotions.

18

Some Relationship Advice

Only time can heal your broken heart.
Just as only time can heal his broken arms
and legs.

—Miss Piggy

You will never know true happiness *until you
have truly loved,* and you will never understand what pain really is until you have lost it.

—Unknown

KYLIE AND I TOOK A TRIP to Myrtle Beach during my 1L summer. I got into a timeshare presentation where they offered me a free stay. I took it. I pretended to be interested in buying but the truth was, I wasn't going to buy anything, I just wanted the free room next to the beach. They gave us a nice suite overlooking the beach at Myrtle Beach where we could see the sunrise over the horizon.

Throughout the vacation, I could tell something was bothering Kylie. She wouldn't laugh when I cracked a joke. She didn't smile at me anymore. It was like she was a ghost that I shared a room with. It felt like I couldn't make her happy anymore. I still wanted her, though. There was something on her mind. One night, we went walking on the beach and she suddenly started to cry. I stopped walking and turned to her. "Babe, what's wrong?"

"Nothing."

"Ah, okay. For some reason I thought something was wrong. I just see that you're crying. But silly me."

"I said nothing's wrong!" she screamed. She started stomping back to our hotel room. I was startled. I only could think that if she wasn't happy during a nice vacation, she wouldn't be happy in another setting. I stayed quiet and followed her back to the room.

We returned to DC, and the minute we got back to her apartment she told me, "I'm breaking up with you."

I thought it was a joke. Then I looked into her eyes and saw she meant it. I didn't want to break up. She started crying. I shed a tear. I didn't understand what was in her mind, but I didn't need to. There was nothing I could do. I tried to have a conversation and she would not tell me much. "Just tell me why. Did I say something, did I do something?" She would just say, "I don't think we are good for each other." Without an explanation I walked out of her apartment with questions in my head and pain in my soul.

Over the next several days we were broken up; however, we kept texting. A few weeks passed and I went over to her apartment to talk about things. One conversation led to another, and next thing we knew, we ended up in bed. We became friends with benefits; no titles, no drama, just fun and freedom. I enjoyed the benefits of her friendship while not dealing with her drama. Slam, bam, thank you, ma'am. I felt like *The Man*.

A few days later I texted Kylie again. She was cooking at her apartment, and I decided to come over. She made brownies. We ate the brownies, but she perceived that I wanted to eat something else.

"Let's watch a movie."

A movie? Why is she beating around the bush?

I didn't want to wait much. All I wanted was one thing and then to leave and sleep alone. Halfway through the movie I made a move and the deed was done. It took us a little longer than I had anticipated but now I could leave in peace. I grabbed my shirt and she yelled at the top of her lungs, "You are staying here!"

"What?" I said.

"You're my boyfriend and I'm telling you to stay!"

"Okay..." Then we were together again.

I had intense feelings for her, and I liked her. Truth was that I would take whatever affection she would give me. If she would give me a few hours, I gladly took it. If she wanted a relationship, I was there. I thought that this American girl just wanted sex, like in the movies. I liked the macho *conquistador* persona I created during our sporadic visits, but I liked it better to be in a relationship with this one girl.

That summer Kylie went to upstate New York for an internship. I went there to visit her. I met her mother, sister, and brother-in-law. She showed me her town that reminded me of the 1950s. Kylie was warm with me in private, but she was busy and distant when she was with her family. By the end of the weekend, I was anxious to leave. I drove back to DC alone. I wanted some quiet time away from Kylie.

I felt love for her but this thing was not healthy. We both had issues and got together to comfort each other's loneliness. Later that year we finally decided to end the on-and-off relationship. It hurt to see her around school, but life moves on. Like Robert Kiyosaki says in *Rich Dad, Poor Dad*: "Who has been in love that has never gotten his heart broken?"

Kylie started dating another guy outside of school. That crushed me. I met Kylie during happy hour and we caught up.

"Are you dating someone?" I asked.

"I knew that question was coming at some point." She continued, "Yes, and I'm also taking him to the Barrister's Ball. He drives a Lexus and just took me out for dinner in an expensive restaurant. You know, he doesn't mind spending money, unlike a guy I know."

That hurt. I realized I was wasting my time with someone who stopped valuing me. This time I decided to stop pursuing her. I sat there in silence. I said goodbye to her, and this time there was no turning back. I withdrew quietly into the night.

A Single Dude

Again, a lonely guy. I took shelter in the books. My twelve-hour study days were my shelter. I hung out at a local bar with a few friends on Friday and Saturday evenings to keep my sanity. I went out with friends and talked to girls. I implemented some tricks I learned from Nile Strauss in his book *The Game*. I read this book after college, and it gave me confidence. I recommend this to you if you're a guy and want to learn a few tricks to catch a girl's attention. I was out and about. I wasn't emotionally available, but I liked the sport. A couple lucky nights came my way.

One evening during my drinking rampage I met Allison. She was a nice Midwestern girl from Wisconsin. When I first saw her at the bar, I saw a gorgeous girl. She had an angel's face. Beautiful hair. We talked and exchanged numbers. The following day I saw Allison's number on my phone. I texted her and made plans to meet again. I met her a day later and I saw a not-so-good-looking girl.

I went with her on a date and thought, *I'm here already, I might as well learn something from this human being.* Surprisingly, she was funny, and we laughed. I was also attracted to her personality, not her physique. That was a new concept for me. Little by little she grew on me. I perceived a good heart. This good girl had such a beautiful inside that attracted me so much.

I stayed over at her place, and she stayed over with me. While Lenny was in Florida during the winter months, I had a nice apartment to impress a girl. I had the apartment for myself, and I could bring a friendly companion over. Allison taught me to look past physical appearances. At the end of the summer, she had to leave DC to go back to Wisconsin. By then it was too late, I didn't want her to go. But she did.

I was empty inside again. All alone I needed family, and Dad opened his arms to me. I'd called him to check on him. To tell him that I was still alive and well. He was so happy to hear from me. He told me to come back and visit. We spent Thanksgiving and Christmas together with his new extended family. He was proud of me, showing off his law student son to all the new family he was building with a new life partner. I perceived a positive change with Dad. If we lost time together, now was the time for us to build the relationship we needed to have. From that moment on I kept in touch with him and we got together for important holidays and birthdays.

Now I'll tell you when I was about to die for the second time. This time I was really close. But this was the best thing that happened to me.

SUCCESS FORMULA

1. There is always an opportunity. Keep thinking about opportunities to provide the solution to a problem. If money is an issue, keep thinking about money and the solution will eventually pop in. Whatever the issue, keep thinking and thinking at all times, and the solution will come. You'll be surprised about the problems that humans have solved while on the toilet.

2. If she wants to be with you, she will be with you. Love is a game. In order to succeed you must fail.

3. Eventually physical appearance fades. Losing physical attraction over time is natural. After two years of having the same pheromones with your partner, the chemical attraction fades. Mental attraction stays longer and evolves if you cultivate it. People may remember a little how you look or what you say, but as Maya Angelou said: "they will remember forever the way you made them feel."

19

Like the Phoenix

In order to rise from its own ashes a phoenix
first must burn.
—Octavia E. Butler

Whether we remain the ash or become the
Phoenix is up to us.
—Ming-Dao Deng

I SURVIVED TWO YEARS OF LAW school. I even got As in some courses. If I was behind the curve during my 1L year, I was at the same level as everyone else during my 2L year. People made fun of my accent, but that didn't bother me. Little did I know that my weakness would turn into my strength after graduation. I noticed I was editing the work of classmates. I was changing the words and sentence structure of a native English speaker. That hit me—I dominated the English language at a level where I could say, *Hey, this writing needs to change.*

The Clinic

It was the summer of 2011 right after my 2L year, and I could not afford to work for free in an unpaid internship like most law students do in order to get experience and get a good job offer after gradua-tion. Unlike some of the other students, I needed money to pay for my 3L year. Lenny gave me a place to sleep and a few hours of work on his bookkeeping. This money was my beer money. I got another job working at the law clinic as a teacher's assistant for Professor Blair. Professor Blair was great. He went out of his way to care for his students. In the clinic, I took real cases from real people who had real problems owing taxes to the IRS. I represented people before the federal government. The clinic job gave me $4,000 that summer. How did I work? I gave them a copy of the fake ID and didn't look back. It worked in the past, so it had to work again. Nobody asked any questions. I kept on working hoping to get a check at the end of the summer and, luckily, they gave me one.

I worked closely with Professor Blair. One day we had beers after working a long day. He genuinely wanted to know about my journey. I was hesitant to tell him, but I heavily hinted that I wasn't a normal student. I kept on saying, "I don't have the same opportunities that other students here have." He perceived where I was going and said, "How about you tell me why you feel that way."

I could not verbalize it to him; it was a secret I would only tell my closest friends. I kept on saying, "You would not understand. You know, I'm not from this country, I have a heavy accent, I am broke." There was silence and he told me, "You act very confident in front of your classmates and you are doing good work. But I know that you are holding inside something that hurts. I think I know what you are going through." With kind eyes and understanding he just stated, "You are undocumented, aren't you?"

I was relieved he knew about me and had the compassion to understand. A couple of heavy tears dropped to my lap. He put a hand on my shoulder. "It's okay, Jose. You've done a great job for your situation."

I couldn't contain my tears and exploded, "I'm sorry, this is embarrassing. I don't know why I'm crying."

"You don't have to apologize. If you ask me, you're doing so much better than most people ever dreamed about."

"It doesn't matter. I don't even matter," I muttered.

"Don't ever say that again. You matter a lot. Hell, for being undocumented you're out and about. You're involved and active in everything. Other people lay low, but you? You're in the front lines where everyone can see."

His encouraging words made me feel better. "Now, finish your beer. In fact, chug this fresh one, it'll make you feel better." He popped open a new can of beer. That was the best advice I could get that night. The following morning, I came early to work even harder for Professor Blair.

I had four friends in law school who knew about me. Eva, the drinking buddy I spent lots of Saturdays with, going to bars and seeing how other guys picked her up. She was so cool that I treated her like one of the guys. Kylie, you already met her. Ernesto, the other Latino student in school who spoke Spanish and who always was there for me when I needed a beer. And now I had Professor Blair. The cool professor who drank with the students and genuinely cared for the success of his students. These were the only friends I confided my identity to and they genuinely liked spending time with me.

Law Camp Counselor

That same summer I also landed a job as a law camp counselor for twenty-five talented Latino high school kids who came from different US cities and were interested in law school. This counselor job was for two weeks, and I earned $2,000. During the interview for this job, they asked me why they should hire me.

My pitch was a mix of enthusiasm and genuine care. "That's easy. I'm cool and awesome! And the kids will have a great time with me. Trust me, I'm good with kids and they love me. They'll learn a lot from me. The kids will remember this learning experience for the rest of their lives!"

They loved my energy. The hiring committee was sold. During the camp we visited federal judges, big law firms, government agencies, and law schools. We had so many activities and did a mock trial where I trained them on how to present evidence and cross-examine a witness.

We were also supposed to visit the Department of State, where everyone had to provide a government-issued ID and our country of nationality. I panicked. I thought of ways I could tell my boss I had something else to do that day. Or maybe I would call in sick. This was the *federal government* we were talking about and the Department of State with all the sensitive information they had. They knew who I was because I had a visa and now that expired. I saw the end of the road, but I still took a chance.

I did not call in sick. I went to the Department of State. I gave them my Salvadoran passport and told them I was Salvadoran. As I entered the metal detector, I thought a few security guards would be waiting there to bust me in front of the kids. In my mind I saw myself in handcuffs, being thrown into a van and thrown in a jail cell for trying to infiltrate the federal government. I went through the metal detector and to my surprise, nobody cared. I was there with the kids being a chaperone, walking around the press room and walking by the office of Hillary Clinton, who was the secretary of state at the time. Nobody really cared for this undocumented guy.

I had a great time with the kids, and I'm still friends with some of them. I was happy to see that later in life some of them went to law school.

The Internship

That summer I also had a fellowship working for the Latino Economic Development Center, an organization helping small Latino businesses that also advocated for affordable housing in DC. This fellowship gave me another $4,000. The fellowship was a grant given by rich people to help the community. It certainly helped me. My job was to help low-income tenants to know their rights and complain against slumlords. I had a great time telling people that they have rights and empowering the community. I saw some landlord/tenant cases in court and a few tenants got money back and rent-free compensation.

These three summer jobs, plus Lenny's work, gave me $12,000 in three months. I worked my ass off. Life was going so well for me. Now I had enough money to finish law school. I believed in working hard and playing harder. So, to celebrate I went out by myself to the DC bars in Adams Morgan on Eighteenth Street. When I went out on my own, I made friends and had fun meeting new people. I started random conversations and danced around with random girls. I was young and had everything going for me. I didn't have the legal authorization to live in the United States, but that didn't hold me back much.

When Life Knocks You Down

I was at Rumba Café on Eighteenth Street, a place for salsa dancing and great mojitos. I was talking to a couple of lesbian girls laughing and trying to be funny with them. That night was just another night of good fun. The jokes and pickup techniques could only do so much. The evening ended as usual for me—I went home by myself. I headed toward the Metro station in Woodley Park on Connecticut Avenue around 2:30 a.m. I'd had a few mojitos and a good time.

A guy was walking next to me and looked at me with a defying face. I looked back at him with a defying face too. I was thinking, *why is this guy looking at me?* It was a macho contest and I wasn't going to back down. I kept walking to the Metro and he continued walking in the same direction giving me a dirty look. We did not say much, we just watched each other. It was a Mexican stand-off. Then the guy stopped to chat with a friend of his and I continued walking. After I walked a few yards, I looked back at them. Now both guys were looking at me with an angry face. I felt the need to defuse the situation. I could get into a fight with one dude, but two was going to be a challenge. I went back to the guy and changed my tone.

"Hey, man, we haven't done anything. I haven't done anything to you and you haven't done anything to me. We should just leave things like that."

Both dudes nodded like gangsters. I walked away. I walked faster. I noticed they followed me. I suddenly felt threatened. I started running. *I need to get the hell out of here.* The two guys chased after me. They yelled something I could not distinguish. Fifteen seconds into running, another guy waiting for me in front tripped me, and I fell to the ground. Then five guys started to beat the shit out of me. Kicks and punches went directly to my face. I could only cover myself. I kept yelling out: "I didn't do anything to you! I didn't do anything to you! Why are you doing this?!" But my yells went unheard.

Then a guy reached for my pocket, aiming for my wallet. I held on to my wallet inside my left jean pocket with both my hands. That meant that I could not cover my face with my arms. I was not going to let go of my wallet. I actually only had three dollars in my wallet, but I had something much more important there. Something that made my life relatively normal. I had a document that let me board planes and get into bars. I had my driver's license there. They had to kill me before they could take my driver's license away. I took that to the test.

I estimated that they beat me for two to three minutes and they gave me everything they had. Then a police car passed by with the flashing lights right on Calvert Street where I was being assaulted. The five guys scattered like smoke, and I was left on the ground. After noticing that the punches and kicks were not coming anymore, I opened my eyes and stood up. I kept my wallet in my pocket. *Ha, those wimps couldn't get my wallet.* I touched my nose. I saw blood in my hands. *Those bastards made me bleed.* Then I saw my reflection in a car window. I looked like I worked at a haunted house. My face was bloody and swollen. I hailed a cab, but the cab drove away as soon as he saw my bloody face. Then I hailed another cab, and this other cab drove away as soon as he saw me up close. The third cab saw my face and just passed me by. No cab wanted to be part of this.

I walked to the other side of the street and a guy saw me. He immediately came over to me. "What happened, man? Are you okay?"

"Yeah, I'm okay, but no cab would stop for me in these conditions. Would you hail a cab for me?"

He hailed a cab while I waited on the sidewalk a few feet away. A cab stopped, then the Good Samaritan told me to come. I came and then the cab driver said in a thick African accent, "Hell no, I don't want any trouble! I don't want any trouble!"

The Good Samaritan ushered me in. "Hey, he's with me, he was just a victim of a crime, I'll ride with him." We both rode in the cab.

The Good Samaritan looked over at me. "Hey, man, a similar thing happened to me, you'll be fine."

"Yeah, those bastards could not fight me one-on-one like real men. They're faggots," I snapped. When I looked over at the Good Samaritan, I noticed that he might have been gay. I grew up hearing that word over and over, so during my taxi rage I translated the Salvadoran word into English as close as I could. I immediately saw that something got lost in translation by the reaction of the Good Samaritan, and at that moment, I learned a big lesson in my life. Words matter.

I told the cab to leave me at the Friendship Heights Metro. The Good Samaritan did not let me pay for the cab. I thanked him for what he did. From that moment on I decided to stop using homophobic language. I never saw that guy again.

I called the police to make the report. The cops came and saw me all messed up. They called an ambulance and they put me on a stretcher. I was all tied up looking at the ceiling of the ambulance. Then a thought of joy entered my brain. *I qualify for a U visa now.*

During my internship at CASA de Maryland, I learned that people who are victims of a crime qualify to get immigration papers. The government does this to encourage immigrants to report crimes to help the police catch the criminals so that the criminals do not go around hurting others.

I was excited. I thank God for the beat-up. It was like God was looking down at me and saw what a rascal I'd been. As if he said, "This guy needs a beat-up—here you go, dude, enjoy it."

The ambulance took me to Suburban Hospital and they did a

CAT scan on me. The hospital nurses were so professional. They told me I had a fractured nose and major swelling. My face looked like a basketball. The nurse gave me a painkiller and a doctor came in and prescribed all kinds of stuff. Another nurse came to ask me for my insurance information, and I got pissed at him. I had no health insurance. Me getting pissed was my disguise, so I wouldn't have to tell him that I had no insurance.

A couple detectives came to interview me. I started telling them that I was a victim of a hate crime. They told me that it was not a hate crime and rolled their eyes at me. I totally felt like Michael Scott in *The Office*. *"Well, I hated it."*

It was 6:00 a.m. and the nurse told me that I could go home, that I would be fine in ten days. I called Lenny and he came to pick me up. I looked bad but I was glad to be alive. It looked worse than it felt, and it felt really bad. I got to my room and crashed.

That day I could have died. I was given a second chance. From that moment on I realized that every day is a blessing. I try not to take things for granted. I try to enjoy the little things in life. What happened to me was a blessing in disguise.

SUCCESS FORMULA

1. Dare to go places in the name of a good cause. For me it was teaching kids about education at the Department of State. Maybe for you it is to help others in a warzone or as part of the press. If you go to a place for the right reasons, most people will let you help those you intend to help.

2. Tragedy comes to us all unexpectedly. Suffering is inevitable. What you can control is your reaction.

3. During times of imminent peril and danger, the Universe conspires for your success. Call it other people helping you in times of need. Be a force of the Universe for someone else.

4. Ask yourself if what you do or say will benefit others. If so, go ahead even if it is painful. When the pain is gone you will enjoy peace again.

5. We are the product of our environment and it takes time to decode our mental programming. It can be done, but we have to recognize that we all have implicit biases and that change is possible.

Healer

HEALER IS ONE OF THE STRONGEST Fellows I encountered. In the late 1980s she arrived in the US at the age of five and went to live in Santa Ana, California. Her parents worked hard in the fields picking apples and other fruits. She lived in a community of immigrant farmworkers where resources were scarce and they lived in crowded rooms. Healer remembers having running water, electricity, and basic food. She does not remember "knowing" that she was poor. She did not notice she was poor as everyone around her lived in the same conditions.

Just like many immigrant farmworkers, Healer's parents do not speak English despite being in the US for more than thirty years. Healer only speaks to them in Spanish. In 2008, Healer attended college in California and got a degree in developmental neurobiology. Fancy stuff for someone with zero papers. California invests in their youth the smart way. The state has a version of the Dream Act that gives grants to immigrants who want to go to college, regardless of their immigration status. Healer had a dream of going to medical school and she wanted to attend Harvard. People laughed in her face. Healer did not care about people laughing; she knew she was destined for something bigger. She went to Harvard.

Wait a second, how the hell did she go to Harvard!? Just keep reading.

I told you she was poor and went to college in California with some scholarship from the state government. After college she went to work in whatever she could. She even worked selling Mary Kay

door to door for a living. It consumed her inside when she saw her fancy neurobiology degree on the wall while she was working selling Mary Kay. If only she had papers, she would have a decent job related to her field.

Healer was tired of having no papers, so she married her college sweetheart at the age of twenty-two. They were young and in love. The college sweetheart was a US citizen, so they thought their immigration problems would be solved by marriage. What they hadn't counted on was that the dude was broke and did not have enough money to prove to the US government that he could support Healer. That is a requirement in the immigration system. They don't let broke US citizens give papers to broke immigrants. Not only that, he also had to pay for a lawyer and those guys cost a lot of money. On top of it all, they had to prove that the US citizen husband had an extreme hardship in life. The law requires a special waiver to forgive the fact that Healer came through the border without permission. Healer was disappointed to realize that marriage alone did not give papers to her. Some people who enter the US with a visa and overstay can get married and get papers just by proving that the spouse has enough money to support them. Usually for a visa overstay, it is not that hard to come up with a little bit of cash. Sometimes sham marriages happen, but that is another story. Healer was indeed young and in love. Her marriage was real. Her finances were not that real.

Somehow Healer met a doctor who had a laboratory and he hired her as an independent contractor to do research in his lab. To be an independent contractor you don't need papers. She did not have everything that her peers had. She had no benefits or a nice salary, but she had a decent-paying job working in her field. She spent six years doing mundane lab tests assigned to her. She woke up early to be in the lab before everyone else and left the lab after everyone was gone. She was happy doing research. In the lab she could use her brain and express herself through research. She knew more than her colleagues. They asked Healer to give a presentation in Europe about their research. Healer made up excuses: "I can't travel right now. I

like it here. My husband and I don't like to travel. My dog needs me."
Her colleagues asked Healer to apply to medical school. Healer came
up with more lame excuses: "No, I like it here. I like my coworkers.
I don't think that med school is for me." That was bullshit and she
knew it. Deep down she was losing her soul every time she lied about
not wanting to go to med school. Healer's younger colleagues came
to the lab to train and then they went on to med school. Healer saw
these youngsters come and go while she stayed behind. Healer could
only watch. After six years of work, day and night, she was about to
accept her life as it was.

Her break came in 2012 when DACA was announced. Healer,
being a survivor, did not trust the government right away. The government was asking her to disclose all her information so that they knew
where she lived and that she lacked an immigration status, and in
exchange they promised to give her a work permit. It was too good
to be true. Thus, Healer did not apply to get DACA immediately.
She waited for other kids to apply and if they did not get deported,
she would apply too.

It turned out that the government actually kept its word and gave
thousands of young people a work permit with DACA. So, Healer
finally got her DACA work permit in 2014. That meant she could
work legally as an employee, not as an independent contractor. She
got a full-time job at the same lab and this time she got her benefits
package with vacation, bonuses, sick leave, 401(k). Life was getting
better for Healer. She began to live and enjoy her life. She began to
think about her future and remember her dream of being a doctor. She
gained the confidence to apply to Harvard Medical School. Harvard
would not have accepted her to med school if she could not be hired
as an employee of the hospital where she would do her residency after
med school. PhD and medicine programs need to have the students
as employees and thus these programs ask for legal authorizations to
work. They are not like law or social sciences programs where they
don't employ their students, they just take their money.

Healer got into Harvard Medical School. You would think her family would be proud of such an amazing accomplishment. Unfortunately, that wasn't the case here. Her family did not appreciate the magnitude of her success. Healer has five siblings; she is the oldest. Her brother also was born in Mexico, so he does not have papers. Healer's three younger sisters were born in the US. You would think that her siblings born in the US had it easy to succeed, but let me tell you that that is not the case. No sir. Her sisters got pregnant at a young age and they decided that school was not for them. The brother, who was in a similar situation as Healer, just gave up on school. The brother used to tell Healer, "You've been in school all your life and look what that has given you."

The brother did something stupid as a young man and got in trouble with the law. Those with a criminal history do not qualify for DACA, so the brother is doing odd jobs here and there. Healer endured all this suffering and now she is an OB/GYN doctor in San Francisco. She is a big deal. The brother now sees that things are good for Healer. It would be unfair to judge the brother hastily—the reality is that it is so easy to give up when you don't see the light at the end of the tunnel. It is hard to continue suffering when success is extremely uncertain. But my message to you is to keep fighting. Even if you fail in the process, you will give a good fight and earn respect for your effort. A guy by the name of Churchill said it better: "But never give in, never give up, never, never, never."

I was having dinner with Healer in a nice restaurant in San Francisco on Mission Street. She told me that she sacrificed her marriage and having a family to get where she is. Over time, she and her husband grew apart and divorced. She does want to have kids but she tells me that at her age it is very hard. I thought, how hard is it to have kids? I said jokingly, "If you want a kid, you know what you have to do." She looked at me with small eyes and said: "I'm thirty-seven now and it is hard for a woman to have a baby at this age. Trust me, I'm a doctor." "Well, I'm no doctor but if you let me, I can make it happen." Okay, I did not tell her that.

It was Friday night and I wanted to see the nightlife that San Francisco had to offer, so we went to a local bar after dinner. I wanted to hang out more and listen to her. At the bar I made her laugh here and there. Get a beer here and a glass of wine there in the middle of the crowded bar. Then I thought, *Am I flirting?*

We moved to a dive bar close by to have the last beer before we called it a night. But in the process, we had a few more beers. After some more time together, we dug deep into her story, then she broke down. She felt understood and accepted because we both share what it feels like to go to grad school without papers. She told me, "No matter how hard I try or what I do, I will never be accepted by this country." Then thick tears came down. She was letting her pain out. I said, "Healer, you are a superhuman much better than 99% of the human population. You have done unbelievable things. I mean, you can be a US citizen and not a Harvard Medical graduate, I think I'd take the Harvard Medical degree over the US citizenship certificate." We left the bar on a mellow note. I wanted to cheer her up. All I wanted to do was to help this beautiful, smart lady.

The night was ending and I offered to walk her home. I was feeling the beer and wine in my system and I said to myself, why not feel a little with this great human being? I made a move and said, "If you need a good-looking, intelligent, and funny man, here I am." She smiled. I continued, "What if I say that I am serious?" She smiled more and said: "I don't know about intelligent, but you are funny." I smiled. I grabbed her hand and walked down the street holding her. A couple blocks before her place she said, "Stay here." The fantasy was over, she had to go back to her real life. I did my last samurai move and said, "I know that a girl like you deserves a guy like me that is at your level. Just think about it." Healer stopped, looking at the sky in silence for fifteen long seconds. All I could do was watch her think. Her past went through her mind, her future went through her mind. I made the mistake of interrupting her on the fifteenth second. "What did you think about during that long pause?"

She came back to earth. Her smile came to a sharp stop. She said, "I can't. I have sacrificed too much."

I said, "It's okay." *San Francisco and Washington, DC, are far away anyway*—that was me coping with my defeat.

We smiled. I turned around and I left. The following morning, I had to catch a plane and continue on my journey.

This journey became full of emotions. I was hoping that life could be crazy just like in the movies. In the back of my mind, I fantasized about a parallel universe in the future just like Healer did.

After my encounter with Healer, I went to meet Tony in Northern California. Tony went through a living hell, but he became probably the most successful Fellow I met. He has the scars to prove his stories. I consider him my big brother in the law. Because of his success I changed as a lawyer.

20

3L Year

It is by going down into the abyss that we
recover the treasures of life.
Where you stumble, there lies your treasure.
—Joseph Campbell

THE SUMMER OF MY SECOND YEAR in law school was really cool. Not only had I gotten beaten up, which led me to apply for a U visa, but I also made $12,000 in three months. Therefore, I had enough money to pay for my last year of law school. I was convinced that I could graduate.

Enjoy Your Work

Most of the schoolwork I had in my third year was in the legal clinic. UDC has one of the top clinical programs in the nation. Students act like lawyers and work with real people on real cases to help low-income people who otherwise would not have access to a lawyer. A professor supervised our work, and we worked our asses off for the community. This is a great way to do hands-on learning.

Besides the Tax Clinic, I also worked at the Community Development Clinic helping the community organize legally to have a business or to manage their apartment buildings. In this clinic, I had to get certified to practice law before the DC Superior Court. That was another nightmare I went through. Now I was asking the court system to give me permission to practice law (under the supervision of my law professor). It was like applying for a mini bar license. I had to fill out an application, disclose my background, and pretend that I was just a normal kid. The U visa took time to process, so I still did not have papers. I did not have a criminal record, but it always crossed my mind that the court would check with the immigration system about me and that they would deny my license. Not just that, I thought the court would seek revenge and try to deport me. My attitude was to keep going. *Apply and see what happens.* The court didn't have to know I didn't have papers. I gave them all my personal information and whatever they required. Next thing I knew, there was this piece of paper in the mail indicating that I was accepted to practice before the Superior Court under the students-in-court program. I couldn't help it; I laughed my ass off once again.

I remember I prepared one of my cases so thoroughly. I asked the judge to put a woman in jail. This woman was the property manager of this apartment complex, our client, and she took $500,000 from our client's accounts and went to a West Virginia casino to gamble it all. She lost it all, and my client was in the hole. We sued this person, and this property manager was nowhere to be found. So, she didn't show up to court.

Here I was acting like a big-shot lawyer dressed in a suit and looking powerful. I was giving an argument to the judge as to why she should be placed in contempt of court and have a "body attachment," meaning that the US Marshal had to arrest her and drag her ass to court to face the consequences. Here I was, literally practicing law without papers. The judge looked at me like I was arguing in front of the Supreme Court, but it was just a preliminary hearing. He told me he would give her one more chance and instructed another defendant that if the woman did not come next time, he would order her arrested by the US Marshals. I came out like I was a big shot anyway. Not many law students can say they argued in front of a judge asking for the arrest of a criminal.

Partying Hard

I was out and about every weekend. Law school gave me a lot of stress and I had to channel all that energy somehow. Unfortunately, I channeled it into using alcohol as a tool to numb my lonely pain. I overused alcohol. I would start by telling myself that I'd only drink two or three beers. Later it turned out I had eight or nine beers.

Back in law school I started to create an alcohol problem. Even a college friend told me that I had to watch it. When a college friend tells you you're drinking too much, you know you're in trouble. After a rough night of drinking, my accent becomes very thick the next morning. My brain cannot control my speech after I killed so many brain cells. That's how my friend told me that I needed to calm down.

A lot of people blame law school for their alcohol addictions. Even the Muslim girl with her hijab started drinking our 3L year.

∎

I did not know what I would do come graduation time. My best friend in law school, Ernesto, decided to go to the state of Maine for spring break because he wanted to buy land to live on a farm after law school. We had the complete week off. I thought he was joking or went crazy, but that is what he liked to do. I joined him on a road trip to Maine. The weather was getting warmer in DC. I had nothing much going on during the break and Ernesto had a car and paid for the gas. I would help him drive for ten and a half hours from DC to Portland.

We arrived in Maine and saw thick snow in the middle of spring break. We left the spring sunshine of DC to go to a never-ending winter in Maine. We got to the plot of land Ernesto wanted to buy. It was in the middle of nowhere. I saw extreme poverty, which I hadn't seen in a long time—similar to Latin American countries. People around were not that friendly. I'm not sure if they were like that because of their lack of social interaction, as they have to stay indoors during the winter months that never end, or because we were a couple of Latino young men different from what they were used to seeing. Maybe it was both.

On our way back to DC we stayed with a cousin of mine who lived in New Hampshire and another in New York City, and both gave us shelter for a night. I talked Ernesto out of buying that land in Maine. After law school he went on to buy some land in New York relatively close to New York City where he enjoys his farming while also being a judge advocate general working as a lawyer for the Army.

Thanks to this Maine trip, I had a great conversation with an enchanting girl a few weeks later. She was a beautiful blond with caramel eyes who went to the part-time program at my law school. This one girl helped me become human again.

SUCCESS FORMULA

1. Life goes on and so should you. You have to let go of people who are not really there for you. Call them your friends, parents, significant others who stop your dreams or suck your energy. If they go away from your life, let them go. If they want to come back to your life, it is because they really see value in you.

2. Be honest with yourself and recognize your weaknesses. Only by admitting that you need to improve in one aspect of your life will you be able to think about resolving your flaws.

Tony

FROM SAN FRANCISCO I FLEW TO Chico, California, to meet my law brother Tony. Northern California is a whole new world. When you think of California you think of smiling girls and beaches. In Chico, people are conservative. Northern California is to California what the South is to the US. Tony first came to the US from Mexico when he was seventeen months old. His family returned to Mexico when he was nine years old, then went back to the US when he was a teenager.

In Mexico Tony was really poor but managed to do well in school. He almost won a national academic championship. He got second place because he could not stand his hunger in the middle of the final test. He finished the test hours early to look for something to eat. A rich girl took all the time to finish and recheck the test. She won the championship with exactly the same score as Tony. The tie breaker: Tony misspelled one word. Despite him having finished hours early, the judges made up the spelling rule. Not to mention that the rich girl had a rich dad. Tony's teacher/coach was disheartened seeing how a rich family won and the judges did not rule in Tony's favor. Nevertheless, Tony kept doing well in school and was happy living a modest life with scarce resources in Mexico.

When Tony was seventeen, his father told him they were moving back to the US. Tony did not want to go but his father said to him: "I'm not asking you." They put Tony in the back of a pickup truck and covered it up so that nothing would come in or out to cross the

US/Mexico border. The ride lasted for hours and hours and he thought he was going to die. By the time they eventually opened the cover, Tony was severely dehydrated, hungry, and traumatized. Tony still tells that story with watery eyes.

In the US Tony was a pretty insecure kid in high school. He did not like being different in a very white town. He was poor. Tony's confidence was so low that whenever he went to a fast-food restaurant he would speak softly, as he was embarrassed by his accent. He always struggled with the guilt of being forced to lie in order to survive.

Tony took a job at a grocery store to pay his way through college. He had started as a volunteer, but then one day the manager told him they were hiring. Tony said, "No, it's okay, I like it here, don't worry. I am just happy to get the experience." He lied because he did not have papers to be hired legally. But eventually, he got a work application and he filled it out. He wrote numbers and letters in the space asking for his green card; any numbers and letters that came to his head. He got hired. Then he continued working at the grocery store for years and one day he decided to go to the local law school at night. You can read all about his life in his book *Undocumented Lawyer*. I will tell you here the things he does not mention in his book.

How did Tony pay for law school while he was undocumented? Law school is not cheap. Well, he went to an affordable law school—a school that is not accredited by the American Bar Association but is accredited by the California State Bar, which was all he needed. Tony wasn't planning to practice out of state; he always intended to stay in California. The beauty of California is that they let anyone take the bar exam. They don't require people to go to law school, although going to law school helps. Why go to an expensive law school out of state if what you really want is to practice law in your hometown? Tony made the smart move and worked hard in law school. Between working hard at the grocery store and his credit card, he paid for his law school tuition.

Tony interned at a law firm where he met a wealthy lawyer who had a son in the same law school class as Tony. Tony told his struggling story to his classmate, who invited him to come live with him for free in his luxury house. Tony accepted that generous offer. He did not commute much and saved on rent. This meant that Tony could stop waking up at 3:00 a.m. to go work at the grocery store located an hour away. When he used to go to work, he left really early so he did not have to speed and get pulled over and arrested for driving without a license. At that time California did not give driver's licenses to undocumented folks. The money Tony saved in rent by living in this luxury place meant that he could stop working in the grocery store and dedicate his full time to law school.

The son of this rich man, Pamper Boy, was a complete slacker. Pamper Boy had everything he wanted, and his parents would give him anything as long as he stayed in law school. They would give him a Lamborghini when he threw a tantrum threatening that he would drop out of school. The rich parents would say: "No, no, we would do anything for you, we will give you anything you want. Do you want a luxury vacation at the end of the semester? You want a Lambo? Whatever you want, we will give it to you but don't drop out of school." Pamper Boy knew his parents and took advantage of them.

One late night, Pamper Boy made a lot of noise that woke Tony up. Pamper Boy was drunk as a skunk. Tony tried to help him as Pamper Boy was threatening to endanger himself by driving to go meet a girl-friend. Tony called the rich parents and told them that Pamper Boy needed help. The rich parents came and got Pamper Boy to calm down by bribing him with another expensive gift that he didn't deserve. The rich parents talked to Pamper Boy often about the fact that Tony had nothing and he was working hard. All Pamper Boy heard was, "Why can't you be more like Tony?! Tony doesn't even have papers and you have everything!" Jealousy governed Pamper Boy's mind.

Pamper Boy was pissed at Tony for calling his parents. Pamper Boy gave his parents an ultimatum: kick Tony out of the house and fire him as an intern in the law firm or Pamper Boy would drop out of law school and not let them see the baby he was expecting with his girlfriend. Rich Dad came to see Tony and told him he could no longer stay at the luxury place. Tony thanked him for all the time he got to spend there, but ultimately Tony knew this arrangement would not be forever. He went back to living with his parents and continued with his law studies that were about to end anyway.

It was 2008 when Tony applied for the California Bar exam. He passed it on his first try. The California Bar never asked for the immigration status of a person until that year. Tony answered the immigration question as being "pending," since his father, who was a legal permanent resident, petitioned for him in 1994 and the waiting time for Mexicans is enormous. Then Rich Dad, a lawyer too, snitched on Tony, telling the California Bar that Tony had no papers and that they should check into him more. The California Bar admitted Tony but in a matter of months they took Tony's law license back.

Tony was destroyed, depressed, in a dark place in his life. He cried and cried in his loneliness. He'd gone to law school, passed the bar, and was even a practicing lawyer for a few months, but due to the jealousy of a few haters he wasn't allowed to continue with his dream. I'll tell you something, Tony is definitely a man with a pure heart; any other man would be consumed by rage and would seek revenge. Not Tony. Tony eventually got out of his bed and decided to fight his case. A couple of lawyers took his case pro bono and defended him before the California Supreme Court. These lawyers believed in Tony's nobility and just cause. They fought the State Bar to make them let Tony practice.

Tony's case was well publicized, and he received many death threats. He sincerely thought about ending his life at some point. His girlfriend at the time kept nagging him: "Oh, you keep talking about how they're gonna give you your bar license next month or that they will do it at the end of the year, and that never happens!" The girlfriend left him. Tony had no money, no love, no luck, and no mental health. He was fucked up.

This battle for his law license lasted five years. During those years he met with many California legislators and journalists. Tony's quest was to give professional licenses to anyone willing to study hard and be productive. Because of his efforts, California passed a law allowing undocumented people to get professional licenses.

Tony made so many friends throughout his journey. When I was in his office in Chico, he showed me three big binders full of business cards from politicians, reporters, and businesspeople. He became a rock star. Maybe Hollywood will make a movie about him.

Tony told me the story about how his grandfather became so rich but lost it all in Mexico. His grandfather would take his T-shirt off and wash cars for a few cents on the street. Then someone noticed his hustle and offered young Grandpa a job at the train station. Grandpa kept on getting promoted and became an experienced station manager. Later the company decided to sell the station, so his grandpa bought the station with his savings. Grandpa ended up being super rich.

Grandpa liked women. And with his hobby came kids here and there from different entanglements. Grandpa got entangled with the wrong woman. He was murdered when Tony's father was little. Tony's grandmother did not fight for any of her kids' rights, so nothing went to Tony's father. Now Tony is rich on his own merits. I told him he was destined to be rich just like his grandpa and now his offspring will benefit for generations to come. Tony stopped me and told me that he will not have children. When I asked why, he told me it was a personal decision. I persisted. He told me that it was a sad world and he does not want to bring more children to suffer in this world.

I saw Tony and I still detected his broken heart. He got some form of PTSD from the odyssey he had to go through. Tony is a multimillionaire now with a fortune greater than Prince Harry and Meghan Markle, but despite his fortune there is some part of his soul that changed forever. Enduring a trauma like that is not easy, but it turned him into who he is now. He is a motivational speaker and has a foundation to give scholarships to kids who want to continue with their education. He travels around the world and now has it made. Tony is married to the love of his life. They met when Tony was touring the country talking about his case. Tony is now a US citizen with a thriving personal injury practice. Because of his success in personal injury, I myself started working with personal injury cases, and let me tell you, they pay well.

Next, I will tell you about another beautiful doctor. She became a psychiatrist and now she helps a lot of people in need.

PS: Tony's ex-girlfriend regrets leaving him.

21

Last Semester in Law School

*It takes someone very special to help you
forget someone very special.*
—Erich Segal

LAW SCHOOL WAS ENDING AND I didn't want it to end. What was I going to do after school? It wasn't like I had a promising job waiting for me after graduation. School was a shelter for me. It was okay for me to be broke, that's what grad students are. It was okay for me to not work full time or to do odd jobs. For the past three years I changed my way of thinking and the way I processed information. I got used to the new words I learned that nobody uses. My language skills radically improved. My law courses were not as challenging anymore. I was no longer studying twelve hours a day. I was getting bored.

I realized that because of my Spanish language skills, I had a skill not many people had in law school. I could speak directly to the Spanish-speaking population who needed legal help. I realized there were so many clients out there who needed a lawyer to speak to them in their language. I saw an underserved market. I was confident that I was going to be fine if I opened my own law firm right after law school. *Yeah, open your law firm and be your own boss.* Even though I had filed for my U visa to get a work permit, the immigration process takes years to approve the paperwork. I legally could not be employed, but nothing could stop me from opening my own firm.

Everyone in my class made plans to take the bar exam. I wasn't afraid of the bar itself; I was afraid of the Character and Fitness Committee. That committee oversaw evaluating the good morality of each bar applicant. They do an invasive background check on your life. They ask you all kinds of questions. Where have you lived? What traffic tickets did you get? And my favorite question, what's your immigration status?

You had a good run, Jose, don't be disappointed. You tried your best. You almost did it. Your roadblock is here, and it seems it is the end of the line for you. How was I going to explain to the interviewer that I had no papers? For the past twelve years I had no papers and lived a life pretending I was a normal person. I basically faked my life, a thing that the committee doesn't like. One thing that's a big no-no is lying on the bar exam application. It crossed my mind, I had lied to so many people about my immigration status, why should I stop now? But to be completely honest, lying made me so uncomfortable that I was sick of it. At some point in my life, I had to live a real life. I was done. If they didn't accept me as a lawyer, I was okay with it. I had the knowledge. Maybe I would become a professional criminal revolting against the system. I could become a good head of the mafia—drug dealing became an option once again. Not really.

I did not take the bar exam right away after law school like everyone else. My U visa was still pending. I filed my U visa paperwork on my own, acting as my own lawyer. I was proud of the work I did. I showed my friend Ernesto my application and he liked it.

Let me explain to you the law about the U visa. Immigrants can get a U visa for four years which gives them a work permit if they can prove that they have been a victim of a qualifying crime (i.e., one that's on a list of crimes compiled by the government). They also need to prove that they cooperated with the authorities in everything they needed, like testifying in court or doing anything possible to catch the criminals so they don't go hurting others. Lastly, the immigrant has to show that they suffered physical or psychological harm. I had a great case—I got so beat up, I called the police and went to the hospital. I included in the packet full-color pictures of my bloody face. I cooperated with the detective, giving a composite description so that an artist would draw the picture of the assailants and publish their faces. In order to build my case and file the best U visa application I could possibly file, I went to therapy to talk about my psychological harm. I got free therapy from the university, as PhD clinical students worked there to get practice on my emotions. At the time I didn't think it was necessary, all I wanted was to build the best U visa packet, but later it turned out to be one of the best things to help me deal with and heal my traumas. Last, I went to a nonprofit organization asking for help on my U visa application, but they were too busy helping other people. However, a lawyer working there told me that once I was done with the U visa packet, I could come back and she would review it. So, I came back with a complete packet and she gave me a few comments but told me that it was a nice packet.

In my head I was finally going to get papers and then I was going to tell the bar, "Hey, all this time I had no papers but guess what, I just got papers."

To my surprise, this U visa application would take about eighteen months to be reviewed. *Eighteen months!* Talk about an inefficient government agency. I thought, *Maybe I can call USCIS (United States Citizenship and Immigration Service) and get them to hurry up.* I made many phone calls, and it took almost an hour to navigate the automated system to finally get to talk to a real human being. And when I got to speak to a human, that person told me that she could not give me any information because it was a U visa application, and those cases are treated with confidentiality.

"Hey, that's my application. I'm giving you permission to talk to me about my case," I said.

"Unfortunately, we don't do that here, the U visa cases are handled by the U visa center in Vermont."

"Okay, that is good to know. Can you connect me to the Vermont people?"

"All we can do is give you an address and you can send them a letter."

I got the address and I sent them a letter, but that was all I could do. As graduation came, I was more anxious to get a response from the U visa center in Vermont. I made more calls, but there was no success in pushing them to do their job. The answer was always a big "Wait."

I realized that the U visa would not arrive by the summer after graduation. I had to find something to do. Maybe the U visa would come by the next February, just in time for me to take the winter bar exam.

Barrister's Ball

Prom night for law school came in early April 2012. We had all worked hard for the past three years. We became new people. I could no longer watch the news normally. I heard the legal terms that the reporters would spew and knew that most of the things said were not legally possible and it's just a way to give people bullshit. Going to law school is a blessing and a curse. A blessing because you understand complex issues, a curse because you can detect bullshit wherever you go and thus you get annoyed at the fact that some people want to deceive you.

There I was at the Barrister's Ball in my black suit, black shirt, and white tie. I went alone. No date. Kylie had her new boy there. I did my best to not look at them. I did what I did well in times of imminent peril and danger: I hit the bar. That was the best I could do. After a few drinks I was getting into a better mood. Then I started joking around and laughing. I started working the room and talking to new people. I went to speak to the part-time law students gathered in a corner of the bar. I would see them walking by during the evenings in school, but I'd never had a real conversation with them. By the end of the three years, everyone in my class was fed up with seeing each other, so I went to make new friends.

There she was, a gorgeous blonde woman with a beautiful silhouette. She was the most beautiful woman I have ever seen in my entire life. Full makeup, high heels, and a long gown. She was with a group of people close to the bar. I remember her bright red lipstick and her red dress. Her long blonde hair fell to her lower back. She was a Barbie. With the liquid confidence of more than a couple beers, I approached the entire group and talked to the less attractive woman first—a technique I learned to penetrate a group of people. The blonde girl kept her body facing her friends but turned her head and looked at me over her shoulders.

"My name is Jane," she yelled out. The music was very loud. I could barely hear her.

"Nice to meet you, Jane. How was your spring break?"

"It was very nice; I went to Vegas for a few days and won some money."

"You must be a lucky charm. My friend Ernesto and I had a road trip to Maine for spring break a few weeks ago."

"I'm from Maine!" she said quickly.

We talked about Maine all night. We hit it off. Something clicked. I spent most of the night with her. After the party we went to a diner to get something to eat. I was intoxicated; I want to believe I was not that sloppy. We took a cab to my place, and I was trying to be charming. In fact, I was slurring my speech. She wanted to make sure I made it safely to my place. Then she returned in the same cab to where she parked her car. I woke up the next morning and thought, *I met someone special.*

Besides being a part-time law student, Jane worked as a bartender in the bar next to the law school. She was the hot bartender who got hit on constantly by all the men. I thought about my chances with her. I didn't care, I went for it. The day after the party I went to the bar for five minutes to talk to her.

"Are we cool? I know that last night I was a little tipsy and may have said something wrong."

"You were fine. But you were saying, '*Come inside the apartment and spend the night with me, mi amor pero yo te amo tu sabes que yo te amo.*' I know a little Spanish."

"Oh… yeah, that was me telling the truth. I just want to know that we are cool."

She said, "We're cool. Don't worry about it."

"I'm glad. I know you're busy working but we should do something one day."

"We could go watch a movie after I get off in a couple hours."

My eyes widened so big. "Yeah, I'll stop by after you're done working. I'll be back then." I fled the bar right after that.

She just asked me out for a second date. I needed to plan this well. I needed to show her a movie that she would remember for the rest of her life. I got tickets to see *The Avengers*. I felt so cool at the movies seeing the Avengers kick ass with a beautiful girl next to me. I'm not sure if she liked the movie or was being nice to me that night. It got late and she was tired. I told her to come to my apartment and she could rest there. I was sober. She came into the apartment and we talked for hours. We were on a V-shaped couch and were falling asleep. I slept on one side and she slept on the other. We held hands all night and that's all that happened that night. I'm serious, nothing else happened. I just wanted to explore Jane's mind.

We spent a lot of time together. We went to bars on the weekends for drinks and I told her, "I like this."

"Me too but there is something I have to tell you," she said. "I came down to DC and I lived with a man and he is up there in Maine." *Oh no, I knew it, she is married with kids.*

"Wow."

"But I came here because that is over."

"Your past is your past. I like you and if you enjoy this time together, we should be together."

She smiled.

We became a couple. We were in love. I had a great girl once again. Things were going well once again.

We went to Rehoboth Beach in late April and the weather was still chilly. We went in the ocean, and it almost swallowed us. The current was strong and was pulling us in. Luckily, I still had my feet on the ground and pulled her back to safety. That was an adventure that ignited our intense feelings even more. She was so nice, I wondered if she was the one. She had it all. She was smart, good-hearted, and gorgeous. What else could I want? I wanted nothing else. Life right then in the present was all I needed. We were young and reckless.

I told Jane about my immigration problem, and she was sad but then she came up with the original idea that no couple had ever thought about before. She said:

"Why don't you marry me?"

"What?" I never thought a girl would actually propose to me.

"It's to help you out, that is all."

"Don't worry, I'm already taking care of that. I have this thing called a U visa that's coming and my papers will come at some point."

"Okay, let's wait and see, I'm here for you."

A smile was sketched on my face.

Law School Graduation

My entire immediate family came from El Salvador to visit me in Washington, DC, when I graduated law school. Even my grandma came. They were proud. I was proud. It was a big achievement. I introduced them to Jane, and we had a great time at a celebration in the same house where I had my college graduation celebration.

There I was, a law school graduate. I earned my Juris Doctor. I told my siblings, "You don't have to call me doctor but don't you forget I am one." I told my family about the beat-up I got in DC and that everything would be okay. I even showed my mom the graphic video I made while at the hospital. *What dude shows a video like that to his mother?* My mother is a sweetheart and seems docile, but she's tough. She didn't seem surprised about my beat-up and was glad that the experience was leading to me having papers in this country.

Dad was there, proud of his son. He said, "Thank you for bringing everyone in the family together once again. Because of you we all are in the same place."

I gave him a big hug. I told him, "I guess all this time in the monastery was worth it. By the way, thank you for paying for my cell phone bill all these years."

"You didn't call me much, so it wasn't much of a bill." We laughed.

We had a father-son relationship once again. It was time to overcome whatever happened in the past. I was there for him and he was there for me. In whatever we needed. We didn't have much. Dad worked driving a bus for disabled people and he lived paycheck to paycheck. However, now we felt like we had each other.

While I waited to take the February bar, I decided to take a summer job in Chicago. I needed to go away and find myself. I got a job organizing a law camp for middle and high school kids to teach them what law school is all about. While my peers were taking the bar, I took six more months to work random jobs and explore the US.

A Bar Story

Bridgette and Jose walk into a bar during happy hour after a midterm exam.

Jose tells his classmate Bridgette, "You see that bartender. She is hot as hell. I bet you I can get her. I am good with women."

Bridgette says, "Stop it, Jose, you think you are charming but you are not, you will never get anybody."

Jose: "Challenge accepted."

Jose approaches the bartender and says a few things to her that make her laugh. Then Jose comes back to Bridgette.

"What do you think?"

"Anybody can go speak to her, she is the bartender. She was just being nice to you."

Months pass and during a farewell happy hour, Jose and Bridgette walk into the same bar.

Jose says, "Bridgette, you see the bartender, her name is Jane, I bet I can get her…"

She says, "You played me, Jose, and it's not funny."

"Really? I think it is."

"Okay, it is."

SUCCESS FORMULA

1. Seek help. There are professionals out there willing to help. Professionals are expensive. However, money paid to a professional is money invested. If you don't have money, look for organizations that have professionals willing to help. One of those professionals might like your story and help you for free.

2. If you want a real romantic relationship with a person, take it slow. Enjoy the falling in love process. Don't rush. You know when you meet someone special. You want to be with the person and talk to that person. Enjoying each other's minds will give you a higher reward.

3. Don't be afraid to love someone. Loving is never a waste of time because when you love someone, that other person will indeed love you at some level. Maybe not in the way you expect but always in a positive way.

Specialist

I TRIED MEETING SPECIALIST IN PERSON while I was in Chicago, but she was too busy working in her residency. However, I spoke at length with her over Zoom calls.

Specialist came to Chicago from Pakistan at the age of three. Her parents separated when she was five. Her father went back to Pakistan and her mother stayed with Specialist and her seven-year-old brother. Specialist does not speak much about her father since he left the US early in her life. However, she does not dwell on the past and understands that he did what he felt was best for him. She didn't even want to tell me where he was. All she said to me was that her father wasn't in the US. Her mother raised two kids by herself. She emphasized education in her kids. Now Specialist is a psychiatrist and her brother is an employment attorney. A doctor and a lawyer, that is the dream of many parents.

The family came to the US in 1995. Her father asked for asylum and the entire family was part of the immigration package. When he left the country, the asylum application was deemed abandoned. Specialist and her family became undocumented without even realizing it for several years.

Specialist was in the seventh grade when her family moved from Chicago to New Jersey because they had relatives there. Before Mom settled in New Jersey, she tried living in different cities for a few months. The young family went to Kansas City, then Florida for a

couple of months. Her mom wanted to try different environments looking for a good fit for them. It was hard on her; maybe she just wanted to get away for a moment. In New Jersey, Mom had an entrepreneurial mind and worked managing restaurants and beauty salons.

High school was pretty normal for Specialist. She spoke without an accent and had good grades. One day her brother wanted to get his driver's license. So, guess what happened when he wanted to get a government-issued ID? His family told him he didn't have any valid immigration papers and could not get a license. Specialist heard what her brother was going through and she realized that she was in the same boat. Mom had "the talk" with her kids. Specialist is a natural optimist thanks to her mom's positive attitude. Her mom taught her kids that being positive helps confront any problem.

The family faced this undocumented problem with everything they had. They were not allowed to feel sad about it; instead, they had to work hard to find the solution to this challenge. The family's motto was: "Everyone has their struggles and this is going to be our struggle." From that moment on, Specialist had a different perspective on life. She hears other people complaining about trivialities and she realizes that things could be worse for them. She tells me, "People complained during COVID-19 that they could not travel internationally on airplanes. That has been the way I have always lived. I never traveled anywhere." If Specialist goes abroad, just like that, she will get a ten-year penalty prohibiting her reentry to the US.

After high school it was time for Specialist to go to college. She was accepted to a great school in Southern California, but she got a full ride in New Jersey to Rutgers in New Brunswick that included her room and board. All she had to do was show up. However, one week before her school started, Rutgers told her that her paperwork was no good and they pulled her scholarship away. Specialist cried. She had it all but now she had nothing. On top of that, Rutgers classified her as an out-of-state student, which meant she had to pay a tuition that was three times what an in-state student paid. She went from having a full ride to paying three times the cost for her education. Things did not look good. But Mom came to the rescue. She organized many meetings with banks to ask for a loan. Mom said to Specialist: "You are going to school and you are going to school this semester, let's meet with the bankers." Many banks turned her away because they did not have the right papers. But they found one bank that gave her a loan as long as a person with proper papers would cosign on the loan. Mom found a friend cosigner. Also, there is this program in New Jersey called NJ-CLASS, which is neither a federal nor a private loan but a state-backed loan program. New Jersey has this type of loan for people who cannot meet all the expenses with federal financial aid, and Specialist took this loan as well. With struggles, Specialist got her psychology degree. To this date, Specialist is still paying back these loans.

Specialist wanted to be a psychiatrist. Her brother had gone to law school undocumented, and she wanted to go to med school. Big Brother told Specialist that it was more difficult to go to med school without papers than law school because med school requires students to be employees during the residency program. It was 2011, Specialist had no papers but she studied for the MCAT (Medical College Admission Test) anyway. She made her med school application look stunning. In her mind she thought of making her application so good that everyone would overlook the fact that she had no papers. She'd graduated magna cum laude after all. She applied to med schools but only got two interviews. One of them was in Texas. She told the interviewer, "By the way, right now I don't have a Social Security number but President Obama just announced DACA, a program I qualify for, so everything should be okay." Specialist did not hear back from them.

Specialist was not giving up on her dream of becoming a psychiatrist. She took a couple of classes, Anatomy and Molecular Cell Biology, at a community college to continue with her education. She volunteered in an organization to help others instead of staying at home watching TV on a couch. In 2012 she got her DACA work permit and worked at Macy's in the perfume department for a few months.

The following year Specialist tried different med schools. This time DACA was well known. Many med schools wanted Specialist. She had options. She finally went to med school at Loyola University Chicago, and she loved it.

It was 2017, and Specialist was ready to apply to her residency programs, but a big clown in the White House announced he was rescinding DACA. This was stressful. People in residency programs would think twice about hiring a person who may not finish the residency. Med schools did not want DACA to end. What kind of person does not want more doctors to heal others? Thankfully, a team of people in the legal profession sued the federal government and saved DACA for the time being.

When I spoke to Specialist I was irradiated with a sense of peace and calmness. Her words were welcoming. I asked her what message she would have for others who are struggling. She said:

> People have to focus on what they can control; they should focus on the positive rather than the things that they cannot control. . . It's very hard, I'm not going to say it's easy. I've tried to just stay positive by looking at the things that I can control. To be very honest, of course it's in the back of my mind all the time. But if I let it consume me day by day, I'm not going to be able to function and do the things I need to do. If I let it consume me, I would not be here where I am right now finishing up my residency. If I thought much about others telling me that this is impossible, I would not do much. You have to come back and say: "Forget it." [Unfortunately], you were placed into this position as undocumented. It's not your fault. It's no one's fault, it's just an unfortunate circumstance, but now you're going to have to change the trajectory of your life. If I let those other people's opinions really affect me and change

my decisions, then I wouldn't be able to make it where I am right now. So, I would say to those people, do as much as you can to fulfill yourself, try to focus on the positives, and then if you have time, the things that are out of your control. For me, I am a spiritual person, I just leave it up to God, but that's me. It depends whether you are spiritual, or how you could connect with yourself. You have to let go of the parts of your life that you can't control. So let go and focus on the parts that you can control.

She said these words and I felt inspired. This conversation was refreshing.

Specialist's parents had an arranged marriage. It is a cultural practice in Pakistan. Now, the practice continues with a variation in America. Some Pakistani families still introduce the young couple to each other but the couple gets to spend some time dating to make sure they want to get married. Specialist is thirty-three, a busy doctor. She just finished her residency. I asked her if her family had shown her Mr. Right. She said no. She gave me the generic answer: she is concentrating on herself. She told me she was so busy with residency that she forgot what it was to have a hobby.

I'm sure good things will come to Specialist. As a psychiatrist she will dedicate the next four years serving the underserved population of the Chicago suburbs. Maybe she will travel now on advance parole,[4] unless she is "too busy."

Next, I want to tell you about another powerful Fellow, Mighty. The Force is strong with him. He triumphed over his struggles and is using his powers to help other grad students. A biochemist from Yale who worked overnight making sandwiches in a New York deli, he did not sleep much but now is a science professor at Columbia University. I had to meet this man, so there I was on my way to New York City.

---

4   Advance Parole is a special travel document that allows people with TPS and DACA to travel abroad and come back to the US.

22

Chicago

It is better to conquer yourself
than to win a thousand battles.
Then the victory is yours.
It cannot be taken from you,
not by angels or by demons, heaven or hell.
—Buddha

BIG BUILDINGS AND A LOT OF action. I went to Chicago right after law school to take a job as a law camp counselor for the summer. They did not ask me questions about my papers. All they cared about was that I had a law degree. Some distant relatives of mine gave me shelter in a modest place on the west side of Chicago. I didn't have to pay rent, as I crashed on a couch. My distant relatives did not have much, but they welcomed me every night with a hot meal. I love them so much. Despite not having much, they were willing to give me everything without expecting anything in return.

That summer Jane and I did the long-distance thing. It sucked. But I had a job in Chicago that kept me busy. Jane stayed in DC working at the bar and taking summer classes.

I worked in an organization called Just the Beginning Foundation. Their purpose is to help the underrepresented population become lawyers. I was the program director along with Mike. Mike was a fast-talking big guy from New York of Lebanese descent who just finished his second year of law school. He used to be a teacher.

Most of my coworkers were black. I was the only Latino there. It was hard to gain their trust. I was seen as an outsider hired to oversee black people. It was the luxury condo experience all over again. I could hear their minds screaming, *why couldn't they find a black person to be the program director?* There was this girl Brittany who was supposed to be my assistant and when I asked her for a favor, she would give me a dirty look. I asked her to put a simple binder together and it took her three days and a couple reminders to do it. I took it one day at a time.

I enjoyed the fact that we were hosted by a big law firm operating from Willis Tower, the tallest building in Chicago. I enjoyed a beautiful view every day.

The first month of work there was a power struggle between Mike and me. My style was to collaborate with other folks. His style was to confront and excel over others. I tried to implement the organizational skills I developed in my business classes to have good morale with the team, but my techniques did not work.

Our job was to travel from city to city giving a law camp workshop to high school kids for a week. The counselors would take the kids to meet with big corporations and their legal departments. We visited federal courts, state courts, big law firms, and law schools. The point was to give these kids exposure to the legal field. The job was a lot of fun. Traveling and talking to fresh minds. Sharing the journey with good-hearted people was amazing. But the coworkers were there at the end of the day to resent the fact that I was hired last minute to be a co–program director.

∎

Almost halfway into the program, I took my co–program director Mike for a few drinks. I sat down with him and had a heart-to-heart conversation.

"Hey, man, they cut my original stipend they promised me because they wanted two program directors," I said.

"They cut mine too!" Mike responded.

"It sucks but it is what it is. I wanted to chat about the program. You are good at teaching and talking. You're an imposing authority to the kids. I am here to share with the kids and have fun with everyone. This is a three-month gig; we might as well enjoy the time."

"Man, I didn't realize they cut your pay too, I thought they cut mine to give it to you. Everyone else didn't like you because they think they cut everyone's pay to give it to you. Plus, some think you are bossy."

"WTF . . . I'm bossy? If I wanted to be bossy, trust me, I would snap at Brittany and let her have it. She's a piece of work. I asked her for help, and she flat-out refused. Mike, I'm glad you're telling me this, I'm done being the good guy, these brats will know what bossy Jose is like. I'm done with this bullshit."

"Hey, Jose, no, no. You're a good guy. You're a really good man, don't do that, there's no need."

"Fuck no. I'm going to let that little brat have it," I snapped. The few beers in my system started talking.

"Hey, Jose. Let me cut you a deal. From now on let's work together. I'll talk to her and tell her that you indeed are a good guy. Let me talk to her."

I don't know what was said about me before I got to Chicago, but I know that once Mike got to really know me, he changed his mind about me as a person. The moral of the story is to have a heart-to-heart conversation with someone with influence—in this case, Mike. If the other person has a good heart, it will be a productive conversation. If the other person is antagonistic even after you open up, that's a shame and at least you get to find out who that person really is. But don't dismiss people right away. Always give them a chance to prove to you who they really are.

After that conversation we started to work much better together. Sure, we had heated debates from time to time. But in the end, I still remembered Mike as a good guy and I'm sure he thought the same about me.

As for Brittany, I did snap at her one time in front of the kids because I was frustrated. I don't remember what I asked her to do but it was a very simple thing and she looked at me like I had two heads. "Forget it," I said, "don't do anything, just stand there doing nothing. I'll figure it out on my own and I will do it all." I rolled my eyes and looked at the sky raising my hands like I was imploring God to give this girl a brain. Then I left.

That was probably not the best way to handle the situation. Brittany felt ashamed and that day she tried to make amends. For the most part I'm a very docile guy. People can even seem to take advantage of my good heart. But if a line is crossed, I lash out.

Brittany and I teamed up on a project in Minneapolis. Mike was away at a wedding and the others went to another city. It was Brittany, me, and the kids. The kids loved me. I played with them and made friends with them. I was going along for the ride. From time to time, I had to appear like the grown-up program director, especially when we were in front of other adults like judges, lawyers, and rich donors. However, I tried to play as much as I could with the kids, especially when they prepared for a mock trial and a mock appellate argument. I felt like a law professor messing with their brains. I used to give them hard questions and some kids would have that deer in the headlights look. I put them through hard questions so they could get a taste of pressure. Toward the end, a shy kid turned out to be a powerful arguer that amazed the entire group. She won the competition, and I told her, "From now on, you own the world, don't be shy anymore, you are power." She believed it and walked away taller than anyone. Magical moments like these fed my soul and made me enjoy the journey.

Eventually, Brittany got to know me. She came up to me once near the end of the program saying I was a good guy and apologized for the hard time she gave me.

Cultural Insensitivity

While in Chicago a black coworker made a joke. He said, "Here's a joke. What happens when a white woman goes black?"

"What happens?" someone said.

"She turns into a single mother."

I laughed my ass off loud and the entire room looked at me. I was the only nonblack person there. He said, "Well, Jose, I take offense to you laughing at that joke."

What comedian hates the laughter of his audience?

Apparently, I was not his audience. "Okay, I'm sorry that your joke wasn't intended to make people like me laugh. But if it makes you feel better, I can tell you a Mexican joke."

The guy had an unrelenting look on his face. "Alright, I'd like to hear it."

"Why is Mexico not sending an Olympic team to the Olympics this year?"

The room was looking at me with serious faces ready not to laugh at the joke.

"Why?"

"Because everyone who can run, jump, or swim is already here."

Everyone refused to smile for a second. They were holding their breath hard. The dude couldn't hold it anymore and broke out laughing, the others followed.

We all laughed.

I'm not Mexican.

Traveling Job

The summer in Chicago was great. Chicago became my second-favorite city in the US. People were so friendly. Midwestern people rock.

By the end of the summer, my U visa papers were still not ready. Even though DACA came in June 2012 I did not qualify for it because

I came to the US at the age of seventeen instead of fifteen. I met all other requirements of living in the US before June 2005, graduated from high school, but I was too old when I arrived. My only hope was for my U visa to get granted.

The immigration system could say no to my U visa, so my future wasn't certain. Nevertheless, I was done waiting. I was going to take the February bar exam with or without papers. In the meantime, I got another traveling job for the law fraternity of which I was president during law school.

My chapter had done so well recruiting members that the executives of the fraternity wanted me to recruit others around the country. I traveled to law schools in South Dakota, Nebraska, Iowa, Arizona, Michigan, West Virginia, Kentucky, and Ohio. I never would have thought I would go places like that. I had a great time in Vermillion, South Dakota, with some law students playing trivia night.

My job was to go to law schools with a struggling chapter and revive the chapters. I assembled a table with candy to lure students in and told them how great it is to be part of the fraternity. I invited the students for pizza at lunch, where I recruited guys on the spot to become members of the board and lead the chapter. Once a few law students got titles that I made up on the spot, they went along with the fraternity.

During my pitch I showed a video of past US presidents and Supreme Court justices who had been part of the fraternity. I told people to sign up right there and have the opportunity to become a board member like I was. "That's something you can put on your resume." I sold a few students. Then I booked a plane ticket, hotel, and car and moved to the next law school.

Conquering Your Fears

It was Arizona in 2012. That year, Arizona became the epicenter of an anti-immigration bill that allowed cops to stop a person they suspected of being in the country without papers. That was a fucked-up law against the Constitution, but that's another topic.

My point is that I had no papers. As part of my fraternity job, I drove from Phoenix to Tucson. Tucson is sixty-eight miles from the border with Mexico. I thought about making an excuse and not going. I was back living in DC close to Jane, and she told me she didn't like the idea of me going to Arizona. But I had to confront my fears. I decided to stop being such a little bitch. If *La Migra* was going to get me, so be it, I'll have a normal life or no life at all. I was done.

I went to the law school in Phoenix at Arizona State University and then I had to drive two hours south to a law school in Tucson at the University of Arizona. I was within one hundred miles of the border. Per the Supreme Court ruling, there were little to no constitutional rights for me within one hundred miles of the border. *What the hell do I do?* I did that trip back and forth twice. I saw a couple Customs and Border Patrol (CBP) cars pass me by.

All I could say to myself was, *Be cool, act like nothing is happening, and they will not bother you.* One CBP agent looked at me from his car, and I looked right back at him. I waved mildly. Then he looked away. I continued driving. It probably helped that I was driving with a suit and tie. What undocumented person drives close to the US-Mexico border wearing a suit and tie? I got to my hotel without incident. I was glad my Arizona trip was over. It was my way to give a big finger to the Arizona legislature for passing such a racist law. I was proud I didn't chicken out.

Prepping for the Bar Exam

It was December 2012 and it was time for me to study for the bar. I bought the cheapest bar prep course I could find. It cost me $1,000. It was all I needed.

My study program was a military-style regimen. I gave up alcohol entirely. No drinking for the next two months. Jane was not happy that she had to drink wine alone on Saturdays. The good side was that I was the designated driver.

My life for the next two months looked like this:

6:30 a.m. Wake up, take a shower, and go to the study hall close to the apartment.

10:00 a.m. Go to the gym and listen to audio courses while I work out.

11:00 a.m. Study more.

12:30 p.m. Go to Subway to get a sandwich.

1:00 p.m. Study more.

2:00 p.m. Take a power nap on the couch in front of the study hall.

2:30 p.m. Hit the books again.

6:00 p.m. Get something to eat.

7:00 p.m. Hit the books.

10:00 p.m. Go to bed and try to stop thinking about the bar exam. Repeat this Monday to Friday.

On Saturday I left at 7:00 p.m. from the study hall because they closed earlier. Sundays were my days off. Even the Lord rested on the seventh day; otherwise, I would've gone crazy. Go on a hike, take your girl out, but don't do any mental work on Sundays.

The bar exam was the highest pressure I have ever experienced in my entire life. Two weeks before the bar exam I felt like an Oracle. I asked random strangers on the street to ask me any legal question and within ten seconds I was pointing to an answer in my outline. My brain got so much information that I felt like a god. You'll be surprised at the amount of information your brain can hold if you push your limits.

I was ready to take the bar. Two weeks before it was my time to take it, I got an envelope from the US government.

SUCCESS FORMULA

1. Not every leadership position you have will be easy. Learn about what people on your team value and approach them through the things they like.
2. Attempt to have a sincere and genuine conversation with a person who is working with you. Open up and don't be afraid to share your fears. Most decent human beings will welcome you and work with you once they know your humanity.
3. If you know you are facing a big battle, give everything you have. If it is really important, give it your all or you will fail.
4. Work out. Your mind is part of your body. Your brain extends to every cell of your body. The body also needs pressure to grow and to be healthy. Also, sleep. Sleep is the most important thing you can do for your mental and physical health.

Mighty

I WENT TO NEW YORK CITY at Christmastime to meet with one powerful Fellow. The Christmas spirit in NYC is lovely. There is no traffic during the holidays, plus parking is free in Manhattan. That's where I met Mighty. He has a PhD in molecular biophysics and biochemistry from Yale University. He is working in real science stuff.

Mighty was born in Lima, Peru. His family moved to Elizabeth, New Jersey, when he was four years old. Mighty's mother worked in a glass factory from 6:00 p.m. to 6:00 a.m. to provide for the family. His father worked in fast food.

In other ways, Mighty had a normal childhood. His parents were not rich but they loved him and raised him well. In high school, he did well despite attending a rough high school where the teachers did not care much about teaching. It was obvious to Mighty that the teachers did not care for black or Latino students. Mighty told me that at some point the school board gave up on most of the students at Elizabeth High School because they transferred every student with a 3.0 GPA or higher to the Upper Academy. The school board put most of the extracurricular activities into the Upper Academy and those who did not make the cut were given a lot of good luck wishes. Luckily, Mighty made the cut.

While Mighty's parents were working, he was left alone in the home. Mighty was hanging out with the kids from his neighborhood. Some were being arrested for selling weed. Mighty never felt peer

pressure to do weed or cocaine; he was mature at an early age. Mighty appreciated the sacrifices his parents made for him, decided to not be stupid, and he eventually got away from the troublemakers. Mighty stayed home doing homework. Weed and cocaine is alluring to most kids, but Mighty was no dumb guy.

Mighty did not have much guidance on how to apply to colleges. Not like his friends, some of whom had whiteboards hanging in their bedrooms displaying application deadlines at their top-choice schools and their "safe" backup colleges. Mighty went to talk to a high school counselor for help. The counselor was wholeheartedly dismissive, a typical scenario for undocumented students back in 2007. The counselor did not seem interested unless the student was super accomplished or white. Mighty was on his own.

He decided to apply to colleges on his own. While he had the love and support of his parents, they were unfamiliar with the college application process. Unfortunately, Mighty missed several critical application deadlines. No one ever told him about application deadlines.

Another hurdle was that the college applications asked for Mighty's Social Security number. As he completed the application, he called his mother to ask her for his Social Security number. When she told him that he did not have one, the realization of his undocumented status sunk in. Like Mighty, many high school students discover they are undocumented when they begin the college application process and find out they do not have a Social Security number.

The lack of papers did not stop Mighty from pursuing his dreams. He enrolled in community college, where they didn't ask for a Social Security number, to study business. He chose to study business because, growing up, his family lacked money and he wanted to learn the financial skills in order to make money and provide for his family. Good people major in business. To pay for college Mighty worked under the table in restaurants, and his mother helped him as well.

Surprisingly for Mighty, the professors at Union County Community College did care about the students. Mighty focused on math and economics and he was doing even better than in high school. Mighty felt that his high performance stemmed from his professors going the extra mile to make sure that the students understood the material. Mighty took a biology elective class even though biology wasn't his favorite subject in high school. Surprisingly again, he understood everything about Darwin and evolution thanks to the involvement of his professor.

Mighty was fascinated by his biology course, so he stopped by the professor's office. Dr. Fulton, the first black professor Mighty had ever seen. Mighty said to her: "I really like biology and evolution. I want to know more, what can I do?" Dr. Fulton said: "Have you heard about independent studies?"

"What is that?"

"You do research on a topic and at the end of the semester you present it, you write a paper, and then you show your findings at the honors society."

Following the advice of his mentor, Mighty dove into his independent study research. He spent countless hours reading about biology, evolution, and intelligent design. The more he read, the more he stumbled across the same name—Dr. Kenneth Miller. This guy was quoted a lot. At the time, evolution vs. intelligent design was a hot topic and was actively being debated on school boards. Mighty had a strong desire to visit Dr. Miller to ask him about evolution. Mighty calculated that he could reach Dr. Miller, where he worked at Brown University in Rhode Island, after a four-and-a-half-hour Amtrak train ride. Unfortunately, Mighty hit another roadblock due to his immigration status. He could not use Amtrak, which refused service to any customer without government-issued identification. This rule came after the 9/11 attacks. Back then, New Jersey did not give driver's licenses to undocumented people, so Mighty couldn't get on the train.

Mighty had an honest conversation with Dr. Fulton and he disclosed everything to her. "I don't have papers," he explained. "I can't ride the Amtrak train or Greyhound bus. They require an ID; I really want to go see Dr. Miller at Brown University but I can't." Dr. Fulton said: "Let me talk to them." Dr. Fulton grabbed the phone and Mighty heard Dr. Fulton argue with the Amtrak representative.

Dr. Fulton: "Why does he need an ID?!"

Amtrak: "That is the policy!"

Dr. Fulton: "He is just a college student. Can you make an exception? He is undocumented."

Amtrak: "If he is undocumented, what business does he have in college?!"

Dr. Fulton and Mighty eventually found Megabus, which did not require customers to present an ID. The independent study program had some funds, and they were able to pay for the bus and the motel for Mighty to travel to Brown University. He had twenty questions to ask Dr. Miller about evolution. Mighty cold emailed Dr. Miller and asked straight up for an interview. Dr. Miller replied right away. Mighty's email had shown that he read a lot about what Dr. Miller knew. Dr. Miller was intrigued that a college student was asking him such deep questions.

Shortly thereafter, Mighty traveled to Rhode Island. Soon he was in the big college atmosphere of Brown University with its traditional halls and gardens—a majestic university that inspired learning. Mighty and Dr. Miller met in his office for about an hour and a half. Mighty was fascinated. The meeting with Dr. Miller ignited his passion for biology and science. His life's work as a research scientist had officially launched; there was no turning back.

Mighty transferred to Queen's College, City University of New York (CUNY), where tuition is affordable. Unfortunately, the exorbitant rent and cost of living in New York City was a significant stressor. Mighty worked at two restaurants to afford the high cost of living. He could afford only one or two classes each semester.

Mighty could pay rent in a basement but he still needed food to survive. When he attended school events, he observed staff throwing food away when the event ended. Mighty and another undocumented friend snatched the food that was on its way to the dumpster and took it home. They ate that food for the next two weeks. This was Mighty's meal plan for the rest of his college career.

Later, he found a job in a deli on Thirty-fourth Street where he worked from 6:00 p.m. to 6:00 a.m., just like Mom used to do. Still undocumented and without a work permit, he was paid under the table. Following his overnight twelve-hour shift, his class began at 1:00 p.m. He only slept about four to five hours, sometimes on the subway, in between classes. Despite his best efforts, he often fell asleep in biology class, but in the end, he always got an A. His professor asked him, "Mighty, I don't understand, you always sleep in my class but you get straight As."

While at Queens College, Mighty felt that his support system was not there. He was no longer in New Jersey. His family was away, and he was working crazy hours. His academic performance went down. But things started to change for him. Five years earlier, in 2002, New York had become the fourth state to offer in-state tuition rates for undocumented students. After living in NYC for a year, Mighty qualified for in-state tuition. He saved enough money working at the deli to pay for school. However, he did not feel the love at Queen's College, so he transferred to York College, still within the CUNY system. As a point of reference, in 2019 New York began to give financial aid to undocumented students.

Mighty knew that if he wanted to major in biology, he needed to take it seriously. He saved all the money he could from the deli and quit his job. One day, Mighty was at the library doing his physics homework when his friend Omar stopped by his desk to chat. Mighty told Omar his undocumented story. Omar shared that he needed a physics tutor. Omar offered Mighty a free place to stay in exchange for his tutoring in physics. Mighty did not have to pay rent anymore, plus he learned that he could make extra money teaching others.

■

In May 2013, Mighty finally obtained his green card. Then he started grad school in September 2013. His family's journey to obtain their green cards was lengthy. Twenty years prior, in 1993, Mighty's aunt was a US citizen who petitioned for Mighty's father. If you know something about the immigration system you know that a sibling's petition can take fifteen to eighteen years. Eventually Mighty's father's time passed, and his green card was approved. Mighty also got a green card as part of the family package. Right before getting his green card, Mighty received a work permit as part of his green card application, and he landed a job as a lab tech at York College.

■

After obtaining his bachelor's in biotechnology from York College/ CUNY, Mighty applied to Yale University. That's right—the guy who worked the overnight deli shift, slept through classes, and still got straight As, was about to start at Yale. But Yale was hard. It was a different type of hardship. Mighty felt like a fish out of water. Most of his peers already had advanced degrees in biochemistry and biophysics. Even though York College was a good school, at Yale, Mighty's peers already had a history training with private tutors. Mighty began to think he did not belong at Yale. It was like high school all over again, being transferred to the Upper Academy with kids who had private tutoring in math and science. A lot of privileged people at Yale complained that they did not want to spend a weekend on the family's private yacht.

The first semester at Yale, Mighty failed one class and got straight Cs in the rest. The director of the graduate program emailed Mighty and asked him to come into his office. Yale is famous for dismissing their graduate students if they do not perform. In order to stay at Yale, you need a B average, which meant that Mighty needed a couple solid As in order to stay. Mighty was out of his league. He began to struggle with a type of identity crisis. In undergrad, when he didn't perform to his fullest, he had the excuse of being undocumented. Now, he no longer had the undocumented crutch.

Mighty had to decide: either stay at Yale or leave and do something else. Mighty's problem was that he did not like to ask for help; his pride got in the way. It didn't help that he was one of the three students of color in the entire graduate program at Yale. Mighty cared about what others would say—*Oh, you are Latino, and you did not have enough schooling, obviously you need help.* That is what Mighty heard in his head. To the contrary, everyone needs help in graduate school because students are there to learn with the help of professors and mentors. Finally, Mighty realized that there is no shame in asking for help. He finally sought assistance from his professors and peers.

Mighty humbly explained to the graduate program director what he was going through. He promised to seek help in the future. Mighty worked his ass off the following semester, and he got straight Bs. He showed improvement and the program director agreed that he deserved another shot at the third semester. The following semester, Mighty got all As and one B, thus getting his B average and impressing the program director. He turned his academic life around. At that point, the director had asked many students to leave the program, but he spared Mighty. Mighty even got a prestigious fellowship from the Paul & Daisy Soros Fellowships for New Americans, giving him a much-needed stipend for two years.

■

While I sat in a nice restaurant across from Columbia University with Mighty, he told me that he heard the dean say to a professor: "Yale needs more minority applications for grad school." The professor said, "But we had more minority applicants, what is the problem?" The dean said: "None of them are good." Yale did increase the number of applicants but they did not increase the number of minority students they accepted. Then on another occasion the same dean said, "We only want the best of the best of the minorities." Does that mean that Yale is okay with average white students?

While at Yale, Mighty discovered some abnormalities with his blood. I guess that eating recycled sandwiches and free pizza whenever he could did not help his health. That gave Mighty extreme fatigue episodes during school. He thought it was regular grad school stress but he got checked at the doctor. The doctor ordered him to eat better. With a better stipend and funds, he could afford better food and now he takes his time to take care of himself.

Mighty is a postdoctoral fellow at Columbia University and he is doing amazing work. He is a great professor who cares about his students. Mighty's experience as a student makes him relate to the struggles and uncertainties that other students have.

Mighty is the cofounder of Científico Latino, an organization that provides access to resources to prepare students for higher education in the sciences, and they provide a mentorship program for graduate school students. Mighty met with three other scientists to exchange ideas on how they could help the next generation of scientists. They know how it is to be isolated in the scientific world, and their mission is to help alleviate the challenges that grad students in the sciences have.

If you want to help Mighty directly, you can go to cientificolatino. com and make a contribution.

Now Mighty is a US citizen. It took him twenty years to become one. His friend Omar works in the same research lab at York College while he is getting a master's in biology.

Next, I will tell you everything that I learned in my journey talking to all the Fellows I met. I will tell you some common denominators and traits that they possess. Some are obvious but some are not easily recognizable. The last chapter of this book is probably the most important chapter where I tell you how you also can be successful if you cultivate these special habits and skills.

PS: I visited the deli on Thirty-fourth Street where Mighty used to work overnight shifts. The sandwiches were not particularly appealing. I kept on thinking about how the hell Mighty was able to pull all-nighters in this place for years and then become a prominent scientist from Yale. I remember what he said to me.

"When you have twenty impossible things before you, and regardless of their impossibility you still try to accomplish one of those things. You work and work for it, and after a lot of pain you accomplish ONE thing; then you realize that the other nineteen impossible things are also possible."

23

Obtaining Power

Always remember, your weakness is some-
body else's strength.
—Vinaya Panicker

The way to get started is to quit talking and
begin doing.
—Walt Disney

IT WAS FEBRUARY 2013, AND I was feeling like a know-it-all after immersing myself in the bar studies. I took a break and decided to look at the mail. I saw a big envelope from the United States Citizenship and Immigration Service (USCIS).

I held the envelope thinking that my entire existence depended on this one piece of correspondence. I was excited at the possibility; I was afraid of the possibility. I held it in my hands for a couple of minutes, as I could not open it right away. I put the envelope in my pocket and went to a park nearby. *Whatever happens, Jose, you will be fine.* I opened it slowly. It was a reddish piece of plastic with my picture on it. My work permit arrived! They granted my U visa. Instantly, my eyes widened, and my thoughts of power shined through my brain. I felt like Thanos, Mr. Burns, Magneto, Frieza, and Brain, all together in one entity!

Serotonin shot through my brain at an all-time high. The lust for power came to me due to my crazy bar studies and lack of stability. I could finally start laying the foundation for my empire. Even though I didn't qualify for DACA, the U visa was a better option because it leads to a green card after three years of having it. In 2025 DACA people still don't have a permanent solution.

Still, my reality was that I was broke, unemployed, and crashing at a friend's apartment. I had less than $2,000 in my checking account. I called a few family members to give them the news and check in with them after I had disconnected from the whole world because of my bar studies.

I called my dad.

"I got it! I got it!"

"What did you get? Herpes?"

"No! Even better, I got the U visa!"

"Oh shit! I'm so happy for you. Good work, you deserve it!"

"Thanks, Dad, things will be better from now on."

I went to the bar that night to see Jane. I walked up to her and asked her to card me. She raised her eyebrows at me, confused.

"Trust me, just ask for my ID."

She sighed. "Alright, give me your ID, can't you see I'm busy?"

I passed my ID to her and she looked at it. Her eyes immediately widened. "Oh my God, you got it!" She came around the bar and wrapped me in a hug.

That's all I went there to do—I was still on my no-drinking vow.

Taking the Bar

Two weeks later I was in Baltimore checking into the Marriot Hotel getting ready to take the bar. Not many people come to Baltimore in February, since it's freezing cold.

I found myself wide awake wandering the Inner Harbor. The touristy side of town was asleep, not a person in sight to watch the bay. Mindlessly I found myself strolling through the brick roads one last time before having to face the morning.

As I walked, I reflected on the life I'd just lived. I thought about how I had trained for the past twelve years for the exam I would take the next day. I could not believe a person like me pulled this off. I wasn't supposed to go to college, let alone law school, or even exist in this country. Just two weeks ago I was undocumented and tomorrow I'm taking the bar exam.

It was beyond late, and I was still walking. I looked at my cell phone and saw it was 3:00 a.m. I had to go to bed and sleep. I knew all the material. I finished the bar course study program. I was confident.

I am going to kill the bar exam.

I really did not sleep the whole night. After all, I only had to take the most important test of my life the next morning. I tossed and turned all night. Soon enough, it was 7:00 a.m. It was finally time to get up and go to battle.

I was in overdrive. The bar is a two-day exam, each day lasting several hours. The first day they gave us a bunch of hypothetical questions to respond to in essay format. My job was to sound like a lawyer, so I threw as many magic words as I could like Harry Potter: *Nolle prosequi, Res Ipsa Loquitor, Res Judicata, Tu Madre!* We took a one-hour lunch break and then it was back to the test room for another three hours of battling the clock. I left exhausted and went to the hotel. I had dinner at Subway as usual and went to bed early. I slept well. I crashed and didn't open my eyes until the next morning. The following day was round two. Two hundred multiple-choice questions. There I was finding the smallest word they would use to trip me into the wrong answer. The purpose of the test is not to find out whether you can get it right—the real purpose of the exam is to find out whether you can get it right under time pressure. Day two finished and I felt good about it.

I came out with confidence. I knew I gave it my best. That was all that mattered. It would take three months for the results to come.

That night I called Jane to come over and I had to party with a vengeance. I did nothing but study for the past two months. I went to the dive bars at Fells Point. My self-imposed dry days were over. I had two months of retroactive alcohol drinking that I needed to make up for. I drank and danced. The War was over and life was meant to be fun.

■

After the bar exam I had nothing to do. I had no real job waiting for me and I had no desire to go work for someone else. I just waited for the test results. I decided to bum around. I could get a job anywhere with my newly acquired work permit, but I wanted to be a lazy bum. I was tired of working my ass off. I needed a break. Jane didn't like that. Idling was not a thing she appreciated. I enjoyed the peace of waking up without pressure and going to the gym for fun.

I worked a few hours here and there for Lenny, keeping his books, but that was it. I had worked a lot throughout my life, and I was going to take a break. I had all my life ahead of me to work. I was sure that someone out there would hire me in the worst-case scenario. I knew I wanted to open my own firm, but I couldn't do it until I got my law license. I felt I passed the bar exam before the results were up. I just knew it. What worried me was the last hurdle in the process of becoming a lawyer—an interview face-to-face with the Character and Fitness Committee.

The Committee

IN MARYLAND, ALL THE BAR APPLICANTS must go to an in-person interview to determine that they are good, law-abiding people. I patted myself on the back and told myself that I did a good job given my circumstances. I would tell myself, *don't be sad, you did well, I'm proud of you. How many people in your circumstances went as far as you did?*

I was ready to be denied admission to the bar because I lived in the country unlawfully. *Lawyers don't break the law*. If a lawyer breaks the law, that lawyer gets disbarred. If a person breaks the law, that person cannot become a lawyer. I broke the law by merely existing for the past twelve years.

I went to my interview. I opened up about my life journey in the application. My interviewer started flipping through my application.

"Did you work during the time you were undocumented?"

"Yes, I did, sir."

"Did you have authorization to work?"

"I did not, sir. By the written laws of man, I broke the law. But by the laws of nature, I had to work. I needed to eat somehow. I didn't steal the bread I ate; I bought it and then ate it. Look at my belly, I have proof of all the eating I've done."

The interviewer laughed.

If I'm going to be denied, at least I made a good joke about it.

"Did you lie about your status to someone?" he questioned.

"I can only assume," I responded.

"You can only assume what?" *He had to be a lawyer.*

"I can only assume that I did. I surely told people I had papers when I did not."

I admitted to breaking the law to my interviewer. That moment I prepared myself to be denied.

The interviewer was confused about me. I was the first guy he saw with a story like mine. He asked me to come again for a second interview in the future. Not many people get a second interview. I was thinking, *if you are going to deny me, just have the balls to do it to my face.*

I left. At least I did not get a no right there. I came back about a month later and the interviewer asked me a few more questions.

"I thought about your case, and I'll recommend your admission."

I was shocked. I didn't believe he would do that. Had I been in his position I would have denied my own application. I was still thinking as a robot and not as a human. This man taught me the lesson of equity. That concept of doing the right thing and seeking justice despite what is written on a piece of paper. I was so much of a binary humanoid making automatic decisions that I forgot what justice was. I felt like I was Jean Valjean from *Les Misérables* and this prosecutor had let me go. I walked away from the interview thinking, *I'll actually become a lawyer. I will open my law firm and I'll help others.*

A month later the bar results were available. I was working at Lenny's computer and I rushed to the website to match my bar ID with the words PASS/FAIL. There were a lot of PASS and a lot of FAIL. I was going down the numbers and I saw my ID, "195: PASS." I checked again to make sure it was me. Yes, it was! I screamed like a super Saiyan. That was pure euphoric joy. I walked all over telling people in the building I passed the bar. I walked outside and told strangers in the street that I passed the bar. I felt cool and awesome. Humility went out the door that day. I got a lot of congratulations and strangers shook my hand with joy.

The final letter summoning me to the bar admission ceremony came in the mail. I opened it in my bedroom with Jane next to me. I read the words "Congratulations . . . your presence is required to take the oath to be admitted to the bar on June 19th, 2013." I put my face on a pillow and I cried. A grown man was crying at the top of his lungs putting a pillow on his face to suppress the noise. Jane was there not to comfort me but to be there. I was accepted for who I really was and that feeling of acceptance was overwhelming. That represented the culmination of years of sacrifices and hard work. From that moment I knew things were going to get better.

Opening My Law Firm

I opened my own law firm the day after the admission ceremony. In law school, I thought I was never going to be hired by a law firm because I didn't have papers, so I prepared to create my own job. Besides, I didn't want to be employed by anyone. I loved the flexibility of taking off any day I wanted and going to a place far away whenever I wanted to. But in reality, I worked my ass off more than anyone. That's part of having a business. You don't own a business; the business owns you for the first five years. After that, you can take a break here and there.

I worked from 9:00 a.m. to 10:00 p.m. every day of my first year as a lawyer. I didn't notice the clock until it was late and it was dark outside. I had to learn how to be a lawyer, which meant that I had to read a lot and talk to other lawyers, asking them how to handle cases. I was surprised that most lawyers wanted to help me succeed, so they offered their time to give me advice. Most lawyers work because they like to help others.

I rented a desk inside the office of a tax preparer. I paid $500 out of the $2,000 I had in my bank account. I had nothing but time. It was me and my laptop. I had become a lawyer to help people with their problems. I originally set myself up to work on bankruptcy and tax cases because immigration and criminal defense were too sad and depressing. It turned out that nobody wanted help with bankruptcy or taxes and that a lot of Spanish speakers wanted help with immigration cases.

When I was in law school my proficiency in the English language wasn't the best, but I still worked hard at it. Most people saw me as a law student with a disadvantage. I saw that as my strength. I knew that not many lawyers speak a second language fluently. What seemed to be my weakness, with time turned out to be my strength. By the mere force of gravity, I attracted the growing Latino community, and I was happy to help them with their immigration problems. I had some experience with it.

Marcos, the friend that ditched me right before I started law school, called me up to help him with his immigration forms. I sure took his money. It wasn't much but he was a paying client. This friend told two of his friends about me. These friends told another two friends and those friends told others. Six months later I had a healthy number of clients. Cash was coming in. I saved most of the money. I paid myself a salary of $500 a month and saved the rest for this up-and-coming law firm. I was still crashing at Lenny's, so I did not spend much money on rent. The $500 a month was a pay increase. I was making $0 while I was in law school. Six months after I started the firm, I moved to my own office space.

It was a one-man show. I picked up the phone, scheduled interviews, had consultations, and drafted all the arguments on my own. I showed up to court prepared for battle. I had a bunch of clients and I was doing all the work without help. I was burning out. My mood was changing and I had to pay the lease for the new office.

I needed help but I did not have much money. *Who would work for very little pay?* Suddenly, my dad showed up.

He saw me in distress. He saw me worried for my clients. I had bags under my eyes because I kept up at night working on cases that I did not want to lose. For me it was personal. If my client trusted me with her case, I was going to sacrifice myself in order to do anything possible to win her case.

"You need help," Dad said.

"I can handle it on my own," I lied.

"You cannot continue doing this. You are risking a lot. You are risking your health." He pointed at my growing belly.

"I don't know what to do other than keep fighting for my clients."

"You do that but you need someone who can handle the non-legal work."

"I can't pay for help, not yet. I'm growing the law firm."

"Let me help you," Dad said with determination. He saw his time to vindicate himself. He saw the way to get closer with me every day and to finally have a successful business venture. He saw the opportunity to help the family business.

"I don't have much, I can pay you $300 a month." Way below the minimum wage.

"That is enough, let's build something together, son."

I was too tired to shed a tear that night. All I wanted was to sleep, as I had many sleepless nights worrying about the future of the law firm. But that night I slept well, knowing that Dad was next to me.

The next morning there we were, day in and day out. We worked early in the morning until late at night. I practiced law and Dad took care of the books.

We had lunch together almost every day. We talked about strategies and ways to keep the clients happy. We talked about developing a filing and accounting system. After lunch we came back to the office to work more. Dad took phone calls and made appointments, I spent much of my time talking to clients.

During the mornings I would save a client in court charged with a misdemeanor and Dad would manage my calendar to make sure that I missed no court hearings.

Day in and day out. Father and son working. We became unstoppable. Whenever I needed to talk about strategy, Dad had an attentive ear. He never complained and he never asked for a raise. It was his way to pay me back a debt that was no longer alive. I wanted no retribution but Dad wanted redemption. He still wanted forgiveness but there was nothing to forgive. I forgave a long time ago. I was reaching my thirties. Life took us apart for some time and just like that Life brought both of us together again.

I don't think my firm would have grown as fast as it did, had I not had my father next to me. My father, like a wise loving father, helped me in anything I needed even if I had a stressful day and my temper was rough. I appreciate all the hard work that my father did back then. No other person would have been next to me under those circumstances. He was there to love and protect me despite my hot head. He used his accounting training to keep the books of the firm. Sometimes we had great father-son moments. We worked some cases and later went to have a beer watching a soccer match. Most of my temper tantrums with Dad happened during my young lawyer years. I got better over time.

Throughout the years we hired different lawyers and paralegals gradually as the business grew. Being a lawyer provided a lot of stress and great moments of satisfaction knowing that I made a difference in people's lives. I enjoyed going to immigration court to help someone facing deportation remain in the United States. I defended people wrongly accused of a crime. I enjoyed helping people injured in a car accident get the compensation they deserved to pay for their medical bills. Eventually, I helped people get bankruptcy protection when they could not pay for their growing debts. There is no boring moment in the law firm.

I worked for so many people and I saved so many days. That was the reason for me to go to law school. I wanted to be that guy who saved the day. I wanted to be a superhero for someone in need. Where there was injustice, I would come and provide justice.

When I was a child, I wanted to be a superhero. I wanted to use the Force to help others. Now I use the Force by figuring out the solution to a problem. Just like the conversation I had with my father long ago, now I can see the actual outcome of using the Force and I see that I became a superhero to people who came to me seeking help. Anyone can become a superhero if they set their mind to it. After so many years, my childhood dream came true.

A Fellow's Formula

EVERY TIME I INTERVIEWED A FELLOW I felt like Highlander the immortal, the one who chops off other immortals' heads and acquires their powers. But instead of acquiring their powers, I acquired the Fellow's life story. My journey meeting these Fellows was lonely and tiring, but it was also fulfilling. I learned something important from each one.

The following are key traits that most Fellows have. If you made it this far in the book it is time for you to know what common characteristics make a successful Fellow.

1. Entrepreneurs/Hustlers

Some of us have a business now or are leading an organization. Early on most of us learned to survive on our own and not depend on a job to make a living. Yes, we all held a job at some point, but we realized that being employed is a hustle when you don't have papers, so some of us made our own business to make a living. Fighter opened his online business, which he sold later, and now he leads a consulting firm. Sage, Hardy, Fresh, and Tony have written books and they are selling them. I hope to sell a bunch of these books just like I did that summer in law school at the library. Tony owns his law firm and is making so much money.

Those Fellows who are doctors and professors by the nature of their field have to work for different institutions, but before they earned their doctorates, they hustled in what they could find.

2. Volunteerism

Most of us give to those in need. Tony founded a nonprofit to help others. I take pro bono cases for those who can't pay for a lawyer. Sister helps the young college groups outside of her job. Mentalist provides psychological help to the undocumented community. Mighty mentors other students from underrepresented communities to join the scientific field. Matter helps refugees in need.

The concept of giving back to those in need resonates a lot with us because at some point we didn't have much. We got a helping hand when we needed it the most, which taught us how valuable aid is.

3. Leadership Roles

While in college or grad school we got involved in organizations. We were active in our environment. The Arizona Kids got together like gladiators and organized their communities to fight an unjust law. Fighter, Mentalist, Sage, and Hardy were the original gladiators. Bella organized a fundraiser to help a guy continue going to college. Tusk devoted her life to helping those migrant workers to have safe working conditions in the fields. At a young age most of us decided to join an organization and work for a goal. It could be your student organization or your sorority like Sister. The Fellows get actively involved in their communities.

Mentalist, Sage, Hardy, Magnet, and Mighty are top professors at top universities. Healer and Specialist work in one of the best hospitals in the nation.

4. Scholarships

Most of us got some sort of scholarship, whether it was a fellowship working for an organization or a merits academic scholarship. Back in our days it was very hard to find a scholarship that did not require papers. Now, there are tons of scholarships from organizations eager to give money away to those who want to go to college regardless of their immigration status. Just go online and apply to one scholarship every day and I believe you will get your tuition money.

5. Hard Work

This is self-evident. There is no way around it. Success is like academics and the gym. The more you study, the smarter you get. The more you work out at the gym, the stronger your muscles get. You don't get superhuman strength without breaking a sweat or putting your brain through stress. You don't grow if you don't experience discomfort. No pain, no gain. Most of us worked even though we didn't have the legal right to do so. Shocking. We had to earn a living somehow. You can't ask a human being to not work and starve to death. That is unnatural. Some of us used fake papers and told our employer we had papers. Whatever, I will not apologize for working.

Healer swallowed her pride and sold Mary Kay, Specialist worked at Macy's, Mighty worked the graveyard shift at the deli, Magnet did babysitting, Hardy worked years at McDonald's. Mentalist, Tusk, and I worked at Taco Bell. Tony worked in a grocery store. Most of us mopped floors and cleaned toilets.

6. Mental Damage

With any traumatic experience, most of us felt sad for not having the good fortune of having papers. Like a warrior coming home with PTSD, there is a wound in all of us. Some of us have healed more than others. Some of us have worked with a professional therapist to overcome our wounds. All humans have some wounds to heal. Some Fellows are still battling their demons. Writing this book was a great way for me to heal.

Healer heals others but her wounds are still raw. Tusk is tired of the never-ending struggle. Fighter, Fresh, Sister, Magnet, and Specialist have a missing father in their life that has left a void in their spirit.

Tony still sheds a tear to this date talking about the depression he suffered while battling the State of California to earn his bar license. His millions of dollars have not washed the trauma away, yet.

At some point in our lives, we avoided emotions as a defense mechanism. To heal it takes a lot of love, work with a professional, and patience.

7. Sponsors and Mentors

This is one of my favorite common denominators. I will tell you why in the Epilogue. Most Fellows had a free place to live at some point or another. Hardy, Mentalist, Matter, and Mighty lived with their parents while in college. Healer lived with her then-husband. Tony, Fresh, and I found a rich friend who gave us a free luxury place to stay. Sage was couch-surfing from friend to friend in her community. Mighty got free housing in exchange for tutoring. Bella, Tusk, and Fighter got scholarships to pay for their housing. When none of us had a house, someone put a roof over our heads at no cost to ourselves. Without this basic necessity, our stories would have been very different.

Besides financial sponsorships there were always people along the way who mentored us. Hardy, Mighty, and I had a professor who cared about us. Healer had his lab boss mentorship to get into Harvard. Tony had another lawyer teach him how to litigate million-dollar cases. There is always someone out there. Go look for them. Volunteer with that person whom you see as a role model. Offer your genuine help and in return you will get twice the help.

8. Betting on Education

We decided to go to grad school to improve our chances in life. To get stronger and more powerful we invested in ourselves. There is one thing that nobody can take away from you and that is your own brain.

Education has been the number-one proven way to get out of poverty.

And in today's world, it does not have to be a formal education, it can be as simple as reading key books you can check out at the library and assimilating knowledge that you can use to benefit your purposes. This whole book has been about encouraging you to go to grad school and that is one way. It is simple to get the guidance of a professor who can tell you what book you should read next. But even if you cannot have the luxury of a grad school professor, you can still take the long way and research and read and read and then read some more. Then, you will be strong and you will assimilate information on your own. That is the ultimate level that successful billionaires have reached.

9. Luck

The harder we worked the better prepared we were when we encountered luck. There is no other way to explain exactly this recipe for success. I thought and thought about how I could explain the extremely improbable success that we achieved and all I could find was "luck."

Some call it God, the Force, the Universe, Nature, or Energy. But it is also okay to call it luck. I've been a very lucky guy. Most of us have been at the right time in the right place and with extreme amounts of work we were able to catch a wave of lucky strikes. I'm sorry to be simplistic and call this luck instead of giving you a scientific explanation, but sometimes you can't explain it.

10. Living in the US

I'm not sure that our journey could be replicated in another country. I find that only in America can you do things like this. I am not sure if the Founding Fathers were so enlightened as to design a system in which a small percentage of error is permissible and still allowed success. They designed a Constitution that lets people walk away if the government intrudes too much, even if they are guilty of the crime. Maybe because of that margin of error done by design, Fellows exist.

It is the only-in-America narrative. I'm not sure that authoritarian places like Russia, China, or Iran would allow a person without legal documents to be successful.

This success formula is by no means exhaustive. You may be able to detect other traits that will help a regular human become an extraordinary Fellow. I hope that the Fellows have inspired you the way I have been inspired. If you didn't believe that grad school was reachable and now you believe it is, I have accomplished my mission.

Epilogue

If your weakness is love then you are
extremely strong.
—Efrat Cybulkiewicz

TEN YEARS AND ONE MILLION DOLLARS later, here I am in my house somewhere in the Washington, DC area.

When I decided to write this book I'd just gotten out of a long-term relationship. That and a sense of not accomplishing much, a.k.a. a midlife crisis, made me decide to do something to find more meaning in life. It was the era of COVID-19 and isolation was the norm. I was lonely.

I was sitting in my office thinking about what life is really about. After reading a bunch of self-help books such as *The Secret, How to Win Friends and Influence People, The 7 Habits of Highly Effective People, Rich Dad Poor Dad, The 8th Habit, The 4-Hour Workweek, Think and Grow Rich,* among others, I realized that happiness is about the relationships you develop throughout life. By the way, if you have not read these books, do humanity a favor and read them.

I could stare at my computer screen all day long and watch my bank account grow. Was that going to make me happy? Not really. So, I decided to travel all over the United States and make friends. But what kind of friends? I realized that I had the power to befriend anyone I wanted to. Then I thought, how about befriending people like me? People good in nature who have worked hard at something. People who have earned their feathers. People with a sense to help others and understand the struggles that other humans have. How about people who went to law school while they were undocumented? I thought, yeah! I want to meet people who did what I did. That was a hard, seemingly unattainable challenge that not many people have done.

I went on my quest. I met five lawyers who went to law school while undocumented, so I decided to read all about them. I researched their lives and interviewed them. When I asked if I could include them in this book, Fighter and Tony were on board but the other three lawyers were so busy. Or they were scared to open their hearts. For whatever reason, I only had Fighter and Tony. I couldn't write a book with the story of two friends.

I also wanted to inspire the next generation of undocumented students to encourage them to aspire to higher things. I wanted to tell all the struggling kids in America that going to college is possible and that grad school is possible. I wanted to tell all those kids out there that there is hope. I wanted to say, "Hey, look what we have done, look who we were, and this is how we did it. If we did it, so can you." I want to tell all those kids that everything is possible if you are willing to endure.

So, I expanded the scope of the book to "people who went to grad school while undocumented."

That opened the pool of people I could interview in the medical, scientific, and humanities fields. That way I could show that there are other fields that kids can aspire to, not just law. To my surprise, a lot of Fellows were sympathetic to my quest. They wanted to help me. They were first intrigued by my enthusiasm and then they opened their hearts with the stories you have read. I heard so many stories and I selected the few stories to put in this book.

I developed a friendship with these Fellows and I enjoy seeing all the good stuff they are doing. I read the inspirational quotes they share from time to time and I feel connected to them even if they live far from me.

For the past twelve years of practicing law, I had many gratifying experiences. I saved many lives. I fought for people's freedom. I experienced the agony of defeat. I saw an innocent man go to jail. I had many sleepless nights. The practice of law has many highs and lows. When you win, you feel invincible, and when you lose you feel worthless. I will have to write another book to tell you all my adventures of being a lawyer. If I do, I will tell you that one time I tried a case after an extreme night of partying and won despite the hangover. I would tell you that one time a mother cried on my shoulder thanking me for saving her child from deportation.

Practicing law, I saw great lawyers and great judges with incredible wisdom and humbleness. I met great leaders with so much power and a persona that radiates good energy. Also, there are egomaniacs who think that they are all-powerful but have not mastered the craft and are consumed by their limitations.

After I got my U visa, I got my green card four years later, and five years after that I became a US citizen. I've spoken to US senators and representatives in Congress, rich and poor people. I've spoken to upright model citizens as well as low-life criminals. I had the luck of traveling to many parts of the world including Ukraine, Iran, India, Vietnam, Cambodia, and many other countries in Europe, South America, and Asia. As I am writing this book, I am planning a trip to Africa. For years I wanted to figure out how I could stay in this country; now I'm trying to figure out how I could be in another country exploring the world. In my travels I almost died a few times, but more importantly, I lived every day with more intensity. I met people who taught me things by just sharing a meal. I am now blessed to be able to travel anywhere in the world. I am lucky to say that if you give me 120 hours, I can make it to 99% of the globe.

In the years after the ending of this book I became more active in my Masonic lodge acquiring wisdom. I ran two marathons and raised money for a nonprofit helping immigrant children. I went to the Mexico-US border to volunteer in a family detention center helping women and children through the first stages of their asylum journey. For one week I worked nonstop, and I felt like a doctor in a disaster zone where everywhere I turned, someone needed my help. I experienced my first and only migraine there and the experience was humbling.

I learned throughout my journey that the power of love is greater than the power of hate. At first, hatred could seem to give you the strength to challenge any rival, but that is merely brute force that blinds you. If you can love even your enemy and find the positive even in extreme circumstances, then your life will be more rewarding. Even the most uncomfortable places have a positive perspective. If you master the art of positivity, you will find growth everywhere instead of obstacles. You will always see opportunities, and you will learn to love challenges because they will make you stronger. You will see profits instead of expenses.

If you are reading this, it is because you stayed with me through the entire journey in this book and I am sure that you got something out of this. I hope you laughed, cried, felt anger and love. My objective was for you to feel all these emotions.

What happened to some people?

Years later I heard that the complete Stafford Bad Crowd got in trouble with the law. They plotted to rob a convenience store at gunpoint. The police identified them with the security cameras and eventually Bobby snitched on everyone else. Some went to state prison. Francisco wasn't in that incident but last I heard of him, he got deported back to Mexico for carjacking.

Christy, Kylie, and Jane are not their real names. However, years later they all became my social media friends. Had I not gotten beaten up, I would have married Jane. Some people would prefer to get beat-up than to get married. Ask my divorce clients. Things didn't work out with Jane and me for various reasons, but I will say that Jane helped me become a human being once again.

Jack is no longer with us but I will be grateful to him for putting me through college with the money he paid me. I keep in touch with Richard from time to time.

Professor Blair has his own law firm and we collaborate on cases from time to time.

Lenny went to prison for nine years on a conviction for sexual assault of a minor. He touched a couple kids inappropriately and is now out on probation at the age of eighty-nine.

My brother Pepe is going through his immigrant story himself. Decades later his irrational behavior was explained to me. He was diagnosed with bipolar disorder and borderline schizophrenia. His violent episodes now make sense. He never finished college, but he is working physical jobs to support himself.

My sister Pepa lives with her beautiful family in Mexico City. Her husband is a big executive of Grupo Modelo and her US-born son is doing well in school. I enjoyed having her over during her pregnancy.

Mari lives outside of Philadelphia with her husband. She is happily working for an engineering firm drawing and making engineering plans.

Mom spends her time living in El Salvador, Mexico, and the US. I was lucky to take her on a fancy cruise to Greece and a scavenger hunt all over Israel and Palestine chasing Jesus.

Dad still works in the law firm. He is my number one business counselor and is the president of the nonprofit organization that I founded whose purpose is to help other people with life challenges.

As for me, I had many therapy sessions to heal my wounds. Writing this book has been the ultimate healer. At the beginning of this book, I told you that I was going to tell you a secret that not many people know about me, thus here I am telling you that I have an alcohol problem. I don't want to bastardize the word "alcoholic" and call myself one. I like to say that I used to drink a lot. I was going to end this book by promising that one day I would control my alcohol consumption. However, this book project pushed me to take the leap and stop my drinking. It is not that I will never drink again—maybe I'll have two beers some day. But for now, I decided to cut out alcohol altogether because the benefits of not drinking are enormous. Your brain will be more powerful, your productivity will reach new levels, and your wallet will get fatter. I want to encourage you to stop drinking too.

I had to do one final challenge to test my willpower with alcohol. I joined an online class for a thirty-day challenge where a guy teaches you day by day how you can reduce your alcohol consumption and the benefits of quitting. To test this wisdom, I went to New Orleans during Mardi Gras for a bachelor's party. I had fun with the guys in the middle of a packed Bourbon Street without drinking. Throwing beads to people from a balcony was a lot of fun and you don't have to drink to do so. All you do is enjoy people catching your attention so you can reward them with beads. We were there from Thursday to Monday right before Fat Tuesday. Okay, I did have two beers and one of their iconic hand grenade drinks on Friday for a total of three drinks that night. And I had one Bud Light on Saturday. However, I mostly drank non-alcoholic beers, which turned out to be a great substitute for alcohol. The rest of the time I enjoyed the festivities without drinking. I woke up the following days without a hangover and was excited to realize that I conquered this challenge. It's been months since the Saturday at Mardi Gras and I have not had any drinks. I think I will keep it that way for a while. I'm letting go of alcohol now because I am wiser. I did my fair share of drinking when I was younger and I feel more powerful now that I don't drink. Drinking no longer serves a purpose in my socialization. I'm enjoying this newly acquired superpower of a sober life.

At the beginning of the book, I also told you that this journey revealed to me a purpose in life. That purpose is that I need to help people finish their grad school journey despite the challenges that life brings to them. I want to help the next lawyer, doctor, scientist, or professor. As I mentioned, one common denominator for all of the Fellows, including me, was that at some point we received a helping hand that gave us a free place to live. Had these angels not given us a place to live, it is most likely that we would not have finished our grad school programs. That is why I founded **The Philemon Foundation Inc.**, a nonprofit dedicated to giving free housing to a grad student with a life challenge. I want to give a nice place to stay in good condition so that a grad student doesn't have to think about where they will live but rather what paper they will write next.

I defined a life challenge as being undocumented, but you can help me define it in other ways too. Some people may say that a challenge could be having HIV, cancer, a disability, or another medical condition. Some will define a life challenge as experiencing trauma, being homeless, having a near-death experience, losing all your belongings, or surviving war. The purpose of the foundation is to help others and to witness a Fellow overcome their challenges.

If you are a Fellow out there and want to join the cause, whether you made it already or want to continue with your growth, come join me. If you are an ally and want to help, come join me.

Go to www.thephilemon.com and help me give a good livable place for a Fellow. Living in a city like Washington, LA, New York City, or San Francisco is very expensive and your contribution will help the next success story.

For the time being, I will continue with my law practice. However, my next goal is to become a business investor. Eventually I want to become a shark on *Shark Tank* and own a skyscraper. We'll see how things pan out.

I hope you have enjoyed this book. If you did, please make sure to visit www.survivingthelaw.com for pictures and extra content. If you liked this book, drop me a line. Also, donate to the foundation. If you got this book for free, pay it forward and donate to the foundation—$15, $25, $100 will help a lot.

Times have changed once again, and we are living under another administration unfriendly to immigrants. I stand ready to defend those who need help. Whenever someone faces dire legal circumstances, I will be there to help them while they are surviving the law.

Thanks

THIS IS THE PART WHERE I thank everyone who made this book possible. It wasn't that I just sat down and started writing. I needed the help of all those Fellows I interviewed and the army of lawyers and friends with a graduate degree who helped me prepare this book by reviewing chapters and giving me their comments.

First, I want to thank my Fellows who welcomed me into their lives. Fighter, you were the first Fellow who gave me an interview and your clues led me to other Fellows. Mentalist, keep your good heart. Sage, I enjoyed our philosophical debate. Hardy, keep fighting to empower the community. Tony, I follow your example as a big brother. Mighty, I hope you find the cure you are searching for. Matter, you will make a lot of money with your research. Fresh, Del Taco is not real Mexican food. Healer, I had a good time on Mission Street. Specialist, keep healing people's minds. Magnet, thank you for the real tacos in California. Sister, your college students are so lucky to have you. Bella and Tusk, you showed me strong family values.

To my friends who helped me review a chapter and refine my message: Cabo Granato, Esq; Natalia Lorinkova, PhD; Professor Keith Blair, Esq; Adrian Gotcha, Esq; Ernesto Bartels, Esq; Joe Libertelli, Esq; Engineer Jose Roberto Serrano; Tony Fasullo, Esq; Ana Sierra, PhD; Professor Laurie Morin, Esq; Luz Vides, MA; Sara Rager, NP; Joe Lewis; Richard Torres, MS; Roberto Miranda, MS; Jon Rager, CPA, CFP; Ama Lopez; Kimberly Ellis; Mary Beth Craft; Laura Vides; Mo Yassin; and Tina Moerer. Special thanks to Ashley Rodriguez,

Kaylie Escobar-Islas, and Olivia Bourne, my student interns turned creative writing consultants. To my editor, Katherine Pickett, for making me look good; Martin A. Berg for giving this book a final polish; and Peggy Nehmen for coaching me and designing the interior of this book.

I also want to thank the other dozens of Fellows not portrayed in this book who talked to me for hours and showed me around all over America.

Special thanks to Brigette Solatorio, my personal assistant who works from the Philippines and my loyal virtual companion while I traveled America meeting the Fellows.

Lastly, I want to thank my family for allowing me to say things that are uncomfortable. Thank you for giving me that power so that I could share it with others.

It has been a pleasure. That's my time. Thank you.

About the Author

JOSE CAMPOS IS AN ATTORNEY WITH licenses in Maryland, Washington DC, and Virginia. Founder of The Law Offices of Campos & Associates with offices in Silver Spring, Maryland, and Fairfax City, Virginia. He handles immigration, personal injury, and criminal defense cases.

Born in El Salvador, Mr. Campos arrived in the US at seventeen, and completed high school in Stafford, Virginia, and later earned a Bachelor's in International Business from the University of Maryland. He graduated with a Juris Doctor from the University of the District of Columbia David A. Clarke School of Law.

In 2015, he ran the Richmond Marathon, raising funds for a nonprofit. In 2016, he ran the Marine Corps Marathon. In 2018, he completed an Olympic Triathlon.

He has traveled to 35 countries and counting. He enjoys running and hiking in the Washington DC, metropolitan area.

Dear Reader

THANK YOU FOR READING *Surviving the Law.*

I hope you have enjoyed it and that my story will help to inspire you to do the great things I know you are capable of.

Your opinion matters, take a few minutes to leave a quick online review and let us know what you thought. Even a few sentences would be greatly appreciated.

You can reach me on my social media account linked in the QR code below or email me at **jose@survivingthelaw.com**. I'll be happy to come and talk to a group of Fellows like you.

Checkout #survivingthelaw on social media and share your own #survivingthelaw posts. For more information be sure to check out my website at **survivingthelaw.com**.